Marty
from Mother "Dad"
Valentines Day 1969

Esquire's
Book
of Boating

Esquire's Book of Boating

BY ROBERT SCHARFF
AND THE EDITORS OF
ESQUIRE MAGAZINE

Published by Esquire, Inc., New York
in association with
Hawthorn Books, Inc., New York

STAFF

Lewis W. Gillenson, Editor-in-Chief

Arnold Levine, Designer

Philip Doyle, Associate Editor

Charles Fornara, Director of Manufacturing

Sally Weinstock, Assistant Editor

First printing.

TABLE OF CONTENTS

CHAPTER 1
INTRODUCTION

The Golden Age of Yachts 2
Boats of the Future 6
Collecting Antique Boats 9

CHAPTER 2
THE ART OF SAFE YACHTSMANSHIP

Equipment Requirements 14
Rules of the Road 16
For Vessels Under Power 17
meeting head and head or nearly so 18
crossing situation 18
overtaking 19
in narrow channels or canals 19
leaving slips, wharves, docks and piers 19
fishing or special vessels 19
special western river situations 20
For Vessels Under Sail 20
accidents 22
Navigation Lights 22
Requirements 22
Boat Security 25
Fire Prevention 25
Safe Fueling Procedures 26
Other Fire Safety Precautions 27
Know Your Mooring 28
in open water 28
in a slip 29
proper equipment 30
checking mooring 32
guest mooring 34
Weather and the Yachtsman 34
visual indications of the weather 34
clouds 35
storm warning signals 39
small craft, gale, whole gale, hurricane 39
wind barometer indications and table 40
wind velocity and direction 42
when to look for fog 43
foul weather operation 46
Handling Emergencies Afloat 50
Man Overboard 50
First Aid 50
Artificial Respiration 50
In Case of Fire 51
In Case of Fuel Leaks 53
If You Strike a Submerged Object 53
In Case of Shipwreck 55
If You Run Aground 55
On-Board Tools and Spares 56
the hull 56

the engine 57
rigging 57
miscellaneous 57
Recognized Distress Signals 58

CHAPTER 3
GETTING WHERE YOU WANT TO GO

Aids to Navigation 60
Buoys and Waterway Markers 60
types of buoys (spar, can and nun, bell, gong, whistle, lighted, combination) 60
color system 62
numbering system 62
characteristics of lights 63
buoy facts to remember 63
day beacons 64
intracoastal waterway buoys 64
buoyage system for state waterways 69
lighthouses 69
lightships 70
minor lights 70
visibility of lights 70
range markers 71
range lights 72
reduced visibility audio aids 72
radio beacons 72
Basic Navigation Gear 72
Nautical Charts 73
other government publications 74
tide tables, tide current tables, coast pilots, notice to mariners, light lists 74
Marine Compass 76
how to use and read 76
plotting a course 78
Speed Afloat 80
Taking Soundings 83
marking the line 83
using the line 83
using sounding to pilot 84
The Pelorus and Its Use 84
Piloting Techniques 84
the cross bearing 85
the bow-and-beam method 86
the seven-tenths rule 86
doubling the angle on the bow 86
the seven-eighths rule 86
danger bearing 87
the three-point method 88
dead reckoning 88
Locking Through 88
Anchoring and Docking 90
types of anchors 91
rules for anchoring 92
docking procedures 94
Towing 94
Marlinspike Seamanship 95
types of rope 96
knots and their uses 96
how to make fast 102
whipping 102

heaving a line 102
splicing 103
care of lines 105

CHAPTER

4 ELECTRONIC YACHTING

Radiotelephone 107
License information 110
Procedure for Handling an Emergency Call 110
Procedure for Intership Calls 111
Procedure for Ship-to-Shore Calls 112
Procedure for Making a Test Transmission 112
Station Log 113
Rules to Remember 113
Radio Direction Finder 114
Marine Radio Beacons 114
Standard Broadcast Stations 115
aircraft beacons 116
Operation of RDF 116
Loran 118
Radar 118
Depth Sounders 122
Automatic Pilot 125
Electronic Yachting Aids of the Future 126
Non-Electronic Communication at Sea 131
signal flags 131
flashing lights 132
sound 133

CHAPTER

5 THE ART OF CRUISING

A Wife As a Crew Member 134
To the Ladies—how to dress,
children on a boat, etc. 135
Planning a Cruise 135
Where, When, Why, How
Cruising Gear 136
Clothing, Storage Space
Before Shoving Off 138
What to Check Over
Cruising Routine 139
Boatkeeping Afloat—cleaning, storage
A Word to the Galley Detail 141
Laying in Supplies 142
Meat 142
Vegetables 144
Desserts 145
Bread and Cereal 145
Sandwiches 146
Beverages 146

Suggested Menus 146
Stowing of Food 150
Galley Gear 151
Gourmet Cooking Afloat 151
No Fresher Fish (how to clean from scratch) 152
Shellfish Afloat 154
clams 154
crabs—hard-shelled and soft-shelled 155
lobsters 156
oysters 157
shrimps 158
Galley Cleanup Tricks 158
The Cocktail Flag Is Flying 159
Yachting Etiquette 162
flags 162
making colors 164
half-masting flags 164
flag salutes 164
lights 165
the ship's bell 165
Good Manners Afloat 165

CHAPTER

6 BOATING SPORTS

Fishing 168
Using the Depth Sounder 168
Fishing Techniques 172
Crabbing and Clamming 173
Photography Afloat 174
Photo Equipment 174
Taking Pictures Afloat 175
Care of Camera 177
Water Skiing 178
Rules of Safe Water Skiing 181
Skin and Scuba Diving 182
Underwater Photography 183
Spear Fishing 183
Predicted Log Competitions 183
Sailboat Racing 189
Racing Courses 189
The Race Itself 192

APPENDIX A

YACHTING LANGUAGE 194

APPENDIX B

ENGINE CARE AND TROUBLE SHOOTING 205

APPENDIX C

CHART SYMBOLS AND ABBREVIATIONS 212

CHAPTER ONE:
INTRODUCTION:

There used to be a special, often-expressed dream of comfort to Navy men weary of the sea that foretold what they would do when they could finally retire from a life afloat.

"I'm going to take me an anchor," was the way it went, "and I'm going to put it over my shoulder and start walking inland. When I get to a place where somebody asks me what that thing is that I'm carrying, that's where I'm going to drop the anchor and settle down."

It was a pleasant fantasy that sustained many an hour of salt-caked tedium, so old that Homer told it in terms of Odysseus and an oar, but today the retirement-bound tar would have a hard time finding someone to ask him the question. No matter how far inland he wandered his hopeful way, the only questions popped to him would probably be why did he prefer that old Navy anchor to a Danforth or Northill.

No longer is it only in Gloucester, Larchmont, San Pedro, Seattle and other such salty spots that the populace knows an anchor from a hitching post. The whole nation has, in the space of a few years, become one vast pleasure boat "harbor." High in the Rockies, a peak in the Tetons echoes back the whine of an outboard motor on Jackson Lake, while dry winds sweeping the prairies of Kansas carry the "Ready About" cries of Snipe sailors on Lake Quivira. On Arizona roads, the sight of a speedboat on a trailer fails to raise the eyebrow of a single burro.

Someone with a penetrating curiosity about America's most rapidly expanding outdoor sport and an eye for well-rounded figures—the kind that emerge from high-capacity calculating machines—has discovered that approximately 39,325,000 Americans ventured afloat in marine conveyances of one sort or another for at least part of their fun. This same producer of startling statistics turned out 7,865,000 as the number of pleasure boats bobbing about on the bayous, lakes, rivers and coastal harbors of these United States.

He did not classify his boating millions according to their activities—sight-seeing, cruising, fishing, racing, loafing and such—nor did he separate the leaky, flat-bottomed marine-livery-stable skiffs from the fancy motor yachts, equipped with hot and cold running stewards and animated deck decorations, designed to bring every pair of passing binoculars into action. Our researcher was interested only in the number of craft of all kinds used as a medium for recreation, as well as the number of persons who availed themselves of this medium. Conservatively, it may be stated that he found astounding quantities of both; enough to indicate that if the present development continues we soon shall be reading in our Monday-morning papers of bow-to-stern traffic backed five miles up the Wishi-washee River from its junction with the Wotzinit.

1

THE GOLDEN AGE OF YACHTS

Even the landlubberiest landlubber will agree that this is indeed recreational boat's golden age. But what many of us forget is that there was another golden age of boating—or perhaps it would be more accurate to call it a golden age of yachting. By this we refer to the era of really large and unbelievably luxurious ocean-going yachts, an era which reached a dazzling peak during the late 1920's and still retained some of its gilded glory in the decade which followed.

Perhaps typical as any of this highest yacht bracket was Julius Forstmann's *Orion*. She measured 333 feet, which was about as long as the average 28-story building is high. Virtually a sea-going mansion, she had enough bedrooms—each with private bath—for twenty guests. The latter could play *chopsticks* or *Wagner* on the craft's grand piano. They could do Swedish exercises in the gymnasium; play bridge in the card room; toss quoits, practice their golf putting, or acquire a tan on the sports deck. They could drop into the red carpeted library to read any of its hundreds of books. Or they could loll quietly in comfortable chairs on the wide after-deck and enjoy the ocean breezes. The deck chairs cost apiece as much as the poor man's rowboat and somehow the whole setup, according to those who have tried it, provided a feeling of luxury that you just didn't find elsewhere. The *Orion* sported her own complete bakery, laundry, and a dark room for developing snapshots. There were deep rugs in her lounge; and in her huge dining room was a table at which thirty persons could have been seated in high-backed chairs. The entire craft was air-conditioned, and a physician reportedly was in attendance on long cruises to take charge of any medical emergency. Lacking—although Mr. Forstmann doubtless could afford them—were the $25,000 pipe organ, gold-plated guest room fixtures and gold water taps present on many of the other super-yachts of that period.

Many of the old sailing vessels are now used as naval training ships: Indonesia's three-masted barkentine, *Dewarutji*.

2

Actually, the most fantastically beautiful yacht afloat was the square-rigger, *Sea Cloud*. Owned by Joseph E. Davies, she was a 316-foot diesel-powered four-masted auxiliary bark, carried 36,000 square feet of sail and weighed some 2,323 tons. Said to be the largest sailing yacht ever built, the *Sea Cloud* was sent to Russia where Mr. Davies served as ambassador (1936 to 1938) and wrote *Mission to Moscow*. Undoubtedly, the ship was the most costly, if beautiful, white elephant to ever come from the offices of Cox & Stevens, Inc., designers and builders of many of the great yachts of the past. She was designed by this firm in 1931 and was built in Germany. A noted yachting authority once described her as "a cross between the greatest square-rigger ever to grace the China trade and the most sumptuous steam yacht ever to have anchored off Newport for race week." Her interiors were as beautiful as her exterior appearance. The vessel had pink marble bathrooms with gold-plated plumbing fixtures, and was said to contain more teak than any ship then afloat. She had three decks, six master bedrooms and countless other especially designed cabins.

Norway's barque, *Statsrad Lehmkuhl*. Next page, top, is Royal Danish three-masted training-ship, *Danmark*.

The largest yacht built during the golden age of yachting was Richard M. Cadwalader's *Savarona*. Constructed in 1931, she measured 408 feet—which is a lot longer than a football field—and cost about $2,200,000 to build. Her equipment included eleven bulkheads so distributed that any three compartments could be flooded without causing the craft to sink. All doors were watertight and hydraulically-operated from a control on the bridge. Special escape stairways connected the various living apartments with the main deck, to which were lashed four lifeboats and two 30-foot launches for use just in case. In addition to her owner's quarters, consisting of multiple bedrooms, dressing and sitting rooms, she had twelve sleeping rooms and as many extra baths for guests. With a crew of 83 to operate and take care of her, she was practically a full-fledged ocean liner in private use.

Fully as breathtaking, while not so large, was J. Pierpont Morgan's 343-foot, coal-black yacht *Corsair*. Her beam was 42 feet 8 inches, and her steel hull drew 18 feet of water, giving her a gross displacement of 2,181 tons. Built by the Bath Iron Works in 1930, her power was two turbines harnessed to an electric drive. Electric elevators joined her three decks and her corridors, writing, lounging and dining rooms, with their paintings from the Morgan art collection outdid those of the most luxurious metropolitan hotel. But then the craft cost $2,500,000 to build and not a great deal less than $500,000 annually was required for her upkeep. (J. P.'s statement about the cost of yachting will *not* be quoted here—probably for the first time in the history of books on the subject.)

These great yachts, the 200- and 300-footers, which glided majestically through the 1920s and 1930s cruised into oblivion during World War II. Some were scrapped; others were converted to various military use. A couple are—or were—afloat until a few years ago. The *Sea Cloud* was loaned to the United States Navy during the war for a dollar a year. The vessel was assigned to Atlantic weather duty and sailed waters off Greenland and the Azores. After surviving the war, she was subsequently sold to Generalissimo Rafael Leonidas Trujillo Molina, then El Benefactor of the Dominican Republic. At this writing, this yacht which few, if any of the world's millionaires could afford to support, is listed as an auxiliary vessel of the Dominican Navy.

While the beginning of World War II was the deathblow to the golden age of yachting, its end signalled the beginning of modern age of recreational boating. While the "age" may have changed, there's one person who hasn't. We see him almost anywhere there's water. Charts in one hand, tennis shoes, old dungarees, and a battered cap—a man going down to the sea for a week end. He's an amateur, but he knows his boat—fiberglass hull or plywood—because he's been scraping, painting and swearing at it since last winter's snows began to melt. After sandpaper, copper paint, maybe a new nylon sail, or even a complete reconditioning job in the shipyards, the sloop or the runabout or the cruiser is ready to go and so is the skipper.

Subject to more conventional descriptions than home and mother, the boat is always SHE to him. And the combination of skipper, *she*, and the sea—known as yachting—is forever luff and line and Beauty with a capital "B." The words and methods are a part of hallowed tradition—and, somehow, all of the phrases seem to fit. Surely a ship *is* like a woman, with beautiful lines and an exciting mind of her own. Full of whims and close to nature, she's tame—almost—when the right man is at the helm. Ask the skipper of any sailing craft if he thinks there is anything more beautiful than a day when the breeze is up and sails are full across a clear sky. Or ask the motorboat captain if there is anything better than just being out on the water. Man has loved the water since time began.

While most nautical historians called our present era as that of recreational boating, we still like to feel that we're still in the age of yachting—and we have Mr. Webster to back us up. According to the dictionary, "yacht" is a term that applies to a boat used for pleasure, no matter what her size. (The word yacht itself comes from the Dutch *jaghtschip; jaght* means to *pursue* or *hunt*. The jaghtschip was originally a fast sailing ship built to pursue pirates.)

Thus, under modern terminology, if you are owner of a boat of any size, you're a yacht owner, In most cases, you could also be called a "yachtsman." In our modern times, there is one thing that has not changed. The first obligation, or responsibility of a *good yachtsman* —throughout the ages—is the safety of his yacht and crew.

Popular Motor Boat Models

outboard utility

inboard runabout

outboard runabout

inboard cruiser

outboard cruiser

houseboat

stern-drive runabout

pontoon boat

BOATS OF THE FUTURE

Most of us are familiar with the many types and styles of yachts now on the market. Throughout this book the typical present day models are illustrated. But, what will the yachts of the future be like? We found that the majority of manufacturers and designers questioned believe that real change in future boats will be in hull design. In fact, no hotter controversy exists in boating today than that which pits conventional-type hulls (V-bottom, flat bottom, or combination of two of these hull shapes) against those of multi-hull styles —catamaran and trimaran. These latter designs aren't too original—dating back to the time when the caveman found that building his dreamboat with two logs lashed together floated him better than just one.

If you have never seen one of the new powered catamarans, the craft consists of two separate hull units rather than one hull of a conventional boat. When turned upside down, the cat gives the appearance of two broad-beamed planing hulls joined side by side with an indention or a tunnel in the place of the keel of the standard type of construction. Viewed from broad abeam, the catamaran looks like an ordinary boat. However, when viewed from the bow the tunnel between the two hulls can be clearly seen. The majority of the present designs tend toward the use of modified V forms for the two hulls, although some designers stick to the older plan which resembles two toboggans with a tunnel between. There are several variations of these two basic designs; all, however, use the principle of the air passage between two basic hulls. The purpose of the tunnel is to generate lift and produce a smooth, dry ride by trapping air and spray in the forward section of the craft. Trimarans are powered or sailing craft with three hulls.

The big question is: Are two or three hulls better than one? The motor-powered catamarans, like the other hull designs, have assets and debits, but the asset side of the ledger for catamarans is rather impressive. When the giant out board motors came along a

YAWL

KETCH

SCHOONER-GAFF FORESAIL

Classic sailboat rigs.

CATBOAT

6

few years ago they brought with them the problem that at high speeds the conventional-type hulls just became too tricky, jumpy and skittish for safety's sake. At 40 miles an hour water pressure is so great that most would be riding on about one square yard of the after portion of the bottom, and that just isn't enough contact with the water to afford good dynamic and directional stability, control, and good riding. The powered catamarans' wide beam gives greater stability since there's more contact with the water. For this reason they're excellent hulls for the larger outboard motors and are a distinct contribution to safe boating. At present both catamarans and trimarans are essentially boats for high horsepower. They are not, as yet, good general-purpose or fishing boats. However, future plans of some of the manufacturers, which include cabin cruisers and fishing utilities, may change this.

The exceptional speeds available to sailboats of a twin-hull, catamaran configuration have been known from early times in Polynesia, but recently interest in them has increased tremendously, especially so since a recent one-of-a-kind regatta sponsored by *Yachting* Magazine. In a fleet of forty boats, including the newest and fastest of the single-hulled planing boats, catamarans came in first, second, fourth, and seventh. The winner (which in five races took four firsts and one second) was *Tigercat*, designed by Bob Harris. With Frank MacLear he's designed such fast cats as *Va Vite, Jet Cat, DC 14, Aqua Cat,* and *Tiki.* The partners specialize in assignments where "just a little more speed is required" —which nowadays is likely to mean catamarans. How do sailing catamarans, half as wide as they are long, achieve speeds at which they'd trounce a sleek, narrow-beam 12-meter? There are three reasons: (1) light weight (fiberglass construction, no fixed ballast); (2) great stability for size (the windward hull and the crew's weight on it keep the sail upright to use maximum force of the wind); (3) the twin hulls are so narrow they offer minimum resistance to forward motion. MacLear & Harris also design power catamarans: for the Army Corps of Engineers, for instance, they've designed an aluminum 45-footer to

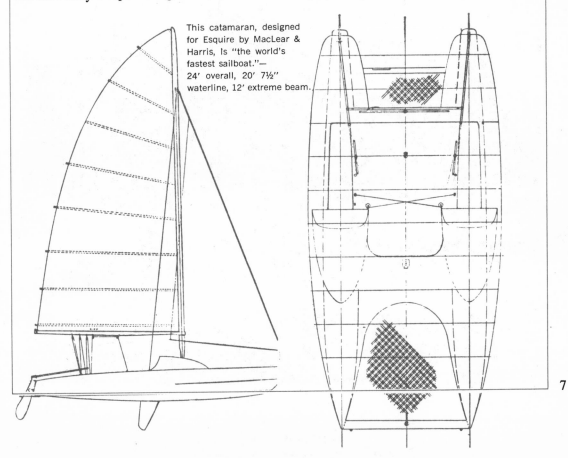

This catamaran, designed for Esquire by MacLear & Harris, Is "the world's fastest sailboat."— 24' overall, 20' 7½' waterline, 12' extreme beam.

7

A 20-foot hydrofoil speedboat, foils submerged, propelled by water jet-stream from stern.

The U.S. Navy's first hydrofoil submarine-chaser with foils wholly submerged.

be used for shallow-water soundings. *Esquire* naturally turned to this company with a request to design for our readers a two-couple, one-design catamaran for yacht-club racing. They came up with "the fastest day-racing sailboat class in existence." You can see it here.

One of the most promising features of the boats of the future is that of hydrofoils. Hydrofoil means "water-wing." And that's just what it is. Like aircraft wings, the foils develop lift from the forward motion of the craft, at cruising speeds, raising the hull completely out of the water. And that creates a whole series of fantastic advantages over conventional displacement boats: Hull friction is reduced from 100% to around 6%. Speed is enormously increased. Fuel costs drop dramatically. Distance traveled per tankful of fuel is greatly lengthened. And riding characteristics are vastly improved, providing much smoother passage. Hydrofoil boats are extremely maneuverable...even at high speeds, and take white water and the rough chop of harbors and bays beautifully...maintaining their high speeds under conditions that would force conventional boats to reduce speed drastically.

This revolutionary new advance is no Johnny-come-lately. As far back as 1919, Alexander Graham Bell (of all people) produced and "flew" the DH-4, most successful of the early models. And years earlier, the Wright Brothers tried their hands at "boat that flies," even before they turned to the experiments that led to the invention of the airplane. Other pioneering efforts were made in Italy. All through the first half of the 20th century, inventors continued to perfect hydrofoil craft. Hydrofoil passenger ferries and transports are currently in regular operation in: The United States, Italy, Switzerland, Germany, Norway, Yugoslavia, Venezuela, Japan, France, Greece, Denmark, The Caribbean, Sweden, Israel, Sicily, The Philippines and Hong Kong. A *few* pleasure cruisers and runabouts are now available with foils, but the principle is still in the experimental stage.

Current foil systems use conventional engines—either gasoline or Diesel powered. Even outboard motors are used on some of the present-day foil runabouts. In most current submerged systems, the power is transmitted mechanically down the foil strut to propellers on the foils. The distance the power is to be transmitted increases as the size of the craft increases, making the design and fabrication of the transmission system increasingly difficult. As an alternative, some manufacturers are developing a water-pump system. Water is taken in by a scoop built into the rear foil, goes up to the foil strut and into a centrifugal pump. With an engine supply power, the water is then pumped out through a nozzle into the air behind the craft. The system, operating under the same principle as an aircraft jet engine, propels the boat.

As a matter of fact, in the smallboat field class, a number of them are powered with water jets. Today such boats are excellent in shallow water areas or where conventional propellers would endanger swimmers and skiers. With no prop spinning below the hull, a skipper using care can ease alongside a fallen skier to get him back aboard. Steering, particularly in reverse, used to be a problem but jet engineers have corrected it. Someday they may also find a way to keep show-off owners from trying to run the boats over dry land; while true that the water jets skim easily over submerged logs and shallows, they still can't climb stone walls and reefs.

COLLECTING ANTIQUE BOATS
In any age which has a pronounced cult of the new, there will be people who insist, and

sometimes insist too much, on the old. They are the conservative of manners, sleeping in trundle beds, shaving with strop razors and smoking Melachrinos or Virginia Rounds. No doubt they make their living as research chemists, discovering startling new bacteria, or as advertising men, persuading the public that new Dizz washes faster, whiter (sic) and so forth; but often they claim the best film they have seen is a faded, flickering print of Tillie Losch in *The Desert Song,* and the car they dream of driving is a 1927 57-C supercharged Bugatti, which did six miles to the gallon and for which most parts would have to be handmade. On the other hand they work in and support a system that creates the quick, the cheap, the mass-produced; on the other, they admire the slow, the expensive, and the particular—objects that were made before meretricious terms like custom-crafted and personalized became a part of the huckster's vocabulary. Indeed, whatever the anti-contemporary fashion of the moment, whether for Stanley Steamers or Hepplewhite chairs, many men have their private refuge in the past. For an increasing number of people, there is no lure like that of old boats.

As antique boat expert, Anthony C. Bailey, tells us, the old boats which arouse enthusiasm today are not, generally speaking, old racing yachts, designed to an ever-changing rule, often out-dated a few years after their launching, and so extreme, expensive and unusuable for anything but racing that before long they were abandoned, their gear removed and their lead keels melted down. Those old boats which have endured and demand allegiance are workboats—pilot boats, fishing vessels, lifeboats, sailing ferries. Boat design is greatly affected by local custom, by the water to be sailed in, and by the temperament and nationality of the designers, builders and sailors. In any country that has a lot to do with the sea, specific types evolved. In the shallow, tidal waters of Holland the apple-bowed and flat-bottomed Dutch leeboard boats, carriers of disproportionately huge cargoes, in the design of whose hulls and sail-plans hardly a straight line could be seen—a sailor's rebuttal to the prevailing flat, linear Dutch landscape. In the stormy waters of the English West Country, the Bristol Channel pilot cutter developed as a plumb-stem, deep-draft vessel which, sailed by two men, could race out to meet incoming ships in heavy weather, remain hove to for days on end, and then be sailed home alone by one man, who—to get the pilot's heavy rowboat back aboard single-handed—would make it fast to the end of his long boom and jibe the boom over (a feat to strike terror into any modern yachtsman who dwells on it). Along the geographically various coast of North America innumerable types of craft were built, and in their heyday, before the introduction of the gasoline engine, it seemed that every little harbor and creek had its own brand of boat. One extreme of the range perhaps was the Cheapeake bugeye, a lean, skinny, ketch-rigged craft made to fish and carry cargo in the thin bay waters; they had raked masts, cheap, canoe-like hulls, and names like *Lola E. Bennett* and *The Brown, Smith & Jones,* the latter the very fast oyster-policing agency's boat. (Can you hear the cry going up on an oyster pirate: "Watch out, here comes the *Brown, Smith & Jones!*"?) At the other extreme, up north in New England, was the Gloucester fishing schooner, a hefty, solid, deep-draft boat, meant to go to sea, stay on the Grand Banks, and then make a fast trip home with the catch.

Old-Boat enthusiasts, like old boats, tend to be found all around the coast. One area, however, in which they are particularly strong is eastern Connecticut around Noank, Mystic and Stonington, all homes of considerable fishing fleets in the Seventies and Eighties of the nineteenth century and still towns in which fishing, sailing and boatbuilding are taken seriously.

On the Mystic River, on the site of a shipyard where clippers once went down the ways, stands the seaport of the Marine Historical Association. There, among many other smaller boats that have been saved from extinction and human forgetfulness, the *Joseph Conrad* (said to be the last full-rigged ship to round Cape Horn) and the *Charles W. Morgan*, a square-rigged whaling barque built in 1841, are preserved—restored as they were in their prime. In his study behind a ship-wright's workshop, we talked one day with Captain James Kleinschmidt, a former merchant-marine skipper, an assistant curator and the marine maintenance superintendent of the seaport, who helped restore many of its boats.

"What you realize after a while," Captain Kleinschmidt said, "is that we haven't come very far in the last hundred years. Maybe we know more about engines and electronics, but not what makes a boat seaworthy. One can learn a lot about that by looking at old boats. You see, they were never a product of slide rules and naval architects. Their builders made half-models—they had to be artists—and the lines of the boat were taken off the models. Moreover, there was a process of continual modification over the years, as things were changed here and there, as sailors and fishermen suggested improvements, and by the time the boat was through as a working craft it was just about perfection in its particular job. Among boats, as among living creatures, the fittest survived."

Captain Kleinschmidt owns a now extinct type, a Kingston, Massachusetts, lobster boat, a twenty-one foot cat-ketch-rigged centerboarder, which he restored. "I suspect I enjoyed rebuilding her more than I do sailing her," he said, "although it tickles me when I sail right through a bunch of modern jib-headed racing machines twice her size. Those old boats had to be fast, because the first man back to market got the best price. They were also seaworthy for two men to handle while they worked. I had to put a new keel in her, and new planks, but she was beautifully built. I have yet to see an old boat—at least fifty years old—which wasn't put together the way it should have been. Fastenings might have crumbled, and the wood might have rotted, but she would be well made. The builder, of course, was close to the men who used her—you don't slap a boat together for people you know and who are going to depend for their lives and their livelihood on the craft."

As with old cars, old furniture and old castles, people easily get carried from enthusiasm into fanaticism, and the results are not always sound. It seems to be a good rule that, if you scale down a large old yacht to build a new small old yacht, you shouldn't reduce it by more than twenty-five per cent if you expect the finished product to behave properly. Nor should one expect to have a perfect boat for inshore racing if one acquires, say, a Maine pinkie, whose bluff bows were designed to keep her decks well above water when anchored, at the end of fathoms of hemp hawser, on the Grand Banks in a gale. The high poop of the *Mayflower* was a bugbear going to windward, but was marvelous in making the ship lie ahull, stripped of all sail, in a fierce storm; most of the seemingly eccentric features of old boats had a definite purpose and, in restoring an original or building a replica, these should not be ignored. Again, in copying an antique design, careful choice should be made among the originals. The urge for speed to make port and thus to get high salt prices was the direct cause for giving clippers such fine lines forward and aft that several sailed themselves right to the bottom. Some fishing boats were overdeveloped in this way, as were the captain's gigs carried by U.S. Navy ships. Competition for the fastest gig in port became so rife that the Navy was forced to standardize these craft so that they weren't rendered too fast and unseaworthy.

A final cautionary note is to be found in a recent design of a small antique schooner. For modern convenience the rigging was made fast with turnbuckles; for antiquey looks the turnbuckles were hidden behind dummy lanyards and deadeyes—something to make Joshua Slocum turn over in his watery grave. Slocum might be called the first old-boat buff, since he was not only the first person to sail alone around the world, but did so in a hybrid vessel that had apparently been a Delaware oyster boat built on the lines of a North Sea fisherman. When Slocum first saw her, in a Massachusetts field in 1892, she was already some hundred years old and dilapidated. He set to work rebuilding her, and soon found that he had more of a new boat than an old one. To date, at least sixteen copies of the *Spray*, as Slocum called his ship, have been built, two of them for American Army officers. *Spray* cost the captain $553.62 and thirteen months of his own labor, which, even if one multiplied the price by ten for the same effort today, would still be cheaper than the $45,000 one man paid for a *Spray* replica two years ago (the price included a 40-h.p. diesel, and Monel and silicone bronze fastenings, which Slocum did without).

A less expensive investment in the past could be made by acquiring a beamy eighteen-foot catboat, such as those G. Frank Carter in East Quogue, Long Island, built for many years until his death a few years ago at the age of ninety-four; or a thirty-four-foot Chesapeake skipjack, which one can buy for $7,000. However, to get the full pleasure out of this kind of thing, old-boat enthusiasts naturally believe one should spend several years combing the fields, backyards and backwaters for a suitable antique wreck, and then take another few years to rebuild it plank by plank and nail by nail.

The antique boat designs can help in the construction of better looking modern craft. Virgil M. Exner, well-known industrial designer, claims that current fashion of cruiser design and styling seems to indicate a very strong trend toward the present day philosophy of automotive styling. This system of style change is too often one of change for the sake of change...and often a "forced" modernism...just to be different. Because of a much more limited volume, this trend is less marked in cruiser and small yacht design than in the motor car industry. However, a pseudo-streamlined flavor is quite apparent in the popular lines of the larger present day boat manufacturers. While this may be a natural trend in the smaller cruisers, we do not see the need or desirability of carrying a non-

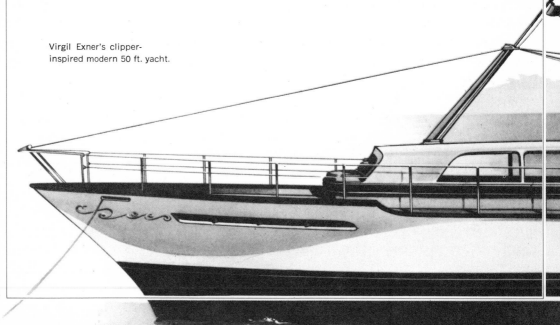

Virgil Exner's clipper-inspired modern 50 ft. yacht.

nautical or "product design" technique into the styling of the larger low volume cruisers and small yacht categories. High volume, low cost, small cruisers need a certain degree of planned obsolescence to feed the growth of their great market potential. This approach need not apply in the small yacht field. These owners want something quite different. They will look for a strong nautical flavor in their boats...both in exterior lines, and in interior treatments. They will abhor the too-softly moulded "product" look. They will strongly criticize a forced so-called modern concept...just to look different.

Mr. Exner believes that present and future large cruiser styles can look fresh, modern, and definitely sea-going if we take a perceptive look at the past. The grace and elegance of countless ships of past centuries have inspired the writer, the poet, the artist, and the romanticist. There should be many sources of inspiration for the modern yacht designer in this back log of great ships. To emphasize his point, he selected the design of the schooner shown here as an example. Although in some respects, similar to the Clipper ships, these schooners were usually somewhat smaller and built in some numbers in the late nineteenth and early twentieth centuries. The very graceful sheer line of these beautiful vessels provides the inspiration for a fresh, new line. However, of even greater importance to style is the "Clipper" type stem with classic decoration. The two cruisers—both approximately 50 feet overall—were designed from the inspiration of the old schooner. Mr. Exner tried to capture some of the nautical appeal of this older ship and has tried to translate this feeling into the present day owners' requirements. While some may feel these designs are too "advanced," they still have a marked traditional origin. For example, the modern sedan cruiser is inspired partly by the decorative Clipper bow of the older vessel. An unusual transom treatment is also inspired by the rear "overhang" often found on older ships. The other cruiser shows an interesting aft cabin treatment. The stern illustrates the ocean racer influence along with "doghouse" cabin treatment in common use in all types of sailing vessels for many centuries.

So much for the giant yachts of yesteryear, boats of the future, and those people who collect antique vessels—let's go about the task of helping you to have more fun aboard your yacht—regardless of size—as well as being a better yachtsman.

CHAPTER TWO:
THE ART
OF SAFE
YACHTSMANSHIP

The comprehensive art of good yachtsmanship embraces many subjects. Perhaps the first and most important is a knowledge of what constitutes the proper equipment for your yacht. This includes not only the equipment required by United States Coast Guard regulations, which specify what equipment *must* be carried, but also a consideration of other equipment without which your yacht cannot be properly, efficiently, and safely operated. Safety is synonymous with good seamanship and yachtsmanship. Remember that as a good yachtsman, your first responsibility is to the safety of your yacht and her crew.

EQUIPMENT REQUIREMENTS

If your yacht operates on any body of water classed as "navigable" by the Federal government, you must comply with equipment regulations of the Motorboat Act of 1940. "Navigable water" is any body of water which is a part of the Atlantic or Pacific Oceans, the Gulf of Mexico, the Great Lakes, and all rivers and their tributaries, upstream to the first lockless dam, which empty into these waters. The navigable waters of the United States also include waterways that are navigable in fact and are inter-state in nature regardless of direct connection with the oceans or the Great Lakes. (Lake Tahoe is an example of this.) When on navigable waters, any Coast Guard patrol vessel or craft may stop you at any time and come aboard to see if you're properly equipped in accordance with Federal law. The chart right shows the "minimum" that must be carried by motorboats up to 65 feet. (Boats without engines on board do not fall under the Motorboat Act, but it is highly recommended that they carry the equipment listed right applicable to their craft. Auxiliary sailboats and sailboats with outboard motors are considered motorboats according to this Act.)

Courtesy Motorboat Examination

MINIMUM REQUIRED EQUIPMENT				
Equipment	Class A (Less than 16 feet)	Class 1 (16 feet to less than 26 feet)	Class 2 (26 feet to less than 40 feet)	Class 3 (40 feet to not more than 65 feet)
BACK-FIRE FLAME ARRESTOR	One approved device on each carburetor of all gasoline engines installed after April 25, 1940, except outboard motors.			
VENTILATION	At least two ventilators fitted with cowls or their equivalent for the purpose of properly and efficiently ventilating the bilges of every engine and fuel-tank compartment of boats constructed or decked over after April 25, 1940, using gasoline or other fuel of a flashpoint less than 110° F.			
BELL	None.*	None.*	One, which when struck, produces a clear, bell-like tone of full round characteristics.	
LIFESAVING DEVICES	One approved life preserver, buoyant vest, ring buoy, or buoyant cushion for each person on board.			One approved life preserver or ring buoy for each person on board.
WHISTLE	None.*	One hand, mouth, or power operated, audible at least ½ mile.	One hand or power operated, audible at least 1 mile.	One power operated, audible at least 1 mile.
FIRE EXTINGUISHER— PORTABLE				
When NO fixed fire extinguishing system is installed in machinery space(s).	At least One B-I type approved hand portable fire extinguisher.		At least Two B-I type approved hand portable fire extinguishers; OR At least One B-II type approved hand portable fire extinguisher.	At least Three B-I type approved hand portable fire extinguishers; OR At least One B-I type Plus One B-II type approved hand portable fire extinguisher.
When fixed fire extinguishing system is installed in machinery space(s).	None.	None.	At least One B-I type approved hand portable fire extinguisher.	At least Two B-I type approved hand portable fire extinguishers; OR At least One B-II type approved hand portable fire extinguisher.
	B-I Type Approved Hand Portable Fire Extinguishers contain: Foam, 1¼ up to 2½ gallons; or Carbon Dioxide, 4 up to 15 pounds; or Dry Chemical, 2 up to 10 pounds; or Vaporizing Liquid, 1 quart.** B-II Type Approved Hand Portable Fire Extinguishers contain: Foam, 2½ gallons; or Carbon Dioxide, 15 pounds; or Dry Chemical, 10 up to 20 pounds.			

*NOTE—Not required by the Motorboat Act of 1940; however, the "Rules of the Road" require these vessels to sound proper signals.
**NOTE—Toxic vaporizing-liquid type fire extinguishers, such as those containing carbon tetrachloride or chlorobromomethane, are not accepted as required approved extinguishers on uninspected vessels (private pleasure craft).

Good yachtsmen also take advantage of the Courtesy Motorboat Examination. This examination offers you the opportunity to have your vessel given a free safety check by a qualified member of the Coast Guard Auxiliary. The special sticker (Courtesy Decal) is awarded to the boat meeting the Federal requirements and certain safety practices recommended by the Auxiliary. The Coast Guard and most State authorities honor the decal and will normally refrain from making any official inspection unless there is an obvious violation of law. In addition to the legal requirements, below are the items the Auxiliary will check in making their examination at *your request*. When completed, the checkoff list is given to you. No copy is retained by the examiner.

Galley stove of recommended type
Galley stove installed as recommended
Fuel tank filler pipe tight to deck plate
Fuel tank filler pipe outside of coaming or within self-bailing cockpit
Fuel tank vents installed leading outboard

Lifesaving devices easily accessible
Fire extinguishers easily accessible
Bilges clean and free from oil and grease
Electrical installation satisfactory
General vessel condition satisfactory
Anchor and sufficient line

In addition to the previously mentioned legally required and officially recommended pieces of gear, the following items of equipment are advisable to have aboard, depending on the size, location, and use of your yacht:

Anchors (1 light, 1 heavy)
Anchor chain or line (long)
Barometer
Bilge pumps
Binoculars
Boat hook
Chamois
Coast pilot
Compass
Course protractor, or
   Parallel rules
Deck swab and bucket
Deviation table
Direction finder, radio (RFD)
Distress signals:
   Flares
   Flashlight
   Signalling mirror
   Smoke signals
   Water dye markers
Dividers

Emergency rations and water
Fenders
First aid kit and manual
Gasoline vapor detector
Heaving line (100 feet)
Insect repellent
Lantern
Lead line (for soundings)
Local charts
Light list
Megaphone
Mooring lines
Motor crank handle
Motor oil and grease (extra)
Nails, screws, bolts, pins,
   washers, wire, tape
Patent log
Pelorus
Radio, portable
Radio telephone
Ring buoys

R. P. M. table
Searchlight
Spare batteries
Spare propeller
Sun glasses
Sunburn lotion
Sunburn preventive
Spare parts:
   Coil
   Condenser
   Distributor head
   Distributor points
   Distributor rotor
   Fuel pump repair
     kit
   Fuses
   Light bulbs
   Spark plugs
Tools
Water pump

RULES OF THE ROAD

A good yachtsman is, in many ways, like a very good automobile driver. He knows the traffic laws (in this case, the Rules of the Road) and obeys them. Therefore, always be sure you know the Rules of the Road, and follow them. It's also wise to review them frequently during the yachting season.

The Rules of the Road are primarily designed to prevent collisions. However, they apply at other times and not only when this danger exists. The Rules additionally specify lights and various signals. They are in effect when the craft is underway; this means any situation where the vessel is free to move; and also when at anchor, or aground, certain signals are prescribed. In the underway conditions the craft having the right-of-way is usually called the *privileged vessel* and is required to hold her course, unless danger of collision is imminent; whereas the other craft is the *burdened vessel* with no rights and is required to keep out of the way. A point to remember is that a good skipper should be always on constant look-out; if he sees that he is on a collision course with another vessel. he will take appropriate action before the danger of collision exists. In other words, although the vessel which has the right of way is obligated by these rules to maintain its course and speed, this does *not* imply that you should keep on your course when you

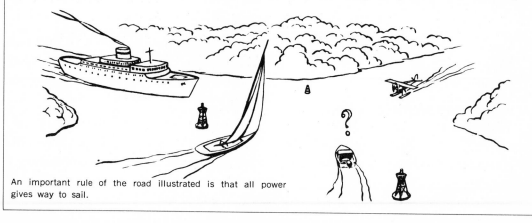

An important rule of the road illustrated is that all power gives way to sail.

have right-of-way to the point of collision with another craft. There may be instances where the other skipper just hasn't seen you, and insisting on your right-of-way could lead to serious consequences. Also, a large vessel usually doesn't have the agility or the stopping power of your boat. It's good to remember the following old verse:

> Here lies the body of Michael O'Day
> Who died maintaining his right-of-way.
> He was right—dead right—as he sailed along,
> But he's just as dead as if he'd been wrong.

While the main provisions of the Rules are similar everywhere, they differ slightly for the high seas, inland waters, the Great Lakes, and certain rivers, as set forth in the following Coast Guard pamphlets:

> CG-169, Rules of the Road, International–Inland.
> CG-172, Rules of the Road, Great Lakes.
> CG-184, Rules of the Road, Western Rivers. (Note: This doesn't mean rivers on the Pacific Coast, but applies to the Mississippi River and tributaries, the Atchafalaya River, and the Red River of the North.)

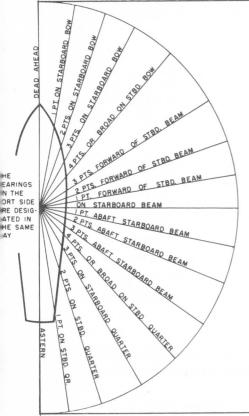

The proper way in which bearings and directions are named on shipboard. The unit is the "point" which is 1/32 of a complete circle or 1/16 of the angular distance from dead ahead to dead astern. Each point has a definite name which is dependent upon the angular distance and the particular direction from the bow, the beam, and the stern of the vessel. The designation—starboard or port—is employed to indicate to which side of the vessel it refers. The "danger zone" is from dead ahead to two points abaft the starboard beam.

You can get copies of these publications without charge from your local Coast Guard office, or from the United States Coast Guard, Washington 25, D.C. But, since most yachts navigate International–Inland Waters, we'll use this booklet (CG-169) as a starting point.

FOR VESSELS UNDER POWER

Vessels under power—either outboard or inboard—must give up the right-of-way to craft not under power—boats under sail or manual operation, except in the not very likely possibility of a craft under sail or oars overtaking one under power. A sailboat using her auxiliary engine is considered a power boat and must follow the Rules of the Road for vessels under power.

Meeting Head and Head or Nearly So

When two vessels approach each other head on, or nearly so, each steers to starboard (bears right, that is) so as to pass port side (left) to port side. Show that you intend to go to the right by swinging the bow of your yacht in that direction—even more than necessary. The proper signal is one blast from either boat, to be answered by one blast from the other.

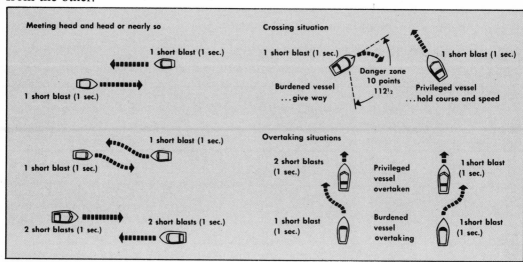

It is the duty of boats meeting head and head or nearly so to pass on the port side of each other as just stated; however, when the courses of these vessels are so far on the starboard of each other and not in danger of meeting head on, either craft can give two short and distinct blasts of her whistle or horn which the other should answer promptly by two similar blasts of her whistle or horn, and they then may pass on the starboard side of each other. (A short blast is approximately one second in duration, while a long blast should last from eight to ten seconds. A four to six second signal represents a prolonged blast.)

In rivers connecting the Great Lakes and on the Western Rivers, because of the strong currents, the vessel going down-stream, or down-current, has the right-of-way over a boat going against the current. That is because it is easier to control a craft going against the current than it is to steer one being carried along by the current.

Crossing Situation

A power boat which has another in her so-called "danger zone" (from dead ahead to two points abaft the starboard beam—roughly translated, this means coming from your right) must give way to her by altering course to go under her stern, by slowing down, or, if necessary, stopping or reversing. By the same token, if you have a craft approaching your port side (coming from your left) you have the right-of-way. The vessel having the right-of-way may sound one blast on her horn or whistle. The other craft should slow down and/or turn and pass behind. *Note:* In the crossing situation, the following signals (in every case one short blast) are incorporated into the Rules:

	Privileged	Burdened
Inland	Optional	——
Great Lakes	Required	Required
Western Rivers	——	——

If for any reason the situation is such as to prevent immediate compliance with each other's signals, the misunderstanding or objections should be made apparent by blowing the danger signal (four or more short and rapid blasts). Both vessels should stop and back off if necessary, until the signals for passing with safety are made and understood.

On Western Rivers, the descending vessel has the privilege of choosing the side on which to pass, but must signify specific intentions in time to avoid embarrassing the ascending vessel. Actually on Western Rivers, there is no blanket privilege extended to the descending vessel in a crossing situation, *except* where the descending vessel has a vessel in tow. Then she will sound three short blasts to signify she has right of way and will maintain it.

Overtaking

When one vessel is overtaking another, the one doing the overtaking must keep clear of the one being overtaken. However, if you are in a narrow channel and are being overtaken by a larger, deep-draft vessel, it will be easier for you in the smaller craft to swing to the side of the channel and let the big gal pass you in the deep water. This is one of the situations in which you don't always insist on your right-of-way. If you want to overtake another boat on her starboard side, give one signal blast with your horn or whistle. Then, wait for her skipper's answering signal of one blast before passing. The same procedure is followed for overtaking on the port side of another boat except that two signal blasts must be given and returned. In either case, if the other skipper considers it unsafe for you to overtake, he should give the danger signal of four or more blasts. Don't overtake him then until he gives either the one-blast signal for passing on his right-hand side or the two-blast signal for passing on his left-hand side. The vessel ahead should never attempt to cross the bow or crowd upon the course of the overtaking craft. *Note:* Four or more short blasts is the danger signal under Inland and Western Rivers Rules. However, five or more blasts is the Great Lakes danger signal.

In Narrow Channels or Canals

When operating a power yacht in narrow or restricted channels, always keep to the starboard (right) side of the channel. When rounding a sharp bend, keep your craft to the right and signal your approach by sounding your whistle, or horn, one long blast. This signal is to be answered by one long blast by any approaching vessel beyond the curve. The usual signals for passing should then be exchanged. On Western Rivers the bend signal is three blasts.

On Western Rivers, most large commercial vessels flash an amber colored light in synchronization with their whistle signals to aid in identification. These whistle lights are required on Western Rivers above Baton Rouge, Louisiana, for all vessels except pleasure boats under 65 feet and all commercial craft under 26 feet.

Leaving Slips, Wharves, Docks, and Piers

Vessels coming out of slips into open, or leaving berths at piers and wharves, have no rights until they are entirely clear. Therefore, they proceed with caution and at low speed. When leaving a slip, float, or pier, always give one long blast on your horn or whistle, regardless of whether you are backing out or running ahead. This is the warning signal for any nearby boats that you are coming out. When leaving dock or berth on Western Rivers, sound three short blasts in lieu of one long blast.

Fishing and other Special Vessels

Pleasure craft should keep clear of vessels fishing with lines or nets or trawls. However, this right-of-way of fishing craft doesn't carry with it the privilege of obstructing fairways or channels used by other vessels. Fishing vessels should display a basket to indicate their occupation.

Although under certain circumstances power vessels have the right-of-way over tugs with barges in tow, it is not only good manners but sound yachtsmanship to yield the right-of-way because your smaller craft is a good deal more maneuverable than a string of barges.

A certain degree of caution should be exercised, when sailing around dredges or other similar floating work plants in a channel. Underwater hoses, lines, or equipment may endanger your own boat and your wash may interfere with the work being done, or might even cause an accident. A long blast of the whistle should be blown to indicate your intention to pass; and the dredge should indicate the side you should pass by, with the same whistle signals as are employed by boats underway. If the channel isn't clear, the dredge should sound the danger signal of four or more blasts; and in such a case you should slow down or completely stop until further signal is given by the dredge. In passing, slow down, and within 200 feet of the dredge, don't exceed five miles per hour. If you should have to pass over any lines or hoses take the engine out of gear to avoid tangling them in your propeller.

Coast Guard craft that are servicing or repairing an aid to navigation should be given a wide berth, and passing boats should reduce speed as necessary to insure the safety of both vessels—slowing to five miles per hour or less when within 200 feet of the operation. During daylight hours, the Coast Guard vessel, while on such missions, may display vertically two orange and white vertically striped balls at the yardarm, and at night, two red lights in a vertical line.

Special Western River Situations

Where two rivers come together, the vessel having the other on the left must give the first signal, and neither should try to pass until full agreement has been reached by means of signals.

A vessel descending a river with tow has right-of-way over a power craft crossing the river, regardless of which side she comes from. The descending vessel should give a signal of three blasts, indicating her intention to cross the bow of the other. The crossing vessel should reply with three blasts and stop or turn to pass astern of the other.

In narrow channels, an ascending vessel should slow down or stop, and lie close to the side of the channel until a descending craft has passed. At a bridge, if the skipper of a descending vessel believes it dangerous for an ascending boat to pass, he should indicate this by sounding the danger signal. The ascending vessel should answer with the same signal, and slow down or stop below the span until it is clear.

The skipper of a vessel descending or ascending the river should not attempt to cross when another descending or ascending craft is so near that it would be possible for a collision to occur.

FOR VESSELS UNDER SAIL

Sailboats always have the right-of-way over powerboats with the exception of when they are overtaking power craft. Sailboats must also keep clear of fishing vessels with lines, nets, or trawls. It is common courtesy of powerboat skippers, when they must pass a vessel under sail, to do so slowly and on the leeward side (the side on which she is carrying her main boom) so as to cause the least possible disturbance from the power craft's wake.

The right of way between sailboats depends upon the direction they are sailing with respect to the wind. A sailboat that is sailing into the wind has the right-of-way over boats that are sailing free or with the wind.

When two boats are sailing into the wind on opposite tacks, the one with the wind has the right-of-way over boats that are sailing free or with the wind.

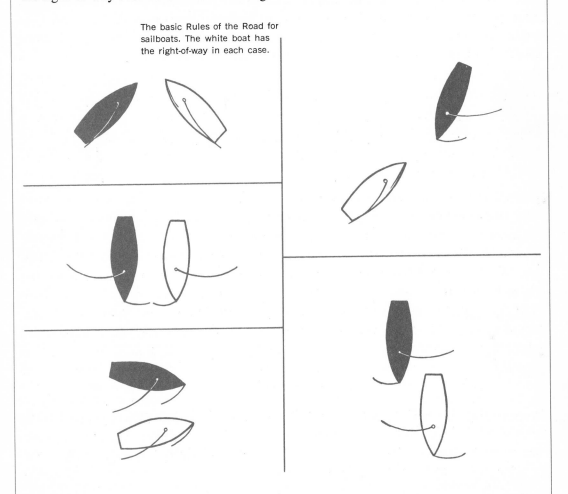

The basic Rules of the Road for sailboats. The white boat has the right-of-way in each case.

When two boats are running free on opposite tacks, the one with the wind coming in over the starboard side has the right-of-way.

When two boats are sailing with the wind, the downwind boat has right-of-way. The reason for this rule is that it is generally difficult for the leeward craft to work up to windward, but the windward boat can run down to leeward easily and so has greater freedom of action.

Whichever the point of sailing the overtaking sailboat must keep clear of the other vessel. Whistle signals are not exchanged between sailboats, or between power and sailboats. Everyone concerned should know well enough what to do to make signalling with sailboats unnecessary.

ACCIDENTS

With any vessel, in cases of collision, capsize, fire or other serious accident, it is the duty of yachtsmen to stand by and render all possible assistance. It is also a tradition as old as the sea itself that mariners always go to the aid of those in distress. The good skipper is always ready and willing to offer a tow, or loan gasoline to a fellow boatman who has suffered an engine breakdown or run'out of fuel. Boats should *not* leave the scene of an accident. In assisting, you are not expected to endanger your craft or take unnecessary chances. You must also give the name of your boat and her port when requested.

When boats are involved in a marine casualty or accident to hull or machinery, equipment, crew, or any persons or when any persons are injured or any lives are lost, immediate notice thereof must be forwarded to the nearest local or district office of the United States Coast Guard, or the United States Cost Guard Headquarters, Washington 25, D.C.

NAVIGATION LIGHTS

Since most of our yachting is done during the daylight hours, we often don't bother to study navigation lights. And if you can't "read" these lights, you should stick to daytime yachting. But, to be a good yachtsman and a responsible skipper, you should know the light requirements for your yacht when operating on Inland or International waters, plus how to "read" lights on craft of all sizes.

NAVIGATION LIGHT REQUIREMENTS

Navigational lights must be displayed while under way from sunset to sunrise. The term "underway," as previously stated, denotes not at anchor or dock, thus vessels trolling or drifting with power off are underway and must show the normal running lights. However, there are two sets of rules for navigation: *Option 1* covers Inland or Federal waters, while *Option 2* is for International waters or the high seas. On yachts which cruise both Federal waters (all navigable of the United States) and high seas, the International rules for the high seas may be followed when navigating inland waters. Therefore, since you're subject to International rules when you move out of a harbor or channel into the ocean (outer-most buoy or other aid to navigation is usually the boundary line between Federal and International waters) your yacht had better carry International running lights.

Navigation light regulations for all vessels use the "point" (abbreviated to "pt.") system. This term is based on the understanding that a light with a completely circular globe—which can be seen from every angle—is said to be a 32-pt. light. Therefore, the globe of a 10-pt. light covers $^{10}/_{32}$nds or $^{5}/_{16}$ths of a circle; a 12-pt. light, $^{12}/_{32}$nds or $^{3}/_{8}$ths of a circle; and a 20-pt. light, $^{20}/_{32}$nds or $^{5}/_{8}$ths of a circle.

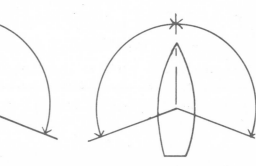

32 POINT LIGHT   **I0 POINT LIGHT**   **20 POINT LIGHT**

The arc covered by various lights employed aflpat. The 32-point white stern light shows all around the horizon; the white bow light ahead through 20-points (Ten points each side) and the colored side lights 10 points on their respective sides.

MOTORBOATS: INBOARDS, OUTBOARDS, AND AUXILIARIES		
Under power alone	**Auxiliaries under sail and power**	**Auxiliaries under sail alone**

INLAND RULES. — These lights may be shown only on inland waters, western rivers, and Great Lakes.[1]

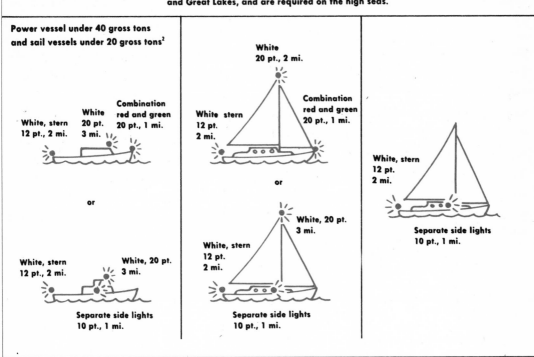

Under 26 feet

White, aft all around 32 pt., 2 mi.   Combination red and green 20 pt., 1 mi.

White, aft all around 32 pt. 2 mi.   Combination red and green 20 pt. 1 mi.

White, stern 12 pt. 2 mi.   Combination red and green 20 pt., 1 mi.

26 feet or over, but not more than 65 feet

White, aft all around 32 pt., 2 mi.   White 20 pt., 2 mi.

White, aft all around 32 pt. 2 mi.   White forward 20 pt. 2 mi.

White, stern 12 pt. 2 mi.

Separate side lights 10 pt., 1 mi.

Separate side lights 10 pt., 1 mi.

Separate side lights 10 pt., 1 mi.

INTERNATIONAL RULES. — Lights under International Rules may be shown on Inland Waters, Western Rivers, and Great Lakes, and are required on the high seas.

Power vessel under 40 gross tons and sail vessels under 20 gross tons[2]

White, stern 12 pt., 2 mi.   White 20 pt. 3 mi.   Combination red and green 20 pt., 1 mi.

White 20 pt., 2 mi.

White, stern 12 pt. 2 mi.   Combination red and green 20 pt., 1 mi.

White, stern 12 pt. 2 mi.

or

or

White, stern 12 pt., 2 mi.   White, 20 pt. 3 mi.

White, stern 12 pt. 2 mi.   White, 20 pt. 3 mi.

Separate side lights 10 pt., 1 mi.

Separate side lights 10 pt., 1 mi.

Separate side lights 10 pt., 1 mi.

[1] A motorboat under sail alone on the Great Lakes is not required to display a stern light. All motorboats under sail alone must on approach of another vessel display a white light in the direction of the approaching vessel.

[2] Under International Rules powerboats of 40 gross tons or over must carry separate sidelights, visible 2 miles, and a 20-point white light visible 5 miles. Sailing boats of 20 gross tons or over must carry separate sidelights, visible 2 miles. Those less than 20 gross tons may use a combination lantern, if under sail alone.

Lights for the various pleasure craft are illustrated here. As you'll note, motorboats under 26 feet in length, operating under Option 1 (Federal Waters), must have a single red-and-green combination bow light, shining 10 points on each of the color sides (red on port, green on starboard), plus a white light aft, visible all around the horizon. Motorboats ranging from 26 through 65 feet must have a white bowlight, visible only from the beam forward, screened red and green sidelights, and an all-around white light set higher than the others on the aft section of the cabin top. On Federal waters, sailboats alone show a red-green combination light forward (or screened sidelights on boats from 26 to 65 feet long), and a white light in the stern as nearly as practicable the same height as the sidelights, visible only from astern (actually 12 points). (On the Great Lakes, sailboats when under sail are not required to display a stern light, but such craft should show a flare-up white or electric torch [a small spotlight flashed on a sail will do] in the proper quarter astern when approached or being overtaken.) Auxiliary sailboats up to 26 feet, under power, must display a white light aft, showing all around the horizon, in addition to the combination red-and-green at the bow. Larger auxiliaries must display separate port and starboard sidelights, and white light aft and on the bow. Small open boats, such as dinghies under oars, should carry a lantern or flashlight which can be shown when necessary to avoid collision.

On International waters (Option 2), sailboats under 40 gross tons must have red and green sidelights (or a red-green combination light forward if under 20 gross tons) and a white light in the stern, visible only from aft, at the same height as the combination or side lights. The same applies for powerboats (including auxiliary sailboats under power) under 40 gross tons, with the addition of an elevated white forward light visible from ahead for a distance of three miles.

White-all-around or 32-pt. anchor lights must be displayed in the forward part of boats at anchor, unless you're in a special anchorage area that is exempted from this regulation. On all waters the light should be visible for two miles.

Being able to interpret the lights you see around you, of course, is as important as carrying the proper lights. This alone will warn you of danger and whether to turn starboard, turn port, or stop. The following verse is worth committing to memory:

> When all three lights I see ahead,
> I turn to *Starboard* and show my *Red:*
> *Green* to *Green, Red* to *Red,*
> Perfect safety—*Go ahead.*

> But if to *Starboard Red* appear,
> It is my duty to keep clear—
> To act as judgment says is proper:
> To *Port* or *Starboard, Back* or *Stop* her.

> And if upon my *Port* is seen
> A vessel's *Starboard* light of *Green,*
> I hold my course and watch to see
> That *Green* to *Port* keeps clear of me.

> Both in safety and in doubt
> Always keep a good lookout.
> In danger, with no room to turn,
> *Ease* her, *Stop* her, *Go Astern.*

BOAT SECURITY

On a strictly legal plane the responsibility of an owner to maintain his vessel in a seaworthy condition has been defined by federal courts as absolute, continuous, and cannot be delegated. A vessel is seaworthy only when she is sound, adequate in design and construction, properly equipped and provisioned, and manned by a qualified crew so that she can perform her intended service with safety. A boat's continued seaworthiness and hence her relative safety, including the safety of those she carries, is appreciably related to the care and protection provided for her during what may be called her periods of idleness. In the interest of better boating safety, the purpose of this section is to discuss some aspects of protecting and caring for boats during such periods.

During navigating seasons the average boat is in idleness from one week-end to the next. She may be secured to a mooring, dock or float, closed up and left alone. A substantially similar condition may frequently prevail during vacation or week-end cruises for reasonable periods of time. Extreme idleness characterizes the out-of-commission period when she may be laid up afloat, on shore in a shed, or on shore in the open. If a boat is worth having she deserves thoughtful protection and care during these periods. She will make full return in safe pleasure afloat.

FIRE PREVENTION

The greatest hazard about a boat is fire. The chief causes of motor boat fires are: improper design (you should check this before buying), poor maintenance, and careless operation —the latter two being things you had better guard carefully against if you want to continue to be captain of your ship as well as master of your soul.

Fire-prevention safeguards for pleasure craft. (1) Fill pipe—good size, straight—connection at deck tight and labeled—sections separated by hose electrically bonded. (2) Tank vent—from top of tank—of good size—inverted U—bend to prevent intake of water—flame arrester at hull. (3) Tank rigidly secured —holding straps insulated from tank surface. (4) Fuel cutoffs—one at tank accessible from cockpit— one at engine. (5) Flexible feed-line section—separates engine from feed line secured to hull. (6) Carburetor—upturned horn type with integral drip collector (other updraft types require separate self-stripping drip pans)—flame arrester on air intake. (7) Battery—accessible, ventilated location— equipped with protecting cover. (8) Ventilation—two intake and two exhaust duals of equal and large diameter terminating in large cowls or equivalent fittings—exhaust blower installed as high above bilge as possible.

Proper equipment properly installed is the starting point for protection against gasoline fires. The following fire prevention safeguards are recommended for pleasure craft by the Yacht Safety Bureau, Inc., 21 West Street, New York, New York 10006:

1. *Fill Pipe*—good size, straight—connection at deck tight and labeled—sections separated by hose electrically bonded, should extend to within 1″ of tank bottom to prevent spillage.

2. *Tank Vent*—from top of tank—of good size—inverted U-bend to prevent intake of water—flame arrestor at hull.

3. *Tank Rigidly Secured*—holding straps insulated from tank surface.

4. *Fuel Cut-offs*—one at tank accessible from cockpit—one at engine.

5. *Flexible Feed Line Section*—separates engine from feed line secured to hull.

6. *Carburetor*—upturned horn type with integral drip collector (other updraft types require separate self-stripping drip pans)—flame arrestor on air intake.

7. *Battery*—accessible, ventilated location—equipped with protecting cover.

8. *Ventilation*—two intake and two exhaust ducts of equal and large diameter terminating in large cowls or equivalent fittings—exhaust blower installed as high above bilge as possible.

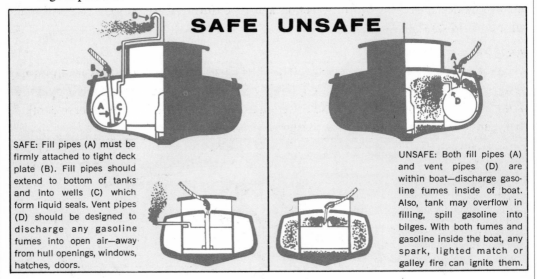

SAFE   **UNSAFE**

SAFE: Fill pipes (A) must be firmly attached to tight deck plate (B). Fill pipes should extend to bottom of tanks and into wells (C) which form liquid seals. Vent pipes (D) should be designed to discharge any gasoline fumes into open air—away from hull openings, windows, hatches, doors.

UNSAFE: Both fill pipes (A) and vent pipes (D) are within boat—discharge gasoline fumes inside of boat. Also, tank may overflow in filling, spill gasoline into bilges. With both fumes and gasoline inside the boat, any spark, lighted match or galley fire can ignite them.

Safe Fueling Procedures

Many boat fires are caused by carelessness in fueling operations. Here are a few common-sense precautions that should always be followed:

1. Fuel up before dark, if possible. Be sure your boat is moored securely.

2. Shut down engines, motors, fans—anything that might remotely cause a spark —and pull the main switch if there is one.

3. Put out that fire in the galley.

4. Forbid all smoking and the striking of matches.

5. Close every last port, window, door, and hatch.

6. Make sure a filled extinguisher is handy.

7. Find out how much fuel you will want and advise the attendant. Don't fill tanks to full capacity—allow at least 2 per cent of the tank contents for air space so that the gasoline can expand. It is important to know your fuel-tank capacity and the cruising radius of that supply. If it is necessary to carry additional gasoline do so only in proper containers, and take special precautions in stowage to prevent the release and accumulation of explosive vapor in confined spaces.

8. Make sure the nozzle of the hose or fuel can makes metal-to-metal contact with the fill pipe and maintains that contact during the entire period of fuel flow. Otherwise, you run the risk of a static electric spark.

9. Avoid any spillage and be sure that no gasoline—nary a drop—gets below decks except inside the fuel tanks.

10. After the refueling operation has been completed, open all ports, hatches, and doors. Allow the boat to air out for at least five minutes. If any fuel spilled, wipe it up. Sniff in bilges and below deck spaces for any smell of gasoline before starting electrical equipment, stove, and so on.

Other Fire Safety Precautions

If you—or your first mate—plan on doing any cooking aboard your yacht, give a little thought to the equipment you might use. First, here are a few "don'ts."

1. Don't use gasoline for cooking, heating, or lighting purposes aboard your cruiser.

2. Don't use a portable stove or heater while under way.

3. Don't use any stove or heater that has a wick or bubble-type burner.

All stoves aboard a cruiser must be fastened securely in place and thoroughly insulated. It a stove's burners must be primed by burning liquid fuel under them, they should be equipped with catch pans no less than ¾-inch deep, fastened inside the frame of the stove.

Alcohol-burning galley stoves: A two-burner model (above) and a three-burner type (left). Note how both are set on gimbals. This is almost a requirement if you plan to cook while underway in a sailboat.

Keep all electrical equipment and wiring in good condition. To begin with, all such equipment should be located as high up in a boat as possible—well above the low-lying areas where gasoline vapors might collect. It is also a good idea to inspect your boat's electrical circuits regularly to be sure all connections are tight and that there are no breaks or signs of wear on insulation. No knife switches or other arcing devices should be in fuel or engine compartments. Storage batteries should be located in a well-ventilated place, free of any possible sparking.

Each electrical circuit on a boat should be equipped with a fuse or circuit-breaker and never should be overloaded. Overloading also should be considered before adding more accessories to a circuit. If a fuse does blow, don't just replace it. Try to find out first why it let go and correct any defect you may discover. Then and only then, replace the fuse— using one of no higher amperage rating than the circuit calls for. Also, in replacing a fuse, be sure there is no load on the circuit—and the best way to be sure is to pull the main switch at the battery.

Check your fire extinguishers frequently to be sure that they are in their proper stowage brackets and free of any damage. Any cracked or broken hose should be replaced, and nozzles should be kept free of obstructions. Once a year have the extinguisher checked by a qualified person. Carbon dioxide extinguishers need refilling if they are 10 per cent under the weight marked on them. For the other types, follow the manufacturer's instructions as to when they need recharging. Working fire extinguishers are required by Coast Guard regulations and they should be a type approved by the Coast Guard.

KNOW YOUR MOORING

No one would be so foolish as to infer that all boats damaged by the severe storms that rip both coasts each year could be saved. However, the record does show that many craft damaged totally or badly during such storms were equipped with inadequate or unreliable ground tackle, or they were damaged by others that had dragged or broken free from moorings. Every year produces its own crop of paralleling instances, some minor, some quite serious, whose causes are similar.

When Selecting a Mooring in Open Water

When there were fewer pleasure craft almost all had permanent moorings consisting of one or more heavy anchors, chain, and rope pendant on which they swung freely to wind and current. In a good harbor, a properly-equipped mooring of this kind is safer in really heavy storms than a slip or "marina."

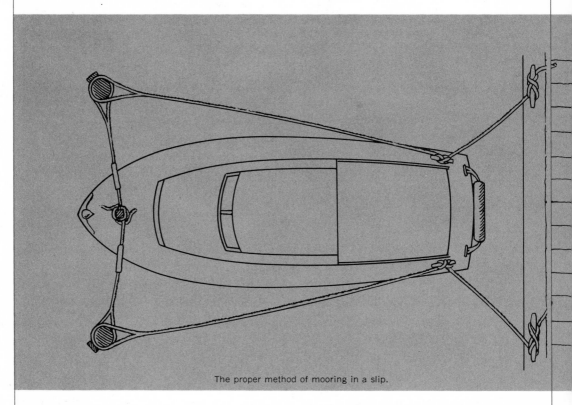

The proper method of mooring in a slip.

To put out such a mooring, inquire of yachtsmen, club officials or boatyard personnel as to local practices, which vary with conditions such as available room, depth of water, prevailing winds, natural protection from storm winds and seas, nature of the bottom, and other factors. In many areas the U. S. Coast Guard or local authorities have designated certain mooring areas. These are generally in charge of a harbormaster—often an official of the local yacht club, or of the town, county, or whatever. These areas are laid out and regulated as to equipment required and other factors. Some points to keep in mind in placing a mooring:

1. Choose a location sheltered from a long sweep of wind from any direction, which could build up a big sea.

2. Make sure you have swinging room, clear of all other moored boats under all conditions of wind and current.

3. Consult an up-to-date government chart as to depths of water, nature of the bottom and location of channels. Remember, charts give depths at "mean low water."

4. When your mooring is down, take soundings over the whole circular area bounded by the longest scope of your mooring line, to be sure there are no uncharted rocks, wrecks or other obstructions.

5. Don't moor near the edge of a channel. If the boat should drag or swing into the channel she might be run down at night. In many anchorages the boats along the outside of the fleet must show anchor lights every night, while those inside need not.

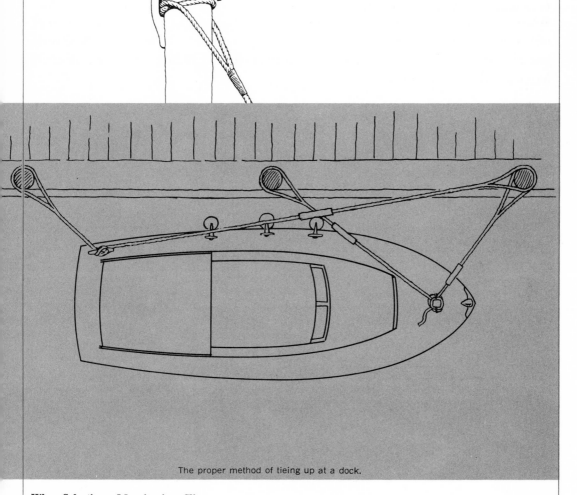

The proper method of tieing up at a dock.

When Selecting a Mooring in a Slip

Many boats today have their permanent moorings in slips alongside piers or floats. These are generally snug and well protected. Convenience for getting on and off the boat and services such as fresh water, electric current, dockside telephones, etc., make them popular. Points to keep in mind when selecting a marina mooring:

1. Pick one well-sheltered from wind and sea, and from current-borne drift-wood and other flotsam. If practicable, moor bow-on to the prevailing wind.

2. Make sure—especially if you're new at boat handling—that there is ample room for you to get in and out of your slip safely.

3. Bitts, cleats or pilings should be so located that your lines lead well forward and aft. (See illustration here.)

4. Where there is more than a three- or four-foot range of tide, it is easier and safer to moor to floats that rise and fall with the tide than to fixed bulkheads or piers.

5. Be sure the piers, floats and piling around you are well fendered to protect your boat. Particularly effective is a "fender board," which consists of two fenders hung over the side a few feet apart with a wooden plank (hardwood 2 x 3 or the like) hung horizontally across and beyond the two fenders.

6. Mooring lines (preferably nylon) should have fairly long leads to permit rise and fall with the tide and to impart some spring. They should never make sharp bends around corners, at chocks, etc., and should be protected by chafing gear.

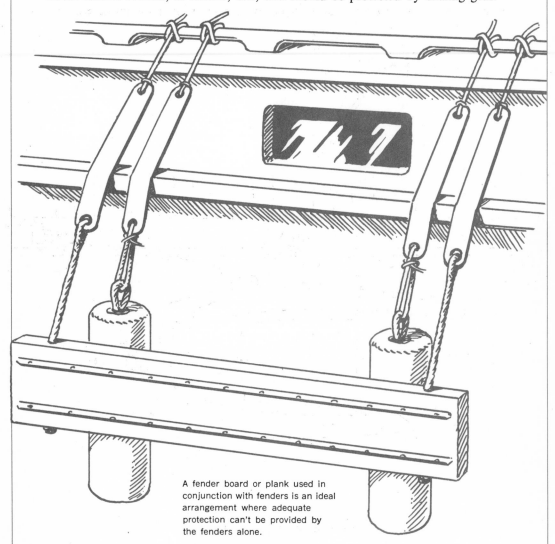

A fender board or plank used in conjunction with fenders is an ideal arrangement where adequate protection can't be provided by the fenders alone.

Proper Mooring Equipment

Returning to the subject of open-water moorings, in a regulated mooring area the harbor master will tell you the requirements. Regard these as absolute minimum specifications. Skimping them is false economy; added weight and strength will pay off in greater peace of mind when a hurricane is heading your way.

The mushroom anchor—ideally the type with a bulb at the upper end of the shank—is the most satisfactory permanent mooring anchor. Old engine blocks, railroad car wheels, heavy slabs of stone or concrete and other makeshifts have proved inadequate.

Local advice from experienced yachtsmen, club dock captains, service yards or the harbormaster will tell you the weight of mooring anchor for your size and type of boat. A rule-of-thumb of 10 pounds of mushroom for every foot of boat length is fairly safe in a protected harbor. One authority suggests: for a boat 25 feet long overall, 150 to 225 pounds; 35 feet l.o.a., 200-300 pounds; 45 feet l.o.a., 300-400 pounds; 55 feet l.o.a., 450-550 pounds. He depends on very heavy chain to bring up the holding power.

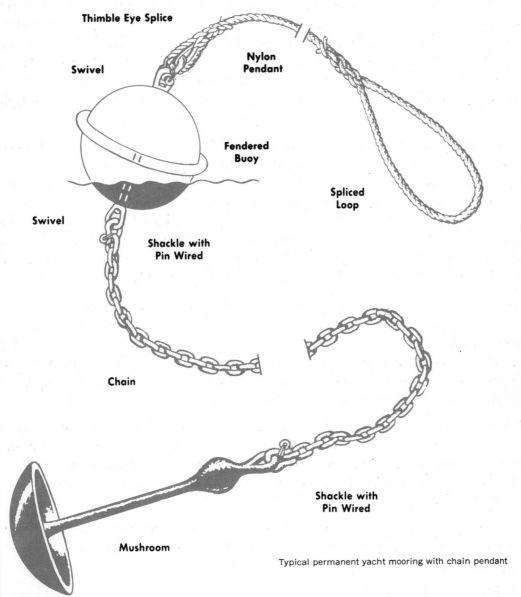

Typical permanent yacht mooring with chain pendant

Heavy chain imparts spring when a boat pitches and yaws. It has a tendency to lie flat and keep the pull on the anchor horizontal. Therefore, chain much heavier than needed to take the actual pull of the boat is recommended for the lower part of the rig, next to the anchor. Lighter chain will be used for the upper end which must be picked up by the buoy or the rope pendant.

Scope, vital in permanent moorings, is the relation of the length of the mooring cable from boat to anchor to the vertical depth from the bow chocks of the boat to the bottom when the tide is as high as it can get. Example: If the bow of your boat is 5 feet high and the highest water at your mooring is 15 feet; and if you have 60 feet of rope and chain from boat to anchor, your scope ratio is 3:1 (60 feet:20 feet).

Most authorities would call 3:1 the irreducible minimum and all will agree that 5:1 is a lot safer—i.e., 100 feet of chain and rope in the example above. Sometimes in crowded ports two anchors are set out in opposite directions so that the boat lies between and above them, making her swinging circle smaller for an adequate riding scope. Only solid forged-link, galvanized chain should be used. Shackles should be of screw type with the pin set up with a wrench and wired in. Use wire of the same metal as the shackle to avoid electrolysis—never a copper wire on a steel shackle, for instance. A swivel must be used in the chain to avoid its kinking up as the boat swings and should be extra heavy because of wear. If the chain goes up to a float, rather than directly to the rope pendant, and the latter is secured to the top of the float, they must be connected by a solid steel rod running through the float.

Nylon rope is popular for mooring pendants because it is strong, has great elasticity which eases the jerks on the mooring in a sea, outlasts manila, and will not absorb water. A main fault is that nylon is so slippery that it is hard to make a splice in it that won't pull out. It's usually wiser to have a yard do your splicing. But when you make the splice, be sure each strand is tucked at least five or six times instead of the usual three for manila and that the ends of the strands are then secured with a sailmaker's needle-whipping. As to diameter see what other boats like yours in your harbor use—then make yours a bit heavier. And put chafing gear on where it leads through chocks or might rub on stem or bobstay.

As to other materials: Dacron is strong, but less springy than nylon. Manila of somewhat heavier diameter than the synthetics is good but will not last as long. Cotton or ordinary hemp should never be used. Stainless steel deteriorates due to electrolysis or galvanic action and can also cut through softer bronze mooring cleats or chocks in a gale, and should never be used. Whatever the material, a thimble must be spliced into the end of the pendant that shackles to the chain or buoy.

Chocks should be of a depth and a design to prevent the mooring pendant jumping out of them in a sea and so placed that the line leads fair in the direction of normal pull. Bitts let through the deck and toed into the keel structure are probably the strongest. Bitts or cleats must never be screwed to the deck, but must be bolted through the deck and through a butt block or backing block under it.

After dropping the mooring, it should be set or "dug in" by towing first in one direction and then another from a husky workboat or launch. This will tend to greatly increase the holding power.

Checking the Mooring

Just because you have a good mooring firmly set in a safe place, don't assume all will be well forever. Moorings get dragged out of position. Rust, chafe and rot are constant enemies and so, especially in salt water, is that insidious malady electrolysis, caused by proximity of dissimilar metals. Here are some things to do:

    1. Several times a season, especially after a blow, check the position by taking bearings on fixed short points, (see illustration) which you should have done when you dropped the anchor. Even swinging at the end of a long mooring cable they won't change much unless the anchor has dragged.

    2. Some moorings are pulled every autumn and stored ashore until the follow-

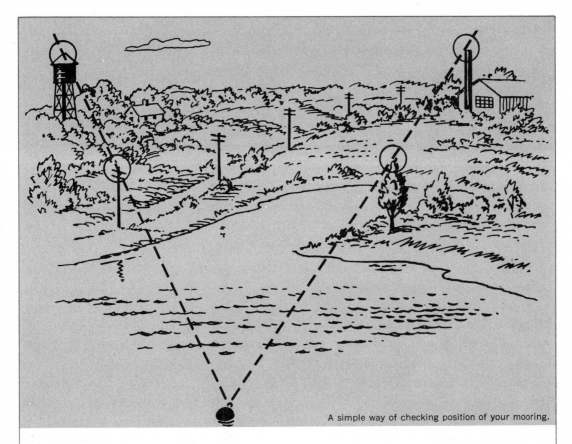
A simple way of checking position of your mooring.

ing season. More are lifted and inspected every two or three years. But it is best to lift and inspect them at the beginning of each season, except for the rope pendant which comes off at the end of each season to be replaced with a "winter stick." (Follow local practice on this.) This annual inspection is particularly important where underwater chemical or electrical conditions accelerate corrosion of the anchor and lower chain. Such conditions may differ in various parts of the same harbor.

3. An anchor that spends practically all its time in the mud will rust less than one that is hauled and left out in the weather all winter. But it will rust, and the shackle especially should be inspected for rust, corrosion, or erosion from friction with sand. The eye that holds the shackle in the end of the shank is also sensitive to these troubles, and swivels often have to be examined and replaced.

4. All shackles and pins should be checked, pins set up if at all slack, and re-wired.

5. If the chain, shackles or any parts look badly rusted, knock and scrape the rust away. Get down to bright metal wherever you suspect weakness, and if a noticeable amount of solid metal is gone, junk the item. That old saw about a chain being as strong as its weakest link applies literally to moorings.

6. The upper end of a chain—the fathom or two nearest the surface—seems to wear or corrode faster than the lower part. Even if you don't inspect your whole mooring every year, pull up as much of the chain by hand as you can. Look it over carefully to see if the top few feet need replacing.

7. Various schools of thought as to mooring pendants all agree that no mooring pendant can be too strong. One school, while admitting the strength and durability of the synthetics preferred by many, points out that good manila is plenty strong in its first season and is enough cheaper so they can afford to throw away the old pendant and rig a new one each year. Most new pendants are rigged at the beginning of the season, but some people along the East Coast put on their new pendants around mid-summer when the hurricane season is imminent.

33

And as to Guest Moorings. All of us who cruise appreciate the courtesy of guest moorings offered by a yacht club or town in the ports we visit. But never blindly assume that the mooring offered will hold your boat. When you pick up such a mooring, haul up the pendant and some of the top chain and satisfy yourself it's of a size and condition to hold your boat. Check with the yacht club launchman or someone else in a position to know what, and how much of it, is on the bottom of that chain. You might be safer on your own anchor.

WEATHER . . . AND THE YACHTSMAN

Good yachtsmanship demands an awareness of surrounding weather conditions. Without it, you may someday find yourself with less than an hour's warning of bad weather that could quickly trap you on rough waves in a strong gale. Such things could easily be prevented with a little knowledge of weather indications.

Weather forecasts are available in your newspaper and on the radio. If there is a Weather Bureau Station in your area, the most up-to-date forecasts can be obtained by simply telephoning the bureau. But, the uninitiated may wonder why the yachtsman needs more than the general information available to him from the predictions of the weather man. The answer to this question is well known by experienced yachtsmen. The meteorologist's predictions are based upon movements of large air masses and upon local conditions at specific points where weather stations are located. The air masses don't always perform as predicted, and the weather stations are sometimes spaced rather widely apart; therefore, it is necessary for the yachtsman to understand the weather conditions occurring between the stations, as well as conditions he encounters which are different from those indicated by the weather reports.

Visual Indications of the Weather

Nature herself supplies many reliable weather signs. All of us are familiar with some of them. Who hasn't heard the old rhyme, "Red sky at night sailors' delight. Red sky at morning sailors take warning." It's based on the fact that a red sunset is seldom followed by bad weather the next day; but when the sunrise is red, that day's weather is likely to be foul.

There are many other reliable hints about coming weather that can be learned merely by observing the sky. For instance, a bright blue sky usually means fair weather; but a dark, gloomy blue sky means windy weather. Also a gray sky in the morning means fair weather. If the sky is golden, watch for wind rather than rain. But yellow sky usually is followed by rain within 12 to 24 hours. And a dull red sky at sunrise or sunset means both rain and wind within a day's time. A rosy sky at sunrise or sunset and a lavender sky in early morning or late afternoon are signs of good weather.

The sun gives some valuable indications, too. For instance, when the sun rises above a cloud bank, the chances are there will be wind that day, but no rain. Also, when the sun comes up out of a gray horizon, chances are that it will be a fair day. A sunset with diffused and glaring white clouds is a good sign that a storm is on its way. A weak, washed-out-looking sun probably means rain in the near future. The moon gives us help, too—that ring, or corona, around it is a sure sign that a storm is on the way.

Of all nature's signposts, however, clouds are possibly the most accurate. Clouds aren't meaningless blotches that mar the blue of the sky or mere accumulations of water vapor, but they are good harbingers of the weather. As a general rule, all cloud forms are classified according to their height: cirrus, cirrocumulus, and cirrostratus are considered high clouds (16,500 to 45,000 feet); altocumulus, altostratus, and nimbostratus are called middle clouds (6,500 to 23,000 feet); and stratocumulus, stratus, cumulus and cumulonimbus are known as low clouds (surface to 6,500 feet). Each type of cloud form indicates oncoming weather conditions.

IDENTIFICATION OF CLOUDS AND WHAT WEATHER THEY BRING

Predominating clouds in a formation determine code number and classification. The caption forecasts appearing below are based on surface wind direction described on page 42.

Code: H—High clouds; M—Middle clouds; and L—Low clouds.

H1 *Cirrus* clouds with mare's tail formation. Fair weather can be expected for at least 24 hours.

H4 *Cirrus* filament clouds which mean good weather if winds are from W NW to N. Rain can be expected in about 25 hours if winds are steady from NE E to S. If they are moving rapidly, especially from SW, chances of foul weather in about 20 hours is good.

H2 Dense *Cirrus* patches. Fair weather can be expected for at least 24 hours, but precipitation is likely after this period if winds are steady from NE E to S.

H5 *Cirrus* and *Cirrostratus* clouds below 45 degrees in bands converging toward the horizon. Storm may be 18 to 24 hours away, especially if wind from NE E to S.

H3 Dense *Cirrus* from *Cumulonimbus.* Such a cloud pattern needs watching, because a thunderstorm may be near.

H6 *Cirrus* clouds 45 degrees above the horizon generally means good weather for the next 24 to 36 hours.

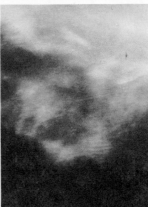

H7 *Cirrostratus* clouds covering the whole sky. Precipitation may be less than 12 hours away, especially if the wind is steady from NE to S. The prismatic effect of the sun or moon through ice crystals of this form of high clouds causes the halo.

M2 Thick *Altostratus* will hide the sun or moon completely and will continue to do so if the wind from any direction other than NE to S. In these directions precipitation is likely in 12 hours.

H8 *Cirrostratus* clouds that do not cover the sky. If the winds are steady from NE E to S, and if they are thickening, rain could be expected within the next 24 hours. Other wind directions will bring overcast or partly overcast sky.

M3 Thin *Altocumulus* clouds mean fair weather unless they thicken. Should this occur and if the wind is blowing from the NE to S, chances are good that it will rain within 15 to 20 hours.

H9 *Cirrocumulus* clouds mean foul weather in 12 to 24 hours if the winds are blowing in a NE to S direction. In late spring and early summer morning such a cloud formation and wind direction often brings afternoon thunderstorms. Other wind direction lead to overcast conditions.

M4 Patchy *Altocumulus* clouds usually mean good weather. But if they should become domed, a thunderstorm is possible.

M1 With thin *Altostratus,* the sun or moon may be weakly visible, as through behind frosted glass. Rain may be less than 12 hours away if the wind is steady from NE to S. Other winds bring overcast sky.

M5 *Altocumulus* in parallel bands usually indicates a storm is coming within the next 12 hours. This is especially true if the wind is from NE to S.

M6 *Altocumulus* resulting from the spreading out of *Cumulus* means that the weather for the next 24 hours is doubtful and needs watching. If the wind is from NE to S chances are good that rain will occur.

L1 *Cumulus* clouds such as these indicate fair weather. Should they grow in size, darken, and thicken across the sky as a warm summer day progresses, a thunderstorm is likely.

M7 *Altocumulus* in two or more layers. The weather will remain fair unless the *Altocumulus* join up with *Altostratus* or *Nimbostratus*. In such a case rain will result.

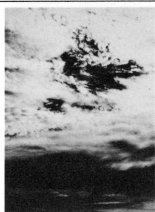

L2 Large *Cumulus* clouds that build up vertically generally indicate that a thunderstorm with gusty winds or just a wind squall will occur within 4 to 10 hours. This is especially true if the clouds are moving from the SW to NW.

M8 Castellated *Altocumulus* clouds are a good sign of clear weather ahead.

L3 *Cumulonimbus* clouds that have grown from *Cumulus*. Could become a thunderstorm in about 30 minutes, usually from SW W to N.

M9 *Altocumulus* of a chaotic sky, generally at several levels as here. Weather will remain fair unless the clouds thicken.

L4 *Stratocumulus* clouds formed *Cumulus*. Continued fair weather for at least the next 24 hours.

L5 *Stratocumulus* that cover the sky means almost immediate bad weather, from a few drops of rain to a heavy downpour.

L8 *Cumulus* and *Stratocumulus* in a foul weather pattern. If the clouds are moving from SW to NW precipitation is likely in about 6 hours.

L6 Low hanging *Stratus* cover which does not indicate immediate bad weather. But, if the wind is from NE to S, it may begin to rain in 6 to 10 hours.

L9 Well-defined *Culmulonimbus* with anvil tops —thunderstorm about to begin.

L7 Low hanging *Stratus* clouds that mean bad weather. Heavy precipitation may be expected in a short while if the winds are NE to S. Other winds may bring only light rain.

While it is important to be able to identify cloud forms, their sequence helps more in making a forecast. The following cloud sequences usually mean the approach of foul yachting weather:

1. Cirrus to cirrostratus (thunderstorm or rain).
2. Cirrus to cirrocumulus (rain).
3. Cirrus to cirrostratus to altostratus to nimbostratus (rain).
4. Cirrostratus to altocumulus (thunderstorm).
5. Cirrocumulus to altocumulus to cumulonimbus (thunderstorm).
6. Cumulus to cumulonimbus (thunderstorm).
7. Altostratus to nimbostratus (rain).
8. Altostratus to altocumulus to nimbostratus or cumulonimbus (thunderstorm).
9. Altocumulus to cumulus (thunderstorm).
10. Stratocumulus to stratus (rain).

Storm Warning Signals

No matter how good you may become at reading nature's weather signs, don't rely on this alone. Get the daily newspaper weather reports and above all, use the radio. A radio set is invaluable for keeping up with local weather forecasts. Even an inexpensive portable that will pick up weather reports from regular broadcasting stations is a big help. And one equipped to receive the mariners' weather reports regularly transmitted by Coast Guard and other government stations is very much worthwhile. Often, your radio can give you tips on weather even when you are not tuned in on a weather report. For instance, when there is static, your radio is telling you there is an electrical storm somewhere within the range of twenty-five miles, and the chances are you can expect it to rain within an hour.

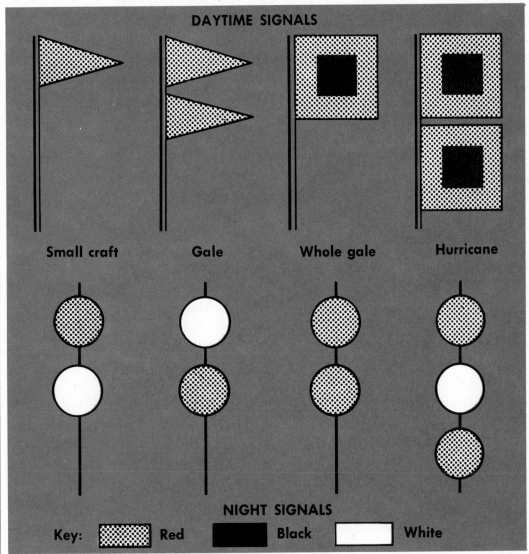

DAYTIME SIGNALS

Small craft   Gale   Whole gale   Hurricane

NIGHT SIGNALS

Key: Red   Black   White

One of the most reliable weather-signs to watch for and respect: The storm signals flown at Coast Guard installations and other places, such as certain yacht clubs, marinas, or boat-yards. Check to see if provisions have been made to fly these signals somewhere in your vicinity. If so, make it a point to look for them on every possible occasion. But, don't get into the habit of ignoring storm warnings if on one or more occasions they prove unnecessary. It is never wise to take storm warnings lightly because they are hoisted only when danger is present, or considered likely to develop. The storm signals are as follows:

Small craft warning. One red pennant displayed by day and a red light over a white light at night to indicate winds up to 38 miles an hour (33 knots) and/or sea conditions dangerous to small craft operations are forecast for the area.

Gale warning. Two red pennants displayed by day and a white light above a red light at night to indicate winds ranging from 39 to 54 miles an hour (34 to 48 knots) are forecast for the area.

Whole gale warning. A single square red flag with a black center displayed during daytime and two red lights at night to indicate winds ranging from 55 to 73 miles an hour (48 to 63 knots) are forecast for the area.

Hurricane warning. Two square red flags with black centers displayed by day and a white light between two red lights at night to indicate that winds 74 miles an hour (64 knots) and above are forecast for the area.

Handy to have aboard is the Coastal Warning Facilities Chart published annually by the Weather Bureau. Its 14 sections cover all U. S. Coastal and Great Lakes waters, including Hawaii, the Virgin Islands and Puerto Rico. For each area, it gives Weather Bureau office phone numbers; the flag warning code and where in the area—yacht clubs, lifeboat stations, boatyards, etc.—these flags are displayed. It lists the special Weather Bureau broadcasts and scores of commercial station radio and TV weather broadcasts in each area, with the times, frequencies, and exact location of each boadcasting station. It costs 10 cents a chart, ordered from the U. S. Government Printing Office, Washington 25, D. C.

Wind-Barometer Indications

Various kinds of instruments are available that will help you in your weather forecasting techniques. One of the most valuable is the barometer which is an instrument used to measure atmospheric pressure. Atmospheric pressure at sea level is approximately 14.7 pounds per square inch; this mean height is expressed as a barometric reading of 29.53 inches of mercury. Variations of the atmospheric pressure serve to indicate changes in weather. In a typical aneroid barometer, the scale is calibrated from 27.5 to 31.5 inches, inclusive. These figures represent inches of mercury which are the standard means of expressing atmospheric pressure. The black pointer indicates the pressure at any given instant: it is actuated by a shaft-and-linkage arrangement from a metal bellows which expands and contracts as pressure varies. The other indicator is a reference pointer which can be turned by hand to any position on the dial by moving the knurled knob located at the center of the dial face. The reference pointer is used to indicate the pressure at the last reading of the barometer. Although the reading must be recorded, use of the pointer allows a quick visual determination of pressure changes between periodic readings and recordings.

The barometer is used in making weather forecasts. A record of barometric readings made at regular intervals will indicate the pressure being exerted on the earth's surface at the instant of observation. If several readings have been logged, as in the following example, significance may be attached to them.

Time (in hours)	Pressure (in inches)	Change (in inches)
0700	30.02	——
0800	30.00	—0.02
0900	29.97	—0.03
1000	29.93	—0.04
1100	29.88	—0.05
1200	29.82	—0.06

Barometric pressure falling at an increasing rate denotes foul weather. A fall of 0.02-inch an hour is a low rate of fall and not particularly disturbing whereas a fall of 0.05-inch per hour is a high rate and normally indicates stormy weather.

Wind directions, plus barometer readings, are a fine way of forecasting weather. For instance, as a rule, winds from the east quadrants and falling barometer indicate foul weather; and winds shifting to the west quadrants indicate clearing and fair weather. The rapidity of the storm's approach and its intensity are indicated by the rate and the amount in the fall of the barometer.

The indications afforded by the wind and the barometer are two of the best guides we now have for determining future weather conditions. As low barometer readings usually attend stormy weather, and high barometer readings are generally associated with clearing or fair weather, it follows that falling barometer indicates precipitation and wind, and rising barometer, fair weather or the approach of fair weather. As atmospheric waves or crests (areas of high pressure) and troughs or depressions (areas of low pressure) are, by natural laws, caused to assume circular or oval forms, the wind directions with reference to areas of low pressure move spirally and counterclockwise inward toward the region of lowest atmospheric pressure, as indicated by readings of the barometer. Areas of low barometric pressure are, in fact, whirlwinds of greater or less magnitude and intensity, depending upon the steepness of the barometric gradient. Areas of high barometric pressure, on the contrary, show winds flowing spirally clockwise outward.

The wind directions thus produced give rise to, and are responsible for, all local weather signs. The south winds bring warmth, the north winds cold. The east winds, in the middle latitudes, indicate the approach from the westward of an area of low pressure, or storm area, and the west winds show that the storm area has passed to the eastward. The indications of the barometer generally precede the shifts of the wind. This much is shown by local observations.

During the colder months, when the land temperatures are below the water temperatures of the ocean, precipitation will begin along the seaboards when the wind shifts and blows steadily from the water over the land without regard to the height of the barometer. In such cases the moisture in the warm ocean winds is condensed by the cold of the continental area. During the summer months, on the contrary, the on-shore winds are not necessarily rain winds, for the reason that they are cooler than the land surfaces and their capacity for moisture is increased by the warmth that is communicated to them by the land surface. In such cases thunderstorms commonly occur when the ocean winds are intercepted by mountain ranges or peaks. If, however, the easterly winds of summer increase in force, with falling barometer, the approach of an area of low barometric pressure from the west is indicated and rain will follow within a day or two.

From the Mississippi and Missouri Valleys to the Atlantic coast, and on the Pacific coast, rain generally begins on a falling barometer, while in the Rocky Mountain and plateau districts, and on the eastern Rocky Mountain slope, precipitation seldom begins until the barometer begins to rise, after a fall. This is true as regards the eastern half of the country, however, only during the colder months, and in the presence of general storms that may occur at other seasons. In the warmer months summer showers and thunderstorms usually come about the time the barometer turns from falling to rising. The fact that during practically the entire year precipitation on the Great Western Plains and in the mountain regions that lie between the Plains and the Pacific coast districts does not begin until the center of the low-barometer area has passed to the eastward or southward and the wind has shifted to the north quadrants, with rising barometer, is an important one to note.

The wind and barometer indications for the United States are summarized in the following table:

WIND-BAROMETER TABLE

Wind Direction	Barometer Reduced to Sea Level	Character of Weather
SW to NW	30.10 to 30.20 and steady	Fair, with slight temperature changes for 1 or 2 days.
SW to NW	30.10 to 30.20 and rising rapidly	Fair followed within 2 days by rain.
SW to NW	30.20 and above and stationary	Continued fair with no decided temperature change.
SW to NW	30.20 and above and falling slowly	Slowly rising temperature and fair for 2 days.
S to SE	30.10 to 30.20 and falling slowly	Rain within 24 hours.
S to SE	30.10 to 30.20 and falling rapidly	Wind increasing in force, with rain within 12 to 24 hours.
SE to NE	30.10 to 30.20 and falling slowly	Rain in 12 to 18 hours.
SE to NE	30.10 to 30.20 and falling rapidly	Increasing wind and rain within 12 hours.
E·to NE	30.10 and above and falling slowly	In summer, with light winds, rain may not fall for several days. In winter, rain in 24 hours.
E to NE	30.10 and above and falling fast	In summer, rain probably in 12 hours. In winter, rain or snow with increasing winds will often set in NE when the barometer begins to fall.
SE to NE	30.00 or below and falling slowly	Rain will continue 1 or 2 days.
SE to NE	30.00 or below and falling rapidly	Rain with high wind, followed within 36 hours by clearing and, in winter, colder.
S to SW	30.00 or below and rising slowly	Clearing in a few hours and fair for several days.
S to E	29.80 or below and falling rapidly	Severe storm imminent, followed in 24 hours by clearing and, in winter, colder.
E to N	29.80 or below and falling rapidly	Severe NE gale and heavy rain; winter, heavy snow and cold wave.
Going to W	29.80 or below and rising rapidly	Clearing and colder.

Wind Velocity and Direction

The anemometer is an instrument used for measuring wind velocity and, in few cases, wind direction. (A separate type wind direction indicator is more popular than a dual purpose style of anemometer.) Readings made under way indicate apparent wind speed and direction; they should be corrected for vessel speed and direction to obtain *true* wind readings. When measuring velocity and direction of wind, the high degree of accuracy usually essential in bearings is not required. It is sufficient if velocity be estimated within one *Beaufort* number, and direction within 5 degrees. Usually, the anemometer is mounted at the masthead or yardarm with indicator located on the bridge. Some units are designed so that the indicator buzzes and flashes a light the number of times per minute that directly corresponds to the wind velocity in knots; others are direct reading units.

THE BEAUFORT SCALE WITH SPECIFICATIONS FOR USE AT SEA

Beaufort No.	Description of wind	Miles per hour statute	Terms used in U. S. Weather Bureau forecasts	Condition of Sea
0	Calm	0- 1	Light	Sea like a mirror.
1	Light air	1- 3		Ripples with the appearance of scales are formed, but without foam crests.
2	Light breeze (Slight breeze)	4- 7		Small wavelets, still short but more pronounced. Crests have a glassy appearance and do not break.
3	Gentle breeze	8-12	Gentle	Large wavelets. Crests begin to break. Foam of glassy appearance. Perhaps scattered whitecaps.
4	Moderate breeze	13-18	Moderate	Small waves, becoming longer; fairly frequent whitecaps.
5	Fresh breeze	19-24	Fresh	Moderate waves, taking a more pronounced long form; many whitecaps are formed (chance of some spray).
6	Strong breeze	25-31	Strong	Large waves begin to form; the white foam crests are more extensive everywhere (probable some spray).
7	Moderate gale	32-38		Water heaps up and white foam from breaking waves begins to be blown in streaks along direction of the wind.
8	Fresh gale	39-46	Gale	Moderately high waves of greater length; edges of crests begin to break into spindrift. The foam is blown in wellmarked streaks along the direction of the wind.
9	Strong gale	47-54		High waves. Dense streaks of foam along the direction of the wind. Water begins to "roll." Spray may affect visibility.
10	Whole gale (heavy gale)	55-63	Whole gale	Very high waves with long overhanging crests. The resulting foam, in great patches, is blown in dense white streaks along the direction of the wind. On the whole, the surface of the water takes a white appearance. The rolling of the water becomes heavy and shock-like. Visibility affected.
11	Storm	64-75		Exceptionally high waves (small and medium-sized ships might be for a time lost to view behind the waves). The water is completely covered with long white patches of foam lying along the direction of the wind. Everywhere the edges of the wave crests are blown into froth. Visibility affected.
12	Hurricane	above 75	Hurricane	The air is filled with foam and spray. Water completely white with driving spray; visibility very seriously affected.

When to Look for Fog

Foggy conditions in a crowded harbor are extremely hazardous. An early prediction that fog will occur may aid in avoiding a dangerous situation. Fog results from the cooling of the air that remains at the earth's surface. Air temperature may be cooled in the following ways:

Warm air flowing over a cold surface. Fog may form, day or night, when warm moist air flows over water or land surfaces which are cooler than the air.

Radiation fog. Radiation fog is a night phenomenon. During the day the earth's surface receives and radiates warmth. At night, the incoming heat ceases but the radiation continues, and the earth's surface gets cooler. Although the lowest temperature is reached just before sunrise, fog sometimes forms soon after sunset. It usually burns off within a couple of hours after sunrise. If mixed with smoke, as often is the case near industrial areas, it will form a heavy, dark, and greasy *smog* that won't quickly burn off.

Air moving from low to higher latitude. Warm moist air moving from a low to a higher latitude may cool to such an extent that fog will form over large areas. This type is called sea fog.

Fog is likely to form as the spread between air temperature and dewpoint (relative humidity) decreases. Dewpoint is the temperature at which the air, when cooled, would be saturated. A simple rule of thumb is that when the temperature and dewpoint spread is three degrees or less, for is likely. When the spread is approximately ten degrees at noon and decreases to three degrees or less late in the day, you have almost a sure bet that there will be a rapid fog development. Other conditions that will help are: The sky must be cloudless or nearly so, and the winds must be light but there must not be a dead calm.

Certain parts of the country have a rather definite fog pattern. Along the Atlantic coast, fog is quite common over cold ocean waters when the wind turns to the south and southwest, and the air becomes warm and humid. Such a fog condition may persist for several days if the winds continue from the south or southwest, but other times when there is a land breeze from west to east, the fog will burn off before noon and fine yachting weather will be available along the shoreline even though you might view a thick bank on the horizon offshore. On the west coast, fog is generally caused when the warm air from the central Pacific is chilled by the cold water near the coast. During the day, surface heating near the shore causes the fog to burn off. When the sun sets, however, the surface heating diminishes and the fog moves in again. In many areas along the west coast, it is almost possible to set a wristwatch by the going and coming of the fog.

The Great Lakes can really have bad fogs at anytime during the yachting season, but generally the highest frequency of thick fogs occurs during the first portion of the season when the lake water is still very cold. Then the moisture in the humid tropical air which comes up the Mississippi River Valley is easily condensed as fog. When the wind is very weak, Great Lakes for can last several days. In the Gulf of Mexico fog seldom exists during the summer months.

When caught out on the water in fog, there are several possible ways in which you may get out of it. Keeping in mind the effect of cold water, it is wise to search out the warmer areas. On the east coast, this can be usually found in shallow water (but remember your draft and make certain that sufficient water is under your boat) or off the mouths of rivers and streams and in areas of bays or inlets where tidal currents are not too strong. Strong currents draw cold ocean water right into the bay. Along the Pacific coast, warmer water will usually be found away from the fresh-water outlets and away from the shore.

If, when cruising serenely along, you should notice that the fog starts closing in, your duty now calls for increased alertness. Check you log and the appropriate chart and light list for the location and characteristics of all buoys and lights within the area, with attention given to those aids specifically useful in fog, such as sound signals, radio beacons, radar, bell and whistle buoys. The boat's whistle (if a motorboat) or foghorn (if a sailboat) should be blown in accordance with the Rules of the Road (see chart here). The speed of your craft should be reduced to a speed that will make it possible to stop her in half the distance of visibility. The running lights should be turned on, and lookouts should be stationed at the bow and on the stern, as well as one far aloft as possible, if sufficient persons are available for such duty.

SOUND SIGNALS IN FOG OR HEAVY WEATHER		
Type of Vessel	Method of signalling	Frequency
*Vessel under sail** (Both International and Inland Rules)		*At intervals of*
Underway, starboard tack	1 blast	1 minute
Underway, port tack	2 blasts in succession	1 minute
Underway, running free	3 blasts in succession	1 minute
*Vessel under power*** Underway (International Rules)	1 long blast	2 minutes
Underway (Inland Rules)	1 long blast	1 minute
Underway but stopped (International Rules)	2 long blasts in succession	2 minutes
Vessel at anchor (Both International*** and Inland Rules)	Ring ship's bell vigorously for 5 seconds	1 minute
*Vessel aground**** (International Rules)	Basic signal—ring ship's bell vigorously for 5 seconds. In addition, strike three separate and distinct strokes on the bell immediately before and after the basic signal.	1 minute
*Vessel towing**** (Both International and Inland Rules)	1 long blast 2 short blasts in succession	1 minute
Vessel towed (International Rules****) Inland Rules*****	1 long blast 3 short blasts in succession 1 long blast 2 short blasts in succession	1 minute 1 minute
Fishing vessel (20 tons or upward) (International Rules)	1 short blast followed by ringing the ship's bell	1 minute

*Signal given on foghorn.
**Signal given on whistle.
***On International waters a vessel longer than 350 feet rings a bell in the forward part of the vessel and a gong, or other different-sounding signal, in the stern, both for about five seconds at intervals of about one minute. To give additional warning of the possibility of collision by an approaching vessel, a boat may also sound one short, one prolonged, and one short blast of her horn.
****Signal given on foghorn or whistle immediately following the signal made by the towing vessel.
*****(Optional) Signal given on foghorn immediately following the signal made by the towing vessel.

When underway in a fog be sure to keep your boat on her desired course and keep a check of your position on your chart. Steer carefully and watch your timing so that you won't overrun the buoy. When creeping through fog, it's a good idea to stop a few minutes before you are due to pick up the next mark and look or/and listen for it carefully. Approach buoys, channel markers, and lightships cautiously, for other craft can also be expected to use such things for check points. If you don't sight your object when your navigation says you should, drop anchor and stay where you are until you can determine what went wrong or until some sound gives you an indication of your position. To continue on in hopes of finding it in another few minutes will surely lead to worse confusion and uncertainty. When you are anchored, keep your fog signal going, and don't wear the ear flaps down on your foul-weather gear.

When in a fog, make sure that you use all the navigational aids you have aboard your vessel: Compass, depth finder, radar, loran, radio direction finder, etc. For instance, charts give water depths, as we know, and thus a sounding lead or depth finder can help you check your position and confirm the shoreward trend of your course. Also remember that a radar reflector, a multi-surface folding metal box hung in the rigging or mast of a wood or fiberglass boat in heavy fog greatly increases your echo on radar scopes of other vessels. In fog, where common sense and the law require that they slow down, they run too fast because they *think* they can see any boat ahead on the radar screen. But radar doesn't always work perfectly; the pilot or watch officer doesn't always use it intelligently, and small boats don't always show up on it. To return a visible echo on the radar screen an object must be a conductor of electricity. Wood and plastics are not. Hence radar reflectors. They are of metal—aluminum usually—of a shape designed for maximum reflection of radar rays. Hung as high aloft as possible, they give back a good solid "pip" on the radar screen of an approaching vessel. They are inexpensive, light and usually come apart and stow flat. If you're out in a fog without one, hang any big metal object high in your rigging. The more flat surfaces and angles it has the better it will serve your purpose.

Foul Weather Operations

When air currents of different temperatures, moisture content or direction come together, storms usually develop. Thunderstorms form when a huge body of warm moist air rises up to great heights. Moisture condenses as it cools on its upward journey, and thunderhead clouds begin to form. At the top of the clouds, the cold air forms a strong downdraft that freezes moisture and forms hail. As hail falls into the warmer regions of the linesquall it melts and rain falls. When a boat passes through a warm or cold front, a noticeable change in the weather may be observed, especially a cold front. A cold front is sometimes acompanied by a sudden shift in the wind and a hard squall from a westerly quarter. Thunder-squalls can be expected any time the weather is hot and humid. Additional warnings are thunder and lightning in the distance, increasing static on the radio, and erratic puffs of cool air.

Since you may very well be caught one day out in the open as a thunderstorm moves threateningly toward you, it is wise to know what procedures to follow. Study the storm carefully to ascertain its direction of movement. Most—but by no means all—thunderstorms cover a limited area. With today's faster boats, it is *sometimes* possible to run to one side of a storm or to get to shelter. But rushing for shelter too fast once the storm has broken can in many cases be foolish. Violent thundersqualls have periods of peak winds,

Warm fronts are preceded by generally southeasterly winds and a slowly falling barometer. noted approaching from *Cirrus* clouds will be a westerly direction and foul weather can generally be expected in approximately 24 hours. The cloud pattern will gradually thicken as it changes from *Cirrus* to *Cirrostratus*, then *Altostratus* (on some occasions *Altocumulus*), and finally to *Nimbostratus* (on some occasions *Cu-* *mulonimbus*). Rain usually begins from dense *Altostratus* clouds before they are obscured by the lower *Cumulus* or *Stratus* clouds. As the front passes the wind will generally become southwesterly, the barometer will rise a little, rain will stop, the sky will begin to clear, and the temperature will start to increase. During the summer months, thundershowers often develop behind a warm front.

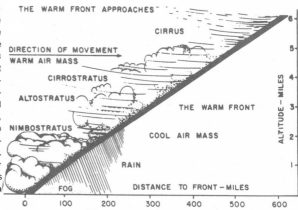

rarely lasting more than an hour or so, after which the wind moderates even though it may continue to rain. Thus, if you are caught out in rough water at the beginning of a storm, it doesn't make good sense to push your vessel recklessly under such conditions, when by waiting where you are for a short time you can come into port a great deal more comfortably and easily only a little later in the day.

There are several tricks for handling your boat in rough water that will help to give a smooth ride. The major one is not to run broadside, or parallel, with the waves. If this should be your course and the seas are rough, it is better to slice into them at about a 45-degree angle, and then when you have gone a few miles, come back on your destination mark still holding a course 34-degrees to the waves. This puts the sea on your quarter, and when steering in this position you do have to spin the wheel back and forth to keep the bow constantly on your course. The important thing to do on this course is to prevent the waves from turning the stern of your boat. Also, by taking the waves on either the port or starboard quarter, the force or momentum of the wave action is not permitted to cause the cruiser to pitch heavily, and at the same time there is little likelihood of a sea pounding over the stern, because this course tends to roll the weather quarter away from the waves. And should the ride still tend to be uncomfortable, the next suggestion is to slacken speed. When you run into a head sea, let the bow rise into each wave instead of being driven into it.

When riding a beam sea all boats have a rolling cycle—the time required for a vessel to roll from side to side. If this cycle coincides with the cycle of the waves there is a danger of capsizing. The cycle can be broken by a change of course. As with head seas, shifting a few degrees off either bow prevents the motion of the boat from being caught by the motion of the sea.

In plotting your course try to work your way into the lee of any land mass that might lie to the windward. Generally, the water will be smooth in such a location in spite of even a howling gale. If there is no such protective land area indicated on your chart, it is always best to follow a deep-water course. Avoid running into areas where the water is shallow; in such places, the waves build up into a dangerously steep chop. The same applies to entrances of channels, harbors, or rivers that are protected by a reef or bar. Before the storm builds up, all unnecessary gear in the cockpit and bridge should go below and loose objects on deck should be lashed down.

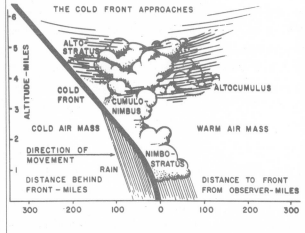

When a cold front approaches, the wind will generally be from a southwesterly direction and the barometer will fall at quite a rapid rate. As a rule, cold fronts move a great deal more rapidly than warm fronts. (The average speed is between 20 to 25 miles an hour, but sometimes they move as fast as 35 miles an hour.) Because of this, the transition from *Cirrus* to *Cirrostratus* and then to *Altocumulus* or *Altostratus* often takes place within a period of a few hours. Rain often begins just after spotting the *Altocumulus* clouds. If the cold front is moving rapidly, clearing will begin fairly quick, but if the front is comparatively slow moving, cloudiness may continue for a few hours. When the front passes the wind will shift abruptly to the Northwest or North, the barometer will rise steadily, and the temperature will fall.

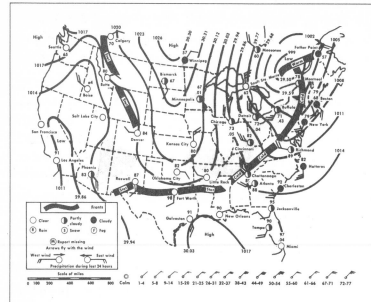

Typical summer's day weather map, notice the various fronts: warm, cold, and stationary. The latter is an air mass boundary which shows little or no movement. The terms *low* and *high* mean low-pressure and high-pressure areas. A high-pressure area is a weather system in which the air pressure or atmospheric pressure is high. The air is heavier, colder, and drier. A low, on the other hand, is made up of a mass of low-pressure air that is lighter, warmer, and wetter. In general, lows bring bad weather, because their air contains more moisture. Our weather, for the most part, flows in a continuous procession from the west to the east. It travels about 500 miles per day in the summer and 700 miles per day in the winter. In other words, as a general rule, tomorrow's weather is always west of us.

When conditions become so intolerable that course or speed changes produce no noticeable improvement, it's advisable to heave to and ride out a storm off-shore, especially one of those quick summer squalls. In such a case, the boat must be anchored to hold it where it is. Anchor with the longest line that can be rigged, because plenty of scope will do more than anything else to make the anchor hold the bottom successfully and also will ease the boat's motion, because it will have the hanging weight of the line to snub it as a cushion against the shock of the sea. A weight added to the anchor will increase the anchor's holding power tremendously, and it will also help the damping action of the long anchor line. If your boat tends to drift, trail a sea anchor from the bow to keep it headed into the waves. (A sea anchor is designed to keep the boat's head into the wind when drifting. It is a canvas cone, open at both ends, with a loop at the larger opening.) If you don't have a sea anchor aboard, a bucket or a shirt with the neck and sleeves knotted together and tied to a line will generally do a good job in an emergency. You can, of course, use your engine to keep the craft headed into the wind with just enough power for steering, if necessary. But remember your fuel supply. It won't last indefinitely, so don't run the engine unless needed. While riding out a storm, make sure to keep the water pumped out of the bilge since this added weight of water can make your boat unstable.

In a sailing craft it is usually wise to reduce the sail area. There are two basic ways in which to reduce the sail area; firstly by taking in one or more sails; secondly to reduce the area of the sails by reefing. In the latter, the method of reefing depends on whether your craft has a roller reefing device or whether your sails are reduced by tying down the reef points. In a real bad storm, it is best to ride it out with bare poles or just enough sail (the jib may do the job) to keep the boat's head to the sea. The actual method of riding out the storm is the same as already described for a powerboat.

If remaining at your mooring, pay out as much extra scope as you safely can and still have clear swinging room, remembering there may be a 180-degree shift of wind in the storm. Run a second strong pendant out to your mooring chain, and protect it and the regular pendant with extra chafing gear. Supplement your mooring by running out your best anchor or your two best set in tandem, with the longest possible scope, in the direction from which you expect the heaviest winds. Don't hang all the strain on your regular mooring bitts or cleat. Carry the lines themselves, or suitable rope "stoppers" from them, to other well-secured bitts, winches, cleats and to the mast. If possible lash pendants and warps down in their chocks, so they can't jump out from pitching in a big sea.

If the approaching storm is a hurricane get all movable objects below decks or ashore to cut windage to a minimum. Unbend sails and stow below and remove most of the running rigging—wrap it a few turns around the mast—leaving one good masthead halyard with which to go aloft and re-rig when it's over. Booms can be lashed flat on deck or put below. Dinghies should be stored ashore. Such objects as life rings, galley stack, removable ventilators, etc., go below. Pump your bilges dry. Make sure all scuppers are clear, all ports and hatches dogged down tight. Engine box covers in smaller craft must be secured solidly. The helm should be secured amidships.

Whether the owner stays aboard during the storm to do what he can for his boat, or does his best in advance and then seeks personal safety ashore is up to him—and to his wife. Boats have been saved by able owners who stayed aboard. And some good men have been

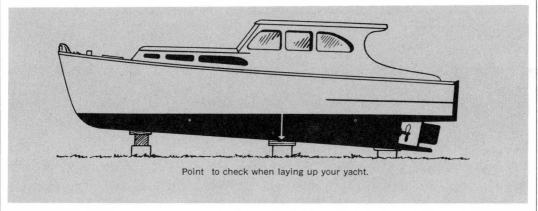
Point to check when laying up your yacht.

drowned trying to do just that. If staying aboard, have your engine ready for action. You may use it to take the heaviest strains off the mooring, but use it sparingly. The worst thing is to run up on your mooring in a lull of the gale until the line hangs slack; then let the boat swing off to one side or falls back to leeward with a yank on the gear. Be sure your fuel tanks are full, oil level up, strainers clear, batteries fully charged. If running the engine in a storm, watch its temperature and keep the intake clear—the water will be full of debris.

If You're At a Dock or Slip. Many of the above precautions will apply, but here are a few extras ones:

1. Secure boat bow-on to the direction of anticipated heaviest seas.
2. Plug exhaust line at the transom to prevent water washing back into engine. You may want to run the engine, so arrange these plugs so they can be pulled out from above.
3. Double up all mooring lines and rig extra chafing gear.
4. If located where anchors can be carried out to hold the boat off the pier or float, do so.
5. Hang all available fenders at strategic points, and contribute a few of your old cushions to the cause. A boat rolling and pitching in a slip may hit piling, bulkheads, etc., with higher-up parts of hull and cabin than it would in normal weather.
6. Mooring lines to pilings should be made fast near the top of the piling, in case of extra-high water.
7. If you aren't going to stay with the boat, or nearby ashore, leave your cabin and ignition keys with the dockmaster. He may shift your berth.

When serious trouble threatens or strikes your boat your best protection is to *be prepared to act quickly*. If you know what to do when the chips are down, frequently you can avoid further damage or personal injury.

MAN OVERBOARD

The procedure given here should be committed to memory. Some day it could save a life:

1. Sing out "man overboard" (so that all on board will know and can help keep the victim in sight).

2. Turn the propellers away from the person in the water (by turning the wheel, and thus the bow toward him—and the stern away from him).

3. Throw him a life preserver (preferably a life ring, but a jacket, cushion or anything that floats will do).

4. Circle around and approach him, heading into the wind or current whichever is the stronger. As soon as he is alongside, shut off the engine or shift to neutral. Hand him a length of line and lead him around to the stern where you can help him aboard.

It is a good idea to hold a "man overboard" drill now and then when your family is on board the boat. Toss over a box or something that will float and sing out "man overboard—this is a drill." The children will get this idea right away.

FIRST AID AFLOAT

Accidents can happen anywhere, afloat or ashore. On land it is often possible to get help quickly, but on a boat it is important to be a "do-it-yourself" skipper. Even seemingly harmless falls, cuts, and bruises should be looked after because of possible infection. One caution though about first aid: No matter how expert you may be, the cardinal rule to remember is—don't overtreat the victim!

If you or someone in your crew have had a course in first aid, all well and good. Even so, a first aid manual (Red Cross or equal) is a must. Every boat should also be equipped with a first aid kit that is adequate for the number of people normally on board. A suggested first aid kit for daily, week-end cruising for a crew of six:

Vaseline Gauze	Benadryl Tablets*	Darvon Compound
Absorbent cotton	Gauze Pads (2"x2", 4"x4")	Eye Pads
Elastic Bandage (3")	Gauze Bandage (2" x 3")	Band-aids
Eyecup and dropper	Adhesive & Scotch Tape	Q-tips
Thermometer & Case	Bandage scissors	Resusitube
Rubbing Alcohol	Safety Pins	Tweezers
Milk of Magnesia	Sunburn Cream	Salt Tablets
Epsom Salts	Hydrogen Peroxide	Aspirin
Aromatic Spirits of	Oil of Cloves	Glycerine
Ammonia	White Vaseline	Merthiolate
Bicarbonate of soda	Pencillin Tablets*	Gantrisin Tablets*
Codeine*	Achrostatin*	Insect Repellent
Paregoric*	Dramamine or Bonine	Burn Ointment

Note 1. Starred items require a prescription from your doctor.
Note 2. Mark all boxes and jars plainly and be sure to keep out of the reach of children.
Note 3. Keep entire kit in one container, easily accessible. The plastic or metal waterproof tackle boxes sold in sporting goods stores make an excellent first aid kit.

Artificial Respiration. You have a good chance to revive the victim if you start artificial respiration within two minutes. You have a very poor chance if you wait ten minutes. But, not matter what the time interval, start breathing life into the victim without delay. Have someone else read the following steps to you while you work if you have not already committed them to memory.

1. Put victim on his back. Check that victim's mouth is clear of obstructions.

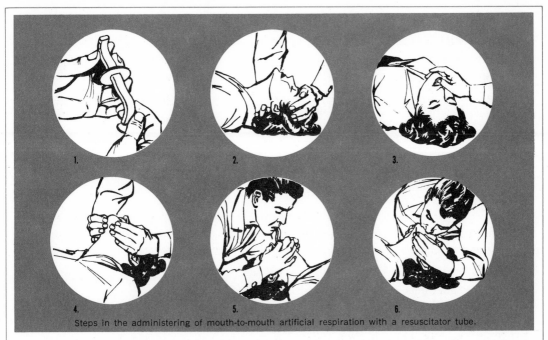

Steps in the administering of mouth-to-mouth artificial respiration with a resuscitator tube.

2. Place a folded coat, blanket, etc., under his shoulders to enable the head to tilt back.

3. Grasp and pull jaw open. Keep open to assure air passage.

4. Pinch nostrils shut, take a deep breath, place your mouth over his mouth (with your thumb in his jaw to keep it open). Blow into his mouth until you see his chest rise.

5. Remove mouth and listen for out-flow of air.

  Adult—rate is about every 5-6 seconds.

  Child—rate is about every 3 seconds. (Use shallow breaths.)

6. If first few attempts are unsuccessful—turn victim on side and give several sharp blows between shoulder blades to remove obstruction.

7. Now do it all over again. Frequently the patient, after a temporary recovery of respiration, stops breathing again. Therefore, he must be watched and if natural breathing stops, artificial respiration should be resumed at once.

IN CASE OF FIRE

Fire is an ever-present danger to boats, especially those with gasoline engines. Alertness to the dangers of highly-volatile fuel will prevent many fires, and an understanding of the types of fires and how to put them out can minimize damage. The Coast Guard, underwriters and other safety officials designate three general types of fires as: Class A, in combustible solid material such as wood, upholstery, fabrics; Class B, in liquids like gasoline, oil and stove fuel; Class C, electrical fires caused by arcing, overheated wires, short circuits.

There are a number of actions to take that apply to all types of fires. One of the first is to determine what type of fire it is and exactly where its base is—not always as obvious as you might expect. Another is to seal off, if possible, the compartment where the fire is, plugging ventilators and other openings, cutting off the air on which fire thrives and preventing its spreading. Reduce wind effect by stopping the boat. If fire is forward, head stern into wind; if aft, head bow into wind. Shut off all flammable engine and stove fuel outlets from tanks and cut off battery switches, regardless of the type of fire. Put all hands in life jackets.

The following is set forth as a guide to fighting fire in specific places aboard a boat:

Engine Compartment. CO_2 dry, dry chemical and foam extinguishers are recommended to fight Class B fuel fires. To extinguish, take the following *possible action:*

    1. Apply proper extinguisher to the base of the fire. CO_2 and dry chemical should be applied as close to base of the fire as possible with a rapid side to side movement. When you think the fire is out, apply extinguisher again to make sure.

    2. If possible, shut off fuel supply at tank.

    3. Shut off battery disconnect switch.

    4. Plug ventilator cowls—seal off compartment as best as you can.

    5. Determine type and base of fire.

    6. Should the heat and smoke force you away, turn the extinguisher on, throw it into the burning area and close the engine hatch.

Galley Fires. This type of Class B fire will usually be galley stove fuel fires or cooking grease fires. This type of fire should be smothered with CO_2, dry chemical or foam. However, alcohol fires can be put out with water. Never carry kerosene or alcohol aboard boat in a glass bottle or breakable container. To extinguish, take the following *possible action:*

    1. Shut off galley stove fuel supply at the tank.

    2. Apply proper extinguisher to the base of the fire with a rapid side to side motion.

    3. Seal off compartment to prevent drafts which will spread and support the fire.

    4. Determine type and base of fire.

    5. Be sure the fire is out.

Electrical Fires. It should be remembered that water and soda acid extinguishers will conduct electricity and should not be used on electrical fires. An electrical fire (Class C type) can start in any compartment on a boat that has electrical wiring. CO_2 and dry chemical extinguishers can be used. To extinguish, take the following *possible action:*

    1. Shut off battery disconnect, or master switch.

    2. Shut off fuel tanks too, just to play it safe.

    3. Look for the source of the smoke. If you see or smell smoke but can't see its source, suspect electric wiring. Don't hesitate to rip out upholstery, etc., if the smoke seems to come from there. Once the base of the fire is found, attempt to extinguish fire.

    4. Seal off compartment to prevent drafts which will spread and support the fire.

    5. Be sure the fire is out.

Class A Fires. These fires are extinguished much the same on boats as ashore. An overheated or overturned galley stove or cabin heater, burning food on the stove, or a carelessly handled match or cigarette can set such fires. They can usually be extinguished with water, under pressure or out of a bucket, and by extinguishers of the soda-acid and foam types. Burning cushions, bedding or pork chops can be thrown overboard. The main thing is to act quickly. However, remember that Class B and C fires will become Class A fires, too, if they burn long enough for the surrounding wood, etc., to ignite. Use the recommended type of extinguisher for the basic cause—electricity or fuel—but be ready to soak the area with water after the first causes are handled.

Carbon tetrachloride extinguishers have not been mentioned because they are no longer approved by the Coast Guard, underwriters, or other safety authorities due to the gas's toxic effect on users and other drawbacks.

Highly recommended for boats with engines below decks are fixed extinguisher systems in engine and tank spaces, actuated automatically by a temperature rise such as a fire would cause. These and all other fire extinguishers should be tested at least once a year by accredited manufacturer's representatives or firefighting authorities, and carry a tag attesting to their working condition.

IN CASE OF FUEL LEAKS

Leakage or spillage of any liquid fuel is dangerous in a boat; that of gasoline, or "LP" gas, is deadly peril. Any odor of gasoline inside the boat indicates danger of explosion and fire. Take every precaution to get the gas vapor out before allowing any open flame or spark on the boat.

Gas leaks inside the boat may be caused by bad fittings, cracked tubing or other mechanical failures. Be sensitive at all times to the distinctive odor of raw gasoline aboard a boat. Before starting the motor after a period of idleness, open the hatches and sniff around in the engine and tank compartments. Be sure there is no gasoline odor, and leave the hatches open a few minutes.

A number of devices to detect flammable vapors in the bilge and warn of their presence by visual or noise signals at the control station are excellent safety devices but not infallible substitutes for your own nose and caution. The same is true of electric blowers which exhaust stagnant air from the engine compartments. Run the blower for five minutes before starting the engines. Have the blower switch tied into the ignition so the engine can't be started until the blower is operating for five minutes or more. If a gasoline leak or the presence of any explosive mixture in the bilge, or other similar enclosure, is suspected, take the following *possible action:*

    1. Shut off *all* machinery immediately—secure the galley.

    2. Shut off battery disconnect switch—which should be a completely-enclosed, vapor-proof, underwriters-approved switch, located outside areas where gas may collect.

    3. Enforce "No Smoking" rule.

    4. Shut off fuel supply at the tank.

    5. Don't attempt to use electric bilge pump to pump the bilges of any gasoline or water.

    6. Open all engine hatches, cabin windows, etc. Allow air to circulate within all parts of the boat.

    7. Gasoline vapor is heavier than air and will seep into and become trapped in every part of the bilge. Don't assume it's gone just because you can't smell it in the cabin. Sniff around the bilge.

    8. Gasoline vapor has a distinct odor—try to find the leak with your sense of smell and try to stop it.

    9. When you feel there is no more vapor, get down in the bilge and inspect all possible places where vapor could be trapped (within the bilge, especially near frames). Don't use a flashlight—they have been known to set off gas vapor, probably due to a defective switch.

    10. Find the source of the leak and try to stop it. If you can repair the leak, make it thoroughly tight and safe, you can get under way after all trace of vapor is out of the boat. But if you can't stop the leak, don't start your engine. Wait for a tow (or sail home if in an auxiliary). Have the tank pumped out and permanent repairs made before you touch an electric switch, light the stove or smoke.

IF YOU STRIKE A SUBMERGED OBJECT

When a boat strikes a submerged object it is usually because of human carelessness. The operator either has not paid attention to his navigation and has run the boat into shallow or foul water, or he has failed to keep a sharp lookout and steer clear of flotsam. Careful piloting and an alert lookout will avoid such trouble. However, you may hit a waterlogged piece of timber floating just below the surface, an uncharted obstruction, or a lobsterpot or fish trawl buoy run underwater by current. So always be prepared to take instant action if the thump and jolt that usually signal such a collision is felt. When this occurs, take the following *possible action:*

1. Stop your engine instantly, take it out of gear and drift or if in close quarters or a hazardous area, anchor.

2. Open up all hatches and floorboards giving access to the bilges and look for leaks. If water is rising, determine where it is coming in. Look around the stern, where the bottom may be holed by a propeller blade, strut or rudder. A twin-screw boat is more prone to this type of damage than one with a single propeller protected by a skeg.

3. If the boat is leaking badly you may be able to start the engine (in neutral) and use its cooling water intake as an emergency pump. A few exceptionally well-equipped boats have valves which, by turning, will pump water from the bilge instead of outside. Lacking such a convenience, you may be able to close the through-hull intake valve, pull off the hose leading from it to the engine circulating pump, and pump the bilge water through the circulating system and overboard. Rig some sort of stiff screen—ordinary metal window or hatch screening can be used—around the bilge intake to prevent debris (most bilges are dirty) from clogging the line. Watch the water level carefully. If the pump removes water faster than it is leaking in don't let it run dry, and "burn up" the engine.

4. If the leak can be reached from inside, try to stop or slow the flow of water with an internal patch. This should consist first of some soft material, like a cushion, clothing or other fabric, backed up by a flat, hard piece of wood or metal. This in

Exterior collision mat in place.

turn may be shored and wedged in place, if it's in an accessible place.

5. It may also be possible to get a "collision mat" over the outside of the hole. This would be a sail, side curtain, mattress or similar object, pulled and held in place under the hull by ropes to its corners, one or more of which must go under the keel to the far side of the boat. Pressure of water will help hold an outside patch in place.

6. If there is no serious leak, or when it's under control, try to get under way with your engine, very slowly at first. The propeller and shaft may be bent by the collision, causing vibration. If there is not too much vibration, run *slowly* to the nearest port. If vibration is excessive, shut off engine, stay where you are and try to get a tow. Use radio or visual distress signal.

7. On making port, if there is any indication of damage to hull or gear, have the boat hauled immediately by the nearest boatyard, or, if none is available, lay her ashore alongside a pier or bulkhead and at low tide inspect bottom, propeller, shaft, etc. Don't leave the boat afloat, unattended, until you are sure she is not leaking. Never depend on an automatic electric bilge pump to keep her dry—pump or battery might fail. Stay aboard or engage someone to do so.

8. Check your strut bolts, rudder posts, stuffing box, and engine alignment, as well as the propeller and shaft.

9. If the boat has been run with a bent propeller or shaft, even though vibration was slight, check the strut bearing or outside stuffing box for excessive wear and loose holding bolts.

IN CASE OF SHIPWRECK

Should this emergency occur, one fact is paramount—stay with the boat. Put on your life preserver immediately. You may have to jump overboard. If you are in the water be sure to remain in the vicinity of your ship.

Many people have tried to swim for the shore when shipwrecked. Distances are deceiving at sea particularly when you are swimming. If there is the slightest doubt in your mind that you can easily swim ashore—stay near the boat.

IF YOU RUN AGROUND

Running aground, also, is usually the fault of the skipper. But most of us make mistakes, and should keep in mind how to get ourselves and our craft out of them. How to do so depends on an infinite variety of conditions. Under the worst conditions, such as grounding

Method of towing a boat from an aground situation. The skipper of the assisting vessel must acquaint himself as fully as possible with the entire problem, including the nature of the bottom, prevailing winds, current and tidal data.

at high speed on jagged rocks, or being driven on shore by high wind and seas, the boat may be lost and the crew be in serious danger.

When you hit bottom with that sickening, solid feeling that means you're really on, not just bouncing or dragging over a shoal spot, stop your engine and/or lower sail. Keep cool and appraise the situation. Is the tide, if any, rising or falling? Is the bottom sand, rock or mud? In which direction, and how far off, is water deep enough to float your boat? Is she aground at bow or stern only, or the full length of the keel? After ascertaining the circumstances, take the following *possible action:*

1. Look below to see if she's leaking, and if so where, and try to stop it.

2. If possible, the first thing to do toward refloating usually is to get out your heaviest anchor on the longest warp available. With your dinghy, or the aid of another boat, plant it out in deep water. With a small boat on a flat shore you may even be able to wade out far enough with it. Once it's out, put as heavy a strain as you can on the line and keep it on. Try to hold the boat end-on—bow or stern—to the deeper water and to any sea there may be.

3. If the boat is aground only on the forward or after part of her keel, move your crew and passengers to the other end of the boat, this may help lift her free as you haul on the anchor line. If the tide is rising and you keep a strain on the anchor she'll usually come off by herself.

4. If she is leaking, or if the weather is getting rough and/or you are aground too solidly to get yourself off, try to get help.

5. In soft sand or mud, suction may hold the hull, especially a flat, wide hull to the bottom. In this case a bit of sea can help break suction. Try to get another motor boat to run by a few times, making a wake, while you haul on your anchor rope.

6. If aground on sand or mud, do *not* run your engine. To do so will plug the cooling system with sand or mud and "burn up" the engine.

7. If the tide is falling and you can't get off within a few minutes, you are probably stuck until the tide floods again. The boat will settle down on her bilge. If she is a wide, shoal hull and is on sand or mud bottom, this may do no harm. But if there are rocks under her, get some kind of padding between the bilge and the rocks —cushions, mattresses, anything thick and shock-absorbent. Better to spoil some equipment than put a hole in the boat.

8. You may be able, with spars and other material at hand, to block up under the bilge so the boat will not lie over. Do this *only* if you can make the blocking solid. Normally it damages a boat less to come down gradually on her bilge, as the tide drops than to fall over suddenly after the cushioning water is out from under her.

9. A deep, narrow-keel sailboat especially is susceptible to filling with water on the rising tide if she is heeled far over. If there seems any chance of this, before the tide comes back plug the scuppers on the low side; close all ports, hatches and other openings watertight; and remove any heavy equipment stowed high up in the boat.

10. If you have to be towed off, take all precautions. The towline should be secured to more than one set of bitts. Carry the strain to several bitts or cleats, and to the mast, if stepped through the deck. If a very heavy strain is expected, lead the towline or bridle all around the hull just below deck level, suspending it at intervals with short pieces of line from the deck fittings. Make sure the line doesn't lead around any sharp corners or through chocks at bad angles. Have the towing boat use as little power as will suffice to do the job, and avoid sudden jerks and surges. Have him pull you end on—bow or stern first, depending on how the boat lies—and never haul her off sideways, especially if there are rocks in the vicinity.

11. Once you're off, get the boat into port, haul out or lie up over a tide to inspect damage. Don't leave the boat before making a careful check for leaks.

"ON BOARD" TOOLS AND SPARES

Every boat needs a kit of tools and spare parts for emergency repairs. The size and make-up of such kits depends on the boat, her equipment, how far she cruises away from repair facilities and, to some extent, on the abilities of her owner.

The Hull. For hull work a few basic carpentry tools may suffice. A hammer or two, a small, all-purpose saw; screwdrivers of two sizes; a sharp, strong-bladed knife; pliers—these are basic. (Drill a small hole in the handle of each hand tool and attach lanyards to help you hold onto them when working over the side, or aloft.) Boatbuilders' C-clamps have a lot of uses, as do a hand drill and bits. From there you can build up, according to your needs and your skills. There must also be assorted nails, screws and bolts of suitable sizes.

For emergency patching, canvas and small sheets of plywood are helpful, along with white lead and copper tacks. Many sealing and bedding compounds, of a variety of chemical compositions, are suitable for this.

In wooden boats, a caulking iron and a few strands of cotton seam caulking should always be aboard, along with a can of seam compound or putty and a putty knife. Desirable also are softwood plugs of sizes and shapes that can be driven into each underwater through-hull opening in case of a failure of sea cocks, scupper pipes, icebox drains, etc.

The Engine. Wrenches, screwdrivers, pliers, and general tools, to fit the engine are essential along with any specialized tools your engine requires. A file, a cold chisel and a peen hammer are pretty close to indispensable as is a roll of electrician's tape. The engine instruction manual, with its trouble shooting guide, is a must aboard any yacht.

The most commonly-needed engine spares are probably spark plugs, points, condensers and pump parts. Get from your engine's builder a list of spare parts recommended to be carried with his particular engine. One manufacturer lists three different kits. The simplest, strictly electrical, includes spark plugs, distributor points, ignition coil, distributor rotor and cap, and condenser. The next larger has these plus gaskets, a fuel pump kit and a *Maintenance Handbook.* Kit No. 1 adds such things as valve springs and complete fuel pump and water pumps. Spare hose and hose clamps may come in handy, as may neoprene tubing. Many owners who cruise far from home or in any driftwood infested waters, carry spare propellers.

Rigging. In the rigging department, a sailboat should have spare fabric for sail patching, a sail repair kit of needles, thread and tools and a coil of rope to replace a sheet or halyard. Wire clamps or U-bolts are handy for temporary repairs to sailboat standing rigging and to steering cable in motorboats. Spare shackles of various sizes are useful.

Miscellaneous. Marine toilets are more prone to get out of kilter than the shore-based kind. Engine tools will do the work, but special spare valves, pump leathers, etc., are required. Several manufacturers put out complete toilet overhaul kits.

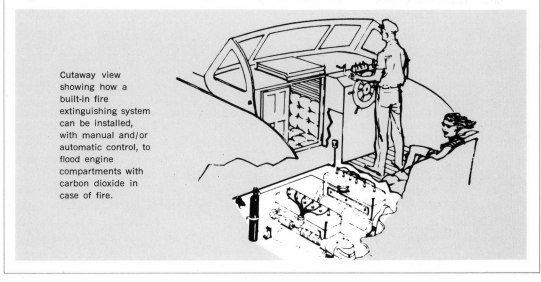

Cutaway view showing how a built-in fire extinguishing system can be installed, with manual and/or automatic control, to flood engine compartments with carbon dioxide in case of fire.

There are some spares so obvious they shouldn't have to be mentioned, but they will be as a reminder. A good-capacity hand pump *and* a bucket should be aboard in case fancier pumping gear fails or a bad leak develops. Spare anchors and warps should be heavy and strong. And if your boat is small—up to 20 feet or so—carry a paddle. Better yet, fit her with rowlocks and keep a pair of oars aboard against the time, in a calm or if your engine fails, when a "white ash breeze" will be welcome.

RECOGNIZED DISTRESS SIGNALS

We have mentioned signaling for help—here's how it's done. The following are the recommended distress signals to use, depending upon the equipment you have on board and upon the visibility at the time:

1. Most widely-recognized distress signal is "SOS." This, in Morse code, is made with three dots, three dashes, three dots. Besides radio, it can be sent by sound signals—three short (space), three long (space), three short blasts on a horn; or by visual signal—three short, three long, three short flashes of a light.

2. Send the emergency signal word "MAYDAY" repeatedly on your radiotelephone and then follow the procedure given on page 110.

3. A gun or other explosive, fired at intervals of about one minute.

4. Continuous sounding of fog horn, bell, or whistle.

5. Rockets or shells burning red flares. In commercial kits, some flares have parachutes attached to keep them in the air longer.

6. Flames at night and heavy black smoke by day, such as from burning oil burned in a metal bucket or equivalent. Use oil or kerosene—*never gasoline*.

7. Reverse your flag or ensign so that it flies upside down.

8. Fly a white cloth from the highest point on your boat. The International Code flags NC, or a square flag with a basket, a box, or a bell-shaped object above or below it on your boat's mast are also well-known day-time distress signals.

9. An old fisherman's distress signal is a pair of oilskin trousers or any other conspicuous and incongruous object hung in the rigging.

10. The most recent distress signal for small craft, as proposed by the Coast Guard, is as follows: the boat operator stands and repeatedly—and slowly—raises and lowers his arms outstretched to each side. This signal is distinctive and not likely to be mistaken for a greeting. As the Coast Guard recommends, "To be as effective as possible, this signal should be given from the highest vantage point on the boat, with consideration given to color contrasts."

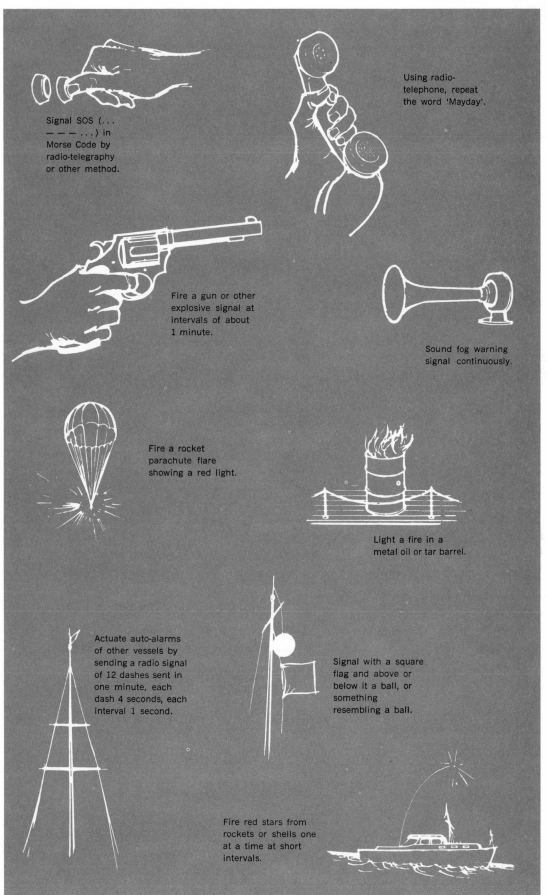

Signal SOS (. . . — — — . . .) in Morse Code by radio-telegraphy or other method.

Using radio-telephone, repeat the word 'Mayday'.

Fire a gun or other explosive signal at intervals of about 1 minute.

Sound fog warning signal continuously.

Fire a rocket parachute flare showing a red light.

Light a fire in a metal oil or tar barrel.

Actuate auto-alarms of other vessels by sending a radio signal of 12 dashes sent in one minute, each dash 4 seconds, each interval 1 second.

Signal with a square flag and above or below it a ball, or something resembling a ball.

Fire red stars from rockets or shells one at a time at short intervals.

CHAPTER
THREE:
GETTING
WHERE
YOU WANT
TO GO

Navigation is the art of getting your yacht where you want her. It doesn't make any difference if your "yacht" is an eight-foot dinghy or a 90-foot schooner. Furthermore, it's not important what kind of boat you're the skipper of; but it's important that you're able to navigate her safely and efficiently, according to her ability and according to waters you're sailing on. This calls for a certain degree of learning; and it also calls for proper gear. But, before going into this, let's look at the "aids to navigation" available.

AIDS TO NAVIGATION

The various aids to navigation are often called the "signposts of the waterways." These aids include buoys, day beacons, range lights, lightships, lighthouses, etc., and they help a skipper to get where he wants.

BUOYS AND WATERWAY MARKERS

A buoy is nothing more than a visual warning device used as a navigation aid for signaling danger, obstructions, or changes in the contours of the sea bottom, and designed to set forth a course of safety for yachtsmen. The coloring and numbering of buoys is determined by their position with respect to the channel as entered from seaward and followed toward the head of navigation. The expression "red right returning" has long been used by the seafaring man to remind him that red buoys are passed on his starboard side when proceeding from the open sea into port (upstream). Likewise black buoys are left to port. Conversely, when proceeding toward the sea or leaving port, red buoys are left, to port, and black buoys to starboard.

Types of Buoys
In addition to several special purpose buoys, having no lateral significance, and used to mark such things as dredging areas, fish nets, quarantine anchorage, etc., the yachtsman can expect to encounter eight different types of buoys marking the nation's waterways. Each kind is marked, shaped and designed to serve under definite marine conditions. Some are equipped with lights for night navigation, others having sounding devices for fog and darkness. Following are the principal types of buoys:

  1. *Spar Buoys* are large shaped logs, trimmed and appropriately painted. They're constructed of steel plates and have no shape significance.

  2. *Can* and *Nun Buoys* are built of steel plates and have distinctive shapes designated by their names.

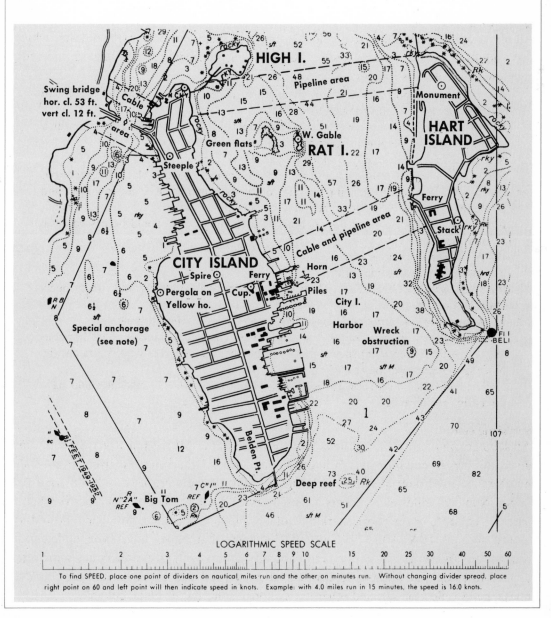

LOGARITHMIC SPEED SCALE

To find SPEED, place one point of dividers on nautical miles run and the other on minutes run. Without changing divider spread, place right point on 60 and left point will then indicate speed in knots. Example: with 4.0 miles run in 15 minutes, the speed is 16.0 knots.

3. *Bell Buoys* are made of steel plates. They float with short skeleton towers attached and fixed with bells. In a few buoys, the bells are struck by compressed air or electrically operated hammers.

4. *Gong Buoys* are constructed similar to bell buoys, but have a distinctive sounding note with alternating tones.

5. *Whistle Buoys* become useful at night and during fog or low visibility. The whistle mechanism is operated by the motion of the water. A variation of sound is also employed by use of a mechanically operated horn.

6. *Lighted Buoys* burn compressed acetylene gas, contained in steel tanks inside the buoy. From the tanks the gas is fed by tube to a flasher set in the lantern at the top of the buoy. A valve mechanism operated by the gas pressure permits a definite amount of gas to pass the burner at intervals, to be ignited by a pilot flame which burns continuously. The period and length of the flash may be adjusted to produce a definite characteristic. An increasing number of these buoys are lighted electrically.

7. *Combination Buoys* have light and sound signal combinations, such as a lighted bell buoy. Most modern buoys have radar reflectors designed to improve radar response, and are easier to locate by searchlight.

Color System

All buoys are painted distinctive colors to indicate their purpose, or the side on which they should be passed. Lateral system buoys, when proceeding from seaward, are indicated by their colors as follows:

Black. Marks the port (left) side of channels, or the location of obstacles which can be passed by keeping the buoy on the port hand.

Red. Marks the starboard (right) side of channels or the locations of wrecks which must be passed by keeping the buoy on the starboard hand.

Red and Black Horizontally Banded Buoys. Mark junctions in the channel, or obstacles which may be passed on either side. If the topmost band is black, the preferred channel will be found by keeping the buoy on the port hand side. If the topmost band is red, the preferred channel will be found by keeping the buoy on the starboard hand.

Black and Vertically Striped Buoys. Mark mid-channels, and should be passed close to, on either side.

White. Marks anchorage areas.

Yellow. Marks quarantine areas.

White Buoys with Green Tops. Used in connection with dredging and survey operations.

White and Black Alternating Horizontally Banded Buoys. Mark fish net areas.

White and International Orange Buoys Alternately Banded. Banded either horizontally or vertically represent special purposes. Neither the lateral-system colors nor the other special purpose colors apply.

Yellow and Black Vertically Striped Buoys. Used for seadrome markings and have no marine significance.

Numbering System

All solid colored red or black buoys (except those in the Mississippi River System), are given numbers or combinations of numbers and letters. Others may be given letters. Odd numbers are used only on solid black buoys, even numbers are used only on solid red buoys. Numbers followed by letters are used on solid colored red or black buoys when a letter is required, or on buoys marking isolated off-shore dangers. Number followed by letters, such as 10A, 10B, 10C, usually indicates that buoys have been added to a channel and the series not at once renumbered. Letters without numbers are sometimes applied to black and white vertically striped buoys; red and black horizontally banded buoys; solid yellow buoys; and other buoys not in solid red or black colors.

Characteristics of Lights

Lights on buoys are either red, green or white. Red lights serve to identify red buoys and are found on red or banded buoys with topmost band of red. Green lights mark only black buoys. Thus entering a channel, red lights mark the starboard buoys; green marks the port buoys. White lights on buoys have no special color significance. Four different light phases are employed on buoys and it is sound judgment to be completely aware of what they represent. They are as follows:

Fixed Lights. These lights don't flash and may be found on either red or black buoys.

Flashing Lights. Placed only on black buoys, red buoys and special purpose buoys. They flash at regular intervals of not more than 30 flashes per minute.

Quick Flashing Lights. Placed only on black buoys and/or red buoys where it is desired to show that special caution is required. The flash rate is less than 60 flashes per minute.

Interrupted Quick Flashing Lights. Placed only on buoys painted with red and black horizontal bands, at points where it is desired to indicate junctions, or obstructions which may be passed on either side. The flashing groups consist of a series of quick flashes, with dark intervals of around 4 seconds.

Short-Long Flashing Lights. Placed only on buoys painted in black and white vertical stripes at points where it is desired to indicate mid-channels, and should be passed close to on either side. The flashing consists of a short flash and a long flash recurring at the rate of 8 per minute. Since perspective is different at night, use a stopwatch to identify all lights by their characteristics.

Buoy Facts to Remember

Since all channels don't lead from seaward, arbitrary assumptions must at times be made in order that the system may be consistently applied. Proceeding from seaward is considered in a southerly direction along the Atlantic coast, in a westerly and northerly direction along the Gulf coast, and in a northerly direction on the Pacific coast. On the Great Lakes proceeding in a westerly and northerly direction is proceeding from seaward; and on the Intracoastal Waterway, proceeding generally southerly along the Atlantic coast, and in a generally westerly direction along the Gulf coast is considered proceeding from seaward. The characteristics of aids to navigation on the Mississippi and Ohio Rivers and their tributaries follow the basic assumption that proceeding from the sea toward the head of navigation will find red on starboard (right side).

Buoys can be carried away, shifted, capsized or sunk as the result of storms, ice conditions, collisions or other accidents. Lighted buoys may become extinguished or their lighting apparatus broken or deranged, causing them to show improper light colors or light phase characteristics. Buoys are moored to chains of various lengths, and in some cases, several times the depth of the water in which they're located. The radius of the swing should be considered. The buoy does not maintain position directly over its sinker. Buoys usually yaw about under the influence of the wind and current, and a boat attempting to pass too close risks collision. Buoys should always be regarded as warnings or guides, rather than infallible navigation marks. Whenever possible, navigate by bearings or angles on fixed objects on shore and by soundings rather than by reliance on buoys.

Local, private channel markers put out by fishermen and local yachtsmen usually are wooden stakes, stone monuments, cage structures of wood or metal, reinforced concrete tripods, or even small trees with the leaves still rattling in the breeze. As a rule, unless you know the local waters, it is risky to pass through such a channel. Sometimes the markers are not channel markers at all but indicate fish traps, nets, or setlines. There is no way of telling, so it's best to keep clear.

Day Beacons

These are aids to navigation in the form of unlighted structures. Design and construction vary. A day beacon may simply consist a single pile with daymark on the top. They are colored to distinguish them from their surroundings and to provide a means of identification. Where they mark the sides of channels, coloring follows the standard color scheme of the United States system of buoyage, i.e., red indicating the right side entering and black the left side entering. Many day beacons are fitted with reflectors to facilitate locating them at night by means of a searchlight.

Intracoastal Waterway Buoys

The Intracoastal Waterway runs parallel to the Atlantic and Gulf coasts from Manasquan Inlet on the New Jersey shore to the Mexican border. Aids marking these waters have some portions of them painted yellow. Buoys have a band of yellow at the top, day beacons have a band or border of yellow, light structures are similarly painted. The coloring and numbering of buoys and day beacons and the color of lights follow the same system as that in other United States waterways. In order that vessels may readily follow this route where it coincides with another waterway such as an important river marked on the seacoast system, special markings are employed. These special marks consist of a yellow square or a yellow triangle painted on the dual purpose aid. The yellow triangle has the same meaning as a nun and indicates the aid should be passed on the starboard side when proceeding in a direction from Chesapeake Bay toward Mexico. The yellow square has the same meaning as a can; in the above direction of travel it would be passed on the port side.

Buoyage system for State Waterways

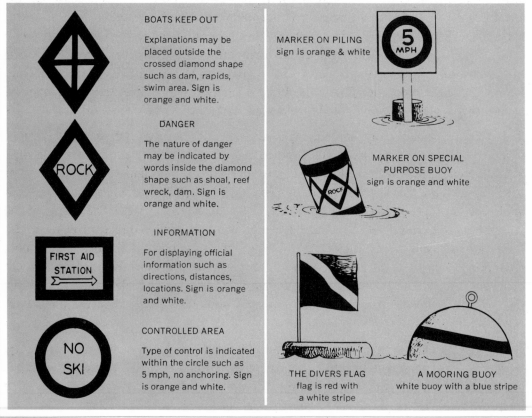

BOATS KEEP OUT

Explanations may be placed outside the crossed diamond shape such as dam, rapids, swim area. Sign is orange and white.

DANGER

The nature of danger may be indicated by words inside the diamond shape such as shoal, reef wreck, dam. Sign is orange and white.

INFORMATION

For displaying official information such as directions, distances, locations. Sign is orange and white.

CONTROLLED AREA

Type of control is indicated within the circle such as 5 mph, no anchoring. Sign is orange and white.

MARKER ON PILING
sign is orange & white

MARKER ON SPECIAL PURPOSE BUOY
sign is orange and white

THE DIVERS FLAG
flag is red with a white stripe

A MOORING BUOY
white buoy with a blue stripe

code flags/running lights/U.S. buoyage/ Intercoastal Waterway aids to navigation

Code Flags and Single Meanings

General Signal

Alfa (Affirm*) *Speed Trial*	Kilo *Stop Instantly*	Uniform *Standing into danger*	1
Bravo *Explosives*	Lima *Stop, Something to Communicate*	Victor *Require Assistance*	2
Charlie *Yes*	Mike *Doctor on Board*	Whiskey *Require Medical Assistance*	3
Delta *Keep Clear*	November (Negative*) *No*	X-ray *Stop your Intentions*	4
Echo *Altering Course to Starboard*	Oscar (Option*) *Man Overboard*	Yankee *Carrying Mails*	5
Foxtrot *Disabled*	Papa (Prep*) *About to Sail (Lights out)*	Zulu *Shore Stations*	6
Golf *Want a Pilot*	Quebec *Request Pratique*	1st Repeat	7
Hotel *A Pilot is on Board*	Romeo *Way is off my ship*	2nd Repeat	8
India (Interrogatory*) *Altering Course to Port*	Sierra *Going full speed astern*	3rd Repeat	9
Juliett *Semaphore*	Tango *Do not pass ahead of me*	*(Decimal Point)* Code and Answering Pennant:	0

• How International Code Flags Are Used In Signaling •

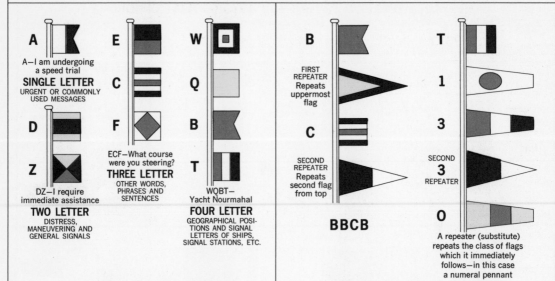

A A—I am undergoing a speed trial
SINGLE LETTER
URGENT OR COMMONLY USED MESSAGES

D
Z DZ—I require immediate assistance
TWO LETTER
DISTRESS, MANEUVERING AND GENERAL SIGNALS

E
C
F ECF—What course were you steering?
THREE LETTER
OTHER WORDS, PHRASES AND SENTENCES

W
Q
B
T WQBT—Yacht Nourmahal
FOUR LETTER
GEOGRAPHICAL POSITIONS AND SIGNAL LETTERS OF SHIPS, SIGNAL STATIONS, ETC.

1, 2, 3, and 4·LETTER GROUPS

B FIRST REPEATER Repeats uppermost flag
C SECOND REPEATER Repeats second flag from top
BBCB

T
1
3 SECOND **3** REPEATER
O
A repeater (substitute) repeats the class of flags which it immediately follows—in this case a numeral pennant

REPEATERS (SUBSTITUTES)

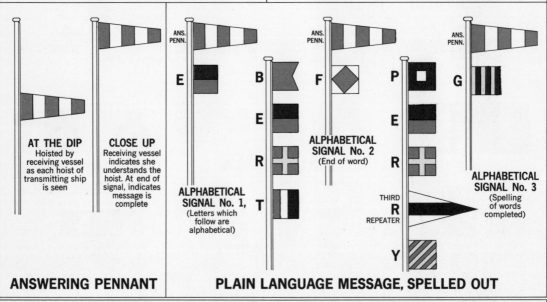

AT THE DIP
Hoisted by receiving vessel as each hoist of transmitting ship is seen

CLOSE UP
Receiving vessel indicates she understands the hoist. At end of signal, indicates message is complete

ANSWERING PENNANT

ANS. PENN.
E
B
E
R
T
ALPHABETICAL SIGNAL No. 1,
(Letters which follow are alphabetical)

ANS. PENN.
F
P
E
R
THIRD REPEATER
R
Y
ALPHABETICAL SIGNAL No. 2
(End of word)

ANS. PENN.
G
ALPHABETICAL SIGNAL No. 3
(Spelling of words completed)

PLAIN LANGUAGE MESSAGE, SPELLED OUT

RUNNING LIGHT RECOGNITION ANY LENGTH UNDER 40 GROSS TONS

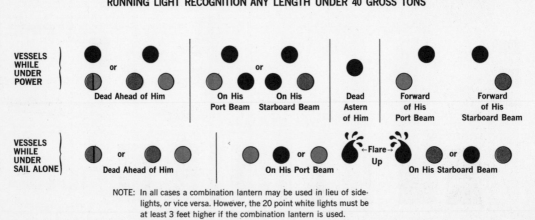

VESSELS WHILE UNDER POWER
or — Dead Ahead of Him
or — On His Port Beam / On His Starboard Beam
Dead Astern of Him
Forward of His Port Beam
Forward of His Starboard Beam

VESSELS WHILE UNDER SAIL ALONE
or — Dead Ahead of Him
On His Port Beam
←Flare→ Up
or — On His Starboard Beam

NOTE: In all cases a combination lantern may be used in lieu of side-lights, or vice versa. However, the 20 point white lights must be at least 3 feet higher if the combination lantern is used.

As per Public Law 552, effective June 4, 1956
Amending Motorboat Act of 1940

AIDS TO NAVIGATION ON NAVIGABLE WATERS
except Western Rivers and Intracoastal Waterway

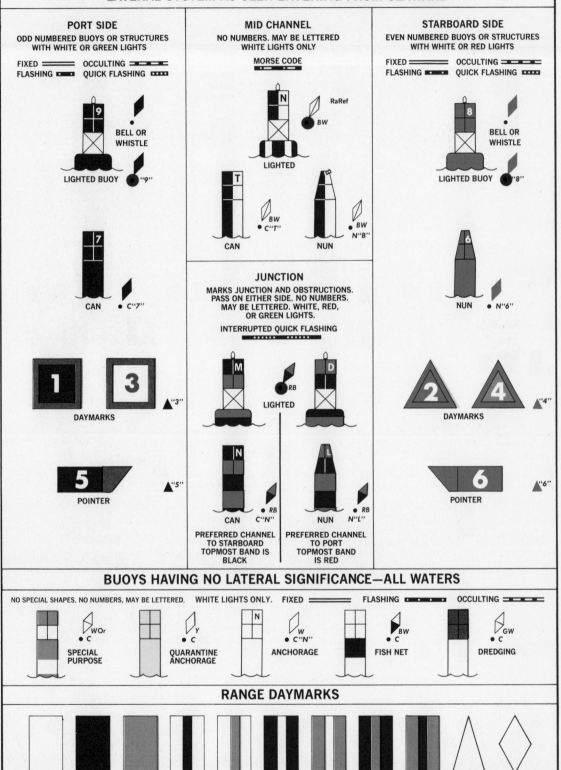

LATERAL SYSTEM AS SEEN ENTERING FROM SEAWARD

PORT SIDE
ODD NUMBERED BUOYS OR STRUCTURES
WITH WHITE OR GREEN LIGHTS

FIXED ════ OCCULTING ══ ▬ ▬ ▬
FLASHING ▬ ▬ ▬ QUICK FLASHING ▯▯▯▯

9

BELL OR
WHISTLE

LIGHTED BUOY   "9"

7

CAN   C"7"

DAYMARKS
1   3   ▲ "3"

POINTER
5   ▲ "5"

MID CHANNEL
NO NUMBERS. MAY BE LETTERED
WHITE LIGHTS ONLY

MORSE CODE
▬ ■ ▬

N   RaRef
          BW

LIGHTED

T   BW
           C"T"

          BW
          N"B"

CAN   NUN

JUNCTION
MARKS JUNCTION AND OBSTRUCTIONS.
PASS ON EITHER SIDE. NO NUMBERS.
MAY BE LETTERED. WHITE, RED,
OR GREEN LIGHTS.

INTERRUPTED QUICK FLASHING
■■■■■ ■■■■■

M   D
          RB

LIGHTED

N   L
          RB   RB
          C"N"   N"L"

CAN   NUN

PREFERRED CHANNEL   PREFERRED CHANNEL
TO STARBOARD   TO PORT
TOPMOST BAND IS   TOPMOST BAND
BLACK   IS RED

STARBOARD SIDE
EVEN NUMBERED BUOYS OR STRUCTURES
WITH WHITE OR RED LIGHTS

FIXED ════ OCCULTING ══ ▬ ▬ ▬
FLASHING ▬ ▬ ▬ QUICK FLASHING ▯▯▯▯

8

BELL OR
WHISTLE

LIGHTED BUOY   "8"

6

NUN   N"6"

DAYMARKS
2   4   ▲ "4"

POINTER
6   ▲ "6"

BUOYS HAVING NO LATERAL SIGNIFICANCE—ALL WATERS

NO SPECIAL SHAPES. NO NUMBERS, MAY BE LETTERED.   WHITE LIGHTS ONLY.   FIXED ════   FLASHING ▬■▬■▬   OCCULTING ══▬▬▬

WOr
C

SPECIAL
PURPOSE

Y
C

QUARANTINE
ANCHORAGE

N

W
C"N"

ANCHORAGE

BW
C

FISH NET

GW
C

DREDGING

RANGE DAYMARKS

MAY BE USED IN SPECIAL CIRCUMSTANCES

NOTES: A. Quick flashing lights mark important turns, wrecks, etc., where particular caution is required.   B. RaRef on chart indicates radar reflector installed.

Published by permission of U.S. COAST GUARD from Vol. I, 1965 Light List

AIDS TO NAVIGATION ON THE INTRACOASTAL WATERWAY

AS SEEN ENTERING FROM NORTH AND EAST AND PROCEEDING TO SOUTH AND WEST

PORT SIDE
ODD NUMBERED BUOYS OR STRUCTURES WITH WHITE OR GREEN LIGHTS

FIXED ═══ OCCULTING ▬ ▬ ▬
FLASHING ▬ ▪ ▬ QUICK FLASHING ▪▪▪▪▪

3
BELL OR WHISTLE
LIGHTED BUOY   "3"

9
CAN   C"9"

5   3
DAYMARKS   ▲ "3"

7
POINTER   ▲ "7"

5
JOINT   • C"5"

6
JOINT   • N"6"

JUNCTION
MARKS JUNCTION AND OBSTRUCTIONS. PASS ON EITHER SIDE. NO NUMBERS. MAY BE LETTERED. WHITE, RED, OR GREEN LIGHTS.

INTERRUPTED QUICK FLASHING ▪▪▪▪▪▪ ▪▪▪▪▪▪

J   N
• RB
LIGHTED

A   S
CAN   NUN
• RB C"A"   • RB N"S"

PREFERRED CHANNEL TO STARBOARD TOPMOST BAND IS BLACK

PREFERRED CHANNEL TO PORT TOPMOST BAND IS RED

STARBOARD SIDE
EVEN NUMBERED BUOYS OR STRUCTURES WITH WHITE OR RED LIGHTS

FIXED ═══ OCCULTING ▬ ▬ ▬
FLASHING ▬ ▪ ▬ QUICK FLASHING ▪▪▪▪▪

8
BELL OR WHISTLE
LIGHTED BUOY   "8"

6
NUN   N"6"

2   4
DAYMARKS   ▲ "4"

6
POINTER   ▲ "6"

6
JOINT   • N"6"

5
JOINT   • C"5"

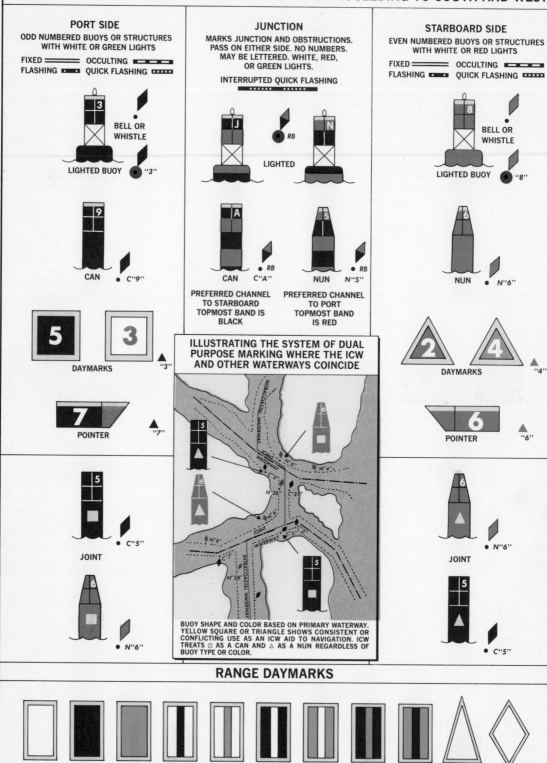

ILLUSTRATING THE SYSTEM OF DUAL PURPOSE MARKING WHERE THE ICW AND OTHER WATERWAYS COINCIDE

BUOY SHAPE AND COLOR BASED ON PRIMARY WATERWAY. YELLOW SQUARE OR TRIANGLE SHOWS CONSISTENT OR CONFLICTING USE AS AN ICW AID TO NAVIGATION. ICW TREATS □ AS A CAN AND △ AS A NUN REGARDLESS OF BUOY TYPE OR COLOR.

RANGE DAYMARKS

NOTE: The ICW aids are characterized by the yellow border

MAY BE USED IN SPECIAL CIRCUMSTANCES

Published by permission of U.S. COAST GUARD from Vol. I, 1965 Light List

Buoyage System for State Waterways

On waters completely within state boundaries (not navigable to the sea) many states have adopted a uniform system of waterway markers. Just as the Intracoastal Waterways markers are distinguished by a special yellow shape, orange and white identify state regulatory markers. On buoys, a 3-inch orange band is *usually* used at the top and bottom, and on the white area between bands, a geometric shape appears, also in orange. A diamond shape indicates danger. A diamond with a cross signifies a prohibited area. A circle denotes zoning or control. A square or rectangle conveys other information. On shore structures, the orange bands are optional.

Lighthouses

Lighthouses are found upon the coasts of the United States and along some of the interior waterways. They are placed where they will be of most use, on prominent headlands, at entrances, on isolated dangers, or at other points where it is necessary to warn or guide the navigator. Each lighthouse has its own distinctive paint job—some are white all over, others are striped in different colors, and still others are spirally painted like a barber's pole. This is done for day identification. At night, these lights flash their warnings in set patterns. With a Government publication called *Light List*, you can identify each light by its characteristic flash. Some lights show green and some show white. Red, unless specifically stated otherwise in the *Light List*, denotes a danger area. You may approach a light at night and see it flashing white or green, then suddenly see it turn red. Look at the chart at once, because when you get into the red sector of a light, you are heading for trouble. A lighthouse may have manned or automatically operated lights. In addition to the visual kind, lighthouses are usually equipped with fog and radio beacon signals.

Buoyage system for State Waterways

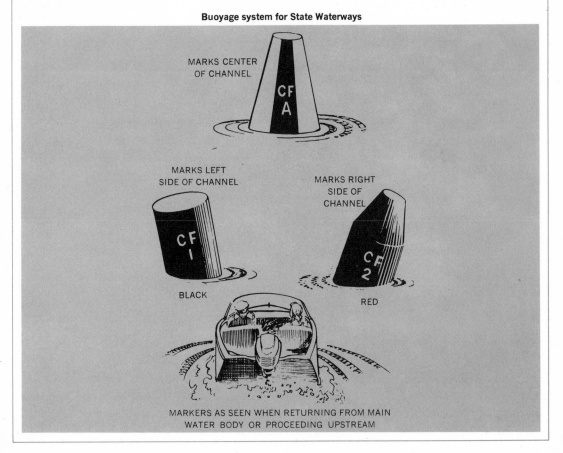

MARKS CENTER OF CHANNEL

CF A

MARKS LEFT SIDE OF CHANNEL

CF 1

BLACK

MARKS RIGHT SIDE OF CHANNEL

CF 2

RED

MARKERS AS SEEN WHEN RETURNING FROM MAIN WATER BODY OR PROCEEDING UPSTREAM

Lightships

Lightships are placed in exposed locations where it's impractical to construct fixed aids to navigation. They provide light, fog, and radio beacon signals and are distinguished from each other by the characteristics of their signals. Lights are displayed from one hour before sunset until one hour after sunrise and at all times when the sound signal is operating. By day, lightships, especially relief lightships, display the International Code signal of the station when a vessel is approaching or is in the vicinity, when there are indications that a vessel is in strange waters or fails to recognize the station, or when a vessel asks for information. The code signal for each lightship station is stated in the *Light Lists*. In addition, the hulls of all lightships, with the exception of the Lake Huron lightship which is painted black, are painted red with the name of the station in white on both sides. The word RELIEF is painted on relief lightships instead of the name of the station.

A lightship underway, or off station, will fly the International Code signal flags "PC." This signal indicates that lightship isn't at anchor on her station. While underway, she won't show or sound any of the signals of a lightship, but will display the lights prescribed by the Rules of the Road. Texas tower lighthouses have not proved successful replacing lightships at many offshore light stations.

Minor Lights

These light structures may be painted similarly to lighthouses. Sometimes, however, they are painted black or red, to indicate the sides of the channel which they mark, following the color scheme of the United States system of buoyage. Minor lights are given distinctive light characteristics for purposes of identification. These lights are occasionally fitted with fog signals and may also be equipped with low-powered, continuously operating radio beacons.

Visibility of Lights

The visibility of lights on navigational charts is given at 15 feet above sea level—the assumed height of the observer's eye. This visibility must be modified proportionately for any other height. For example, when the observer is 20 feet above sea level and observed light is known to be 150 feet above sea level, the distance from the light, using the table below, is:

	Height in feet	Visibility in nautical miles
Observer	20	
Observer's range of vision		5.1
Light	150	
Arc of illumination (light)		14.1
Distance of observer from light		19.2

It must be remembered that atmospheric and other conditions affect visibility appreciably; therefore, it must not be assumed on sighting a light, even in perfectly clear weather, that a vessel's distance from the light is equal to the range of visibility. The range of visibility may be slightly greater or less than it appears because of the refraction of the light rays near the horizon.

DISTANCE BY VISIBILITY

Height in Feet	Distance Nautical Miles	Height in Feet	Distance Nautical Miles	Height in Feet	Distance Nautical Miles
1	1.1	30	6.3	130	13.1
2	1.6	35	6.8	140	13.6
3	2.0	40	7.2	150	14.1
4	2.3	45	7.7	200	16.2
5	2.6	50	8.1	250	18.2
6	2.8	55	8.5	300	19.9
7	3.0	60	8.9	350	21.5
8	3.1	65	9.2	400	22.9
9	3.5	70	9.6	450	24.3
10	3.6	75	9.9	500	25.6
12	4.0	80	10.3	550	26.8
14	4.3	85	10.6	600	28.0
15	4.4	90	10.9	650	29.1
16	4.6	95	11.2	700	30.3
18	4.9	100	11.5	800	32.4
20	5.1	110	12.0	900	34.4
25	5.7	120	12.6	1000	36.2

Range Markers

Ranges are two objects—whether they be range lights, day beacons, lighthouses, minor lights, or one day beacon and a lighthouse—or two of anything identified on the chart as a range. Similar to the principle of rifle-sighting, one of these objects or markers is

A typical range problem.

always nearer to you than the other, and the one closer to you is lower than the one further back. When these markers are in line—one over the other—they indicate to the yachtsman that he is on a safe course within the confines of the channel. If the closer marker of the range begins to shift to the left, you'll know that your yacht is going too far to the right. Correct this with left rudder immediately, and keep the range markers lined up. If the closer marker moves to the right, you're too far to the left, and you must correct it with right rudder. To be valuable in piloting, ranges need not always be established navigational marks; they may be natural ranges, such as a church steeple and a water tower, a tree stump and a fence post, or two hills or mountains. Within harbors, fixed ranges enable small boats to maintain prearranged courses without recourse to navigational aids.

Range Lights

Range lights are the principal night markers of the range system, and they usually are small or skeleton type structures which when in line (i.e., one over the other) indicate to the boatman that he is on a safe course. Generally they are visible in one direction only. By steering a course which keeps these lights in line (range-up) the boatman will remain within the confines of the channel. Remember that quite a few range lights are on shore and that's where you'll be if you don't consult your chart as to where to change course. The range lights may be white, red, or green in color and may also be fixed or flashing.

Reduced-Visibility Audio Aids

Fog signals warn of danger when visibility is limited by fog, rain or thick weather. They also provide a means of determining position when such conditions exist. The devices used for this purpose, generally termed "reduced-visibility audio aids," are as follows:

> 1. Diaphones are devices that produce sound by means of a slotted reciprocating piston actuated by compressed air. Blasts may be of one or two tones; if two tones are used, the second tone is lower than the first.
> 2. Diaphragm horns which produce sound by means of a diaphragm vibrated by compressed air, steam, or electricity. Duplex or triplex horns of different pitch produce a chime signal.
> 3. Reed horns which produce sound by means of a steel reed vibrated by compressed air.
> 4. Sirens operated by compressed air.
> 5. Whistles.
> 6. Bells.

Fog signals on fixed stations and lightships produce, each minute, a specific number of blasts which are interspersed with periods of silence to provide positive identification. The *Light Lists* describes the characteristics of fog signals.

Radio Beacons

There are several classes of radio stations that can be used in radio navigation as beacons. See page 114 for full description.

BASIC NAVIGATION GEAR

The following is considered the so-called basic navigation gear:

> 1. Charts covering in detail all the waters on which you expect to cruise should be aboard—charts made by the U.S. Coast and Geodetic Survey, U.S. Navy Hydrographic office or Lake Survey, depending on where you're going. Charts should be renewed each year or kept up to date by use of the *Notices to Mariners*.

2. A compass—a marine type which, in any but the smallest boats, should be set in a permanent binnacle in front of the helmsman at a level convenient to his eye.

3. Tools for chart work include, at least, parallel rules or one of the various types of course protractors; dividers for measuring distance; sharp pencils.

4. In the book line you'll want *Tide* and *Current Tables* (if on salt water); the *Coast Pilot* for your area; a *Light List*.

5. If you have a radio direction finder you need RDF beacon charts giving location, frequency, signal and "on-the-air" time of each station.

6. An electronic depth sounder is a handy gadget in navigation, but even if you have one, carry a marked leadline aboard and, if you poke around really shallow water, a long sounding pole marked in feet.

7. A taffrail log will give you distance run. Lacking that, for a powerboat, make up a table of boat speeds at various engine revolutions per minute shown on your tachometer; keep a record of your time and speed, and you'll know how far you've run. This information, along with other vital data, should be kept in the logbook.

NAUTICAL CHARTS

To meet our country's need for nautical charts, the "United States Coast Survey" was organized in 1807, during the administration of President Thomas Jefferson. The nautical charts published by the Coast and Geodetic Survey of the United States and its possessions, together with related publications, furnish information necessary for safe navigation. The charts show bottom depths and characteristics, dangers, channels, landmarks, aids to navigation, fish trap limits, anchorage, restricted, prohibited, cable and pipeline areas, wharves, cities, etc. Many charts contain sufficient depth curves to delineate submarine relief for navigation by echo sounder. Loran lines of position are shown on some nautical charts. Nautical charts vary in scales with the importance of the area, purpose for which the chart is designed, and necessity for showing clearly all the dangers within that area.

There are two basic types of charts; so-called conventional charts and small-craft charts. The latter are accordion folded ones which contrast sharply with the conventional charts that were designed for use by large commercial vessels. The small-craft charts emphasize additional navigational information for recreational boating such as large-scale insets of small boat harbors, blue tint to the 6 foot or critical depth curve, facilities and supplies available to small craft, weather, tides, currents, magnetic courses and distances between points of interest, symbols and abbreviations, whistle signals and a wealth of other references. Many a novice skipper is accepting the compact charts with confidence, where in the past he had been intimidated by those 3x4-foot unwieldy conventional charts which more rightly belong in seagoing vessels.

Both types of charts are not the same as maps. They need study. A look at a U. S. C. &.G. S. chart shows that it has a gridwork of vertical and horizontal lines over the surface of the chart. The vertical lines are the meridians of longitude, and the horizontal lines are the parallels of the latitude. These lines run true north and south, and true east and west. Longitude is marked off in degrees, minutes and tenths of minutes in the top and bottom margins of the chart. Of much more importance to the navigator are the scales of latitude found in the left and right margins of the chart, marked in degrees, minutes and tenths of minutes. Each minute of latitude is equal to one nautical mile, thus the scale can be used to measure distance. Just be sure you don't use the scales at the top and bottom (horizontal scale—longitude) for this purpose, as it won't give an accurate reading (except at the equator) because of the way the charts are made. In addition, the following facts pertaining to heights, depths, and visibility of lights must be kept in mind when examining data on a nautical chart:

1. Soundings may be expressed in either feet or fathoms. The navigator must know which unit of measurement was used to record the data on the chart.

2. Heights of land or other conspicuous objects are given in feet above mean high water (unless otherwise noted on the chart) below the title.

3. Elevations of rocks, lighthouses, contours, and hills are also given in feet above mean high water.

4. Elevations of mountain peaks, if underlined, refer to heights in feet above mean sea level.

5. The coastline as charted represents the line of mean high water.

6. Visibility of lights is given in nautical miles and is computed on the assumption that the observer's eye is 15 feet above water level.

7. Dredged channels, with the depth, month, and year of latest examination, are shown by limited dash lines.

8. Chart features which are above the waterline at high water are identified by vertical type. Leaning letters identify features and objects which are in or under the water, or floating. The type of lettering may thus be the only indication that a rock, obstruction, or portion of land can be expected to be found above or below the surface. A rock or piece of land indicated by vertical letters remains above water even at normal high tide, and amounts to a small island; but the same type of formation marked by leaning letters is an underwater obstruction or reef which won't be visible at high water and which may or may not break the surface at low tide.

Caution must be observed with respect to temporary changes which affect lights, buoys, and day beacons. When an aid to navigation has been destroyed or removed, but is to be reestablished (although temporarily replaced by an aid with a different characteristic), its status is indicated in red by the following abbreviations:

D—Destroyed; to be reestablished.

TRB—Temporarily replaced by a red buoy.

TBB—Temporarily replaced by a black buoy.

TFB—Temporarily replaced by a fixed white-lighted buoy.

TFRB—Temporarily replaced by a fixed red-lighted buoy.

T FL B—Temporarily replaced by a flashing white-lighted buoy.

T FL RB—Temporarily replaced by a flashing red-lighted buoy.

T FL GB—Temporarily replaced by a flashing green-lighted buoy.

OTHER GOVERNMENT PUBLICATIONS

The yachtsman is dependent upon accurate charts in navigating unfamiliar waters. However, to supplement this information, he has recourse to a number of other publications issued by the Government. These include *Tide Tables, Tidal Current Tables, Tidal Current Charts, Coast Pilots, Notice to Mariners*, and *Light Lists*. These should be aboard every yacht.

Tide Tables. The predicted times and heights of high and low waters for every day in the year for many of the more important harbors, and differences for obtaining predictions for numerous other places are given in annual tide tables.

Tidal Current Tables. Advance information relative to currents is made available in annual tidal current tables which include daily predictions of the times of slack water and the times and velocities of strength of flood and ebb currents for a number of waterways together with differences for obtaining predictions for numerous other places.

Tidal Current Charts. These publications consist of a set of 12 charts which depict, by means of arrows and figures, the direction and velocity of the tidal current for each hour of the tidal cycle. The charts, which may be used for any years, present a comprehensive view of the tidal current movement in the respective waterways as a whole and also supply a means for readily determining for any time the direction and velocity of the current at various localities throughout the water areas covered. The New York Harbor tidal current charts are to be used with the annual tide tables. The other charts require the annual current tables.

Coast Pilots. Volumes published primarily for navigation use to furnish that information required by the navigator which can't be shown conveniently on nautical charts. They contain general information relative to the coast and harbors, port information, and sailing directions for coasting and entering harbors. Published every seven years with supplements issued each year.

Notice to Mariners. A weekly pamphlet prepared jointly by the U.S. Coast Guard, U.S. Naval Oceanographic Office and U.S. Coast and Geodetic Survey, and is issued free to those who desire copies regularly. It is issued as a safety aid to keep mariners advised of changes so they may keep their nautical charts and related publications up to date.

Note:—Local Notices to Mariners issued by each U.S. Coast Guard District should be used instead of the weekly Notice to Mariners by mariners operating within one U.S. Coast Guard District.

Light Lists. There are six volumes of this publication (CG 158). CG 158 contains the *North Atlantic List, South Atlantic List, Pacific List, Great Lakes List, Intracoastal Waterway List,* and *Mississippi River List.* These lists describe the lighthouses, lightships, radio beacons, and buoys maintained by the Coast Guard in all navigable waters of the United States. The data include the official name of the aid, the characteristics of its light, sound, and radio signals, structural appearance, position, and dimensions for taking angles.

The first five publications are available through the U.S. Coast and Geodetic Survey and information about them, as well as nautical charts, may be obtained from the director of that branch of the Department of Commerce, or from the nearest Coast and Geodetic Survey Field Office. *Light Lists* are published by the U.S. Coast Guard.

A 5-degree card has the advantage of being easy to read (left).
A degree-point card is a practical compromise (right).

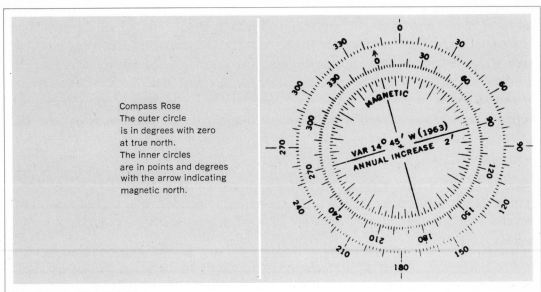

Compass Rose
The outer circle
is in degrees with zero
at true north.
The inner circles
are in points and degrees
with the arrow indicating
magnetic north.

MARINE COMPASS

History has revealed that the property of a loadstone to align itself in a north-south direction was observed over 2000 years ago in the Near East and perhaps 1000 years earlier in China. However, the practical application of this property as a direction indicating source at sea was not observed until about the 13th or 14th century. Today, of course, a magnetic compass is an important fixture aboard any seagoing boat; and like anything aboard a boat, it helps to know how as well as why it functions as it does.

The magnetic compass is a magnet suspended in a manner which allows absolute freedom of movement in a horizontal plane. The magnet alines itself with the earth's magnetic field and thus points to magnetic north and magnetic south. Every marine compass has a lubber's line marked on its case or mounting. This is a fixed reference line set on, or placed parallel to, the centerline of the vessel and indicating the heading of the ship with reference to the compass card. The compass card is marked by degrees in a 360° circle with north as 000. Some compass cards may also be marked in cardinal and intercardinal points such as N, NE, S, SE, W, SW, and so forth.

The magnetic compass is subject to two influences or errors which prevent it from pointing to the geographic North Pole; these must be considered when navigating. One of these errors, called *variation*, is primarily caused by the earth's magnetic poles not being located in the same places as the geographic poles. The housing of the magnetic compass, called a binnacle, is made of nonmagnetic material, usually wood and/or brass, and contains features for compass correction and illumination. (The light bulb for after-dark use should be red—as red interferes least with night vision.) The other error in the magnetic compass, called *deviation*, is caused by magnetic influences of metal in the ship itself. Normally this error changes with every different heading of the ship and is seldom the same for any two headings.

Variation is the difference in direction between the geographic North Pole and the magnetic north. The amount can vary depending upon where you are located and also may change slightly from year to year in some localities. The variation error of the compass is taken care of with one of the compass roses on your chart—the one nearest to your location. As shown in the illustration here, the star at the top of the outer circle of the compass rose points to the true north. The difference between the star and arrow is the amount of variation in the vicinity of this particular compass rose on the chart. To make it easy, the specific data on variation is printed in the center of the compass rose: "Variation 12° 15′ West (1966)."

Variation changes and is normally not constant for any given location. Therefore all compass readings must be corrected for variation unless a yacht happens to be in an area of no variation. Variation, when present, is either easterly or westerly, depending on the location of the compass on the earth. If the magnetic pole is to the west of geographic north at the location, variation is west; if the magnetic pole lies to the east at the location, variation is east. For example, the variation at Southport, North Carolina, is 4 degrees westerly. This means the compass needle while pointing to magnetic north is actually pointing 4 degrees west of true north or 356°. If a ship were steering a course of 360° by the magnetic compass (no deviation considered), the true course would be 4° less than 360° or 356°. When variation is west, the amount of variation should be subtracted from the magnetic course to find the true course. When variation is east, the amount should be added to the magnetic north to find the true course.

Variation is a constant error in all magnetic compasses. This isn't the case with deviation, which is an error caused by the magnetic effect on your compass of anything in your

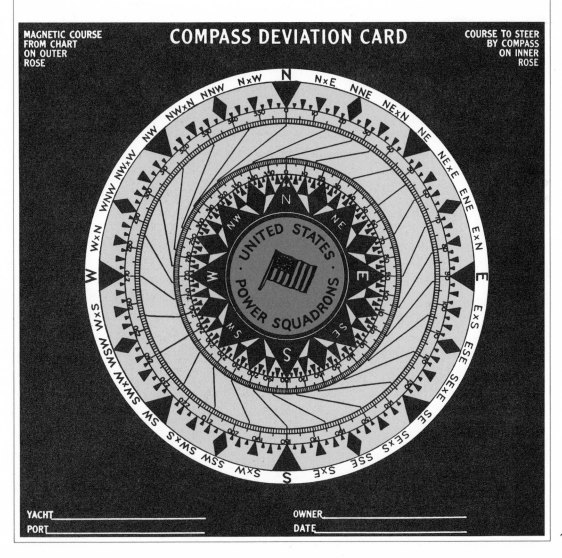

boat that is made of iron or steel. Deviation varies with different boats and also with different directions in which a boat may be headed. For example, a compass may show a deviation of five degrees to the west when the boat is headed one way, and a deviation of two degrees to the east when headed in the opposite direction. Your compass can be compensated for deviation. It's best to employ a professional to do this for you, and at the same time, have a deviation card made up. This card will show how far off your compass is in degrees, and you then can correct easily for your true course.

Deviation is not a fixed figure; it may change when the yacht changes course. Compass deviation cards or Napier diagrams show the deviation for various ship headings. Variation and deviation usually are handled together, their sum comprising the compass error. This error, when correctly applied to the compass course in accordance with the directional symbol of E (east) or W (west), gives the true course. The mariner's rule is: "East, you add; west, you subtract when correcting." This is the method used to convert a compass course to a true course. The procedure is reversed to convert a true course to a compass course. That is, to find a compass course from a true course, add westerly errors, subtract easterly errors.

Plotting a Course

Using the above knowledge, let's plot a course from our point of departure to our destination. First, mark your course (A) on the map with a ruler. Then, using your parallel rules, draw a line (B) parallel to it through the compass rose on the map. Find where this parallel line intersects the compass rose. Let's say it intersects it at 73°. This is your *true course*. Next, make these two corrections:

     1. Note the difference between true north and magnetic north. Let's suppose that in your area this variation is 17 degrees east. So you subtract 17° from 73°, which gives you 56°. This is your *magnetic course*.

     2. Check your deviation card to see to what degree the iron and steel in your boat are affecting your compass. We'll say that your compass deviates 4° West due to this factor. So you add 4° to 56° which gives you 60°—that's your *compass course*. To steer a compass course of 60° just keep the figure 60 right on the lubber line of your compass.

A typical
course plotting
problem.

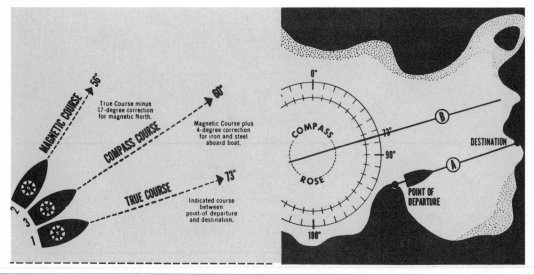

In using a chart with your compass, as just stated, you must first mark two points: where you are, and where you want to go. The best way of reaching your destination is usually apparent. Often, however, you can't run a straight or direct course; instead, you may have to go so far in one direction, then in another, and so on, to avoid land points, shoals, and reefs. Once you have laid out your proposed course in pencil on the chart, then write in the compass direction you must follow on each leg, and for what distance. You can get the compass direction of each leg as just described.

In measuring a course through a channel or other area where it is broken into a series of short legs, here is a method to make it easier: measure the first course line with the dividers. Then, using the end of that first course line as a pivot, carefully swing the arm of the dividers in the opposite direction of the second course line. Using the arm of the dividers away from the course line as a pivot, widen the dividers to the length of the second course line. Next, using the arm of the dividers at the end of the second course line as a pivot, swing the dividers in the opposite direction of the third course line. Using the arm of the dividers away from this course line as a pivot, widen the dividers to the length of third course line. By continuing this process to any desired point, you can then measure the entire distance on the latitude or mileage scale. You'll find this a much easier method than measuring and adding a series of short courses.

When cruising tidal waters, leeway—which affects all types of boats, both power and sail—is sometimes a factor in plotting a course. It's not generally too important if you are traveling a relatively short distance; even where there is considerable wind, wave and current. However, over long courses, making allowance for leeway can mean a worthwhile saving in time and fuel. In making such allowance, the effect of wind and wave are usually matters of personal observation and judgment. On the other hand, the effect of the current in tidal waters can be determined accurately by referring to the *Tidal Current Tables* and *Tidal Current Charts* for your area. But to see how tidal currents affect plotting a course, here's a typical problem: You are going to cruise from point X (point of departure) to point Y (destination), a direction of a compass course of 120° T. You want to make good a speed of 12 knots. Your starting time is 1030 PDT July 6th. By referring to tidal current tables, you find the current flowing across your course in a direction of 065° at 2 knots. You would plot your course as follows:

A typical tidal current problem.

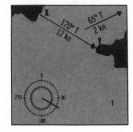 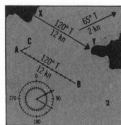 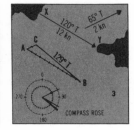 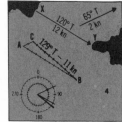

1. Determine your scale, for example, ½ inch equals 1 knot. Then in a free area on your chart draw a line parallel to your intended compass course (120° T.) 6 inches long (equal 12 knots—your speed). Label the ends of this line A and B. Now draw the current line from A, 1 inch long to represent its velocity (equals 2 knots) in a direction of 065°. Label end of this line point C.

2. Draw a line from point C to point B. Line CB is the directional course you'll want to steer and speed you'll want to set your engines. By moving your parallel rules from line CB to the compass rose on the chart, you will determine your course to be 129° T.

3. Then measuring length of line, 5½ inches, show a speed of 11 knots required to make good a 12-knot course speed. So steer a course of 129° T. at 11 knots to get from point X to Y. In this case, if you had ignored your current and simply locked your boat on automatic pilot, you would have landed 9° off course and probably in trouble.

SPEED AFLOAT

Many of us have come to rely so often on the speedometer as a measure of speed and distance that we shall find it difficult without instruments to solve how fast we are going or how far we have gone. Yet on the water we have just such a situation which must be solved and the process must be mastered thoroughly.

The first problem is the difference between land and sea miles. A knot, as you probably know, is the unit of speed in navigation, as opposed to a mile per hour, which is the unit of speed on land. A knot is one nautical mile per hour. (Don't speak of boat speeds in terms of "knots per hour." It's redundant and incorrect.) Master mariners and marine architects always refer to the speed of a vessel in terms of knots. A nautical mile, to which the term "knot" refers, equals 6080.27 feet, or approximately one-seventh more than a land mile. The term "miles per hour" refers to a statute (land) mile, whose length is 5280 feet. Miles per hour, incidentally, is a measurement of speed also used in navigating river and lake vessels.

Here's where an appreciable difference between the units knot and mile per hour comes in: Let's say one skipper says his boat can do 15 miles an hour, and another claims his vessel can do 15 knots. The latter's boat is faster. Fifteen miles an hour is the equivalent of only 13.03 knots, while 15 knots equals 17.27 miles an hour.

CONVERSION TABLES, NAUTICAL AND STATUTE MILES

Statute Miles to Nautical Miles		Nautical Miles to Statute Miles	
Statute	Nautical	Nautical	Statute
1.00	0.86	1.00	1.15
2.00	1.74	2.00	2.30
3.00	2.61	3.00	3.45
4.00	3.47	4.00	4.61
5.00	4.34	5.00	5.76
6.00	5.21	6.00	6.91
7.00	6.08	7.00	8.06
8.00	6.95	8.00	9.21
9.00	7.82	9.00	10.36
10.00	8.68	10.00	11.52
11.00	9.55	11.00	12.67
12.00	10.42	12.00	13.82
13.00	11.29	13.00	14.97
14.00	12.16	14.00	16.12
15.00	13.03	15.00	17.27
16.00	13.89	16.00	18.42
17.00	14.76	17.00	19.58
18.00	15.63	18.00	20.73
19.00	16.50	19.00	21.88
20.00	17.37	20.00	23.03
30.00	26.05	30.00	34.55

Note: For conversions above 20 and 30, either nautical miles or statute miles, you can

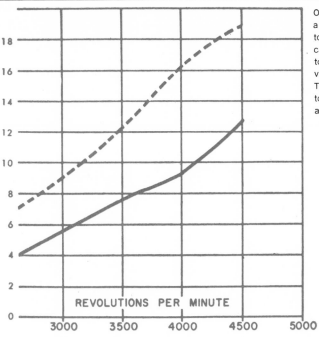

Once rpms are known, a graph similar to that shown at right can be plotted out to show speed with various throttle settings. This is essential to figure time a trip may take.

use these equations:

    (a) *Statute miles to Nautical miles:* 10 (statute miles) is to 8.68 (equivalent in nautical miles, from table) as the statute-mile distance you want to convert is to X (its equivalent in nautical miles). Let's say you want to convert 22 land miles. Here's your equation . . . 10 : 8:68 = 22 : X. You multiply the two outside members, 10 and X, for 10X. Then you multiply the two inside members, 8.68 by 22, for 190.96. Now the equation is 10X = 190.96. All you do is divide 190.96 by 10. The answer is 19.09 nautical miles.

    (b) *Nautical miles to Statute miles:* Same procedure. Let's say you want to convert 36 nautical miles. Your equation is . . . 10 (nautical miles) : 11.52 (equivalent in statute miles) = 36 : X. As before, 10 times X = 10X. Multiplying 11.52 by 36 = 414.2. Dividing by 10 = the answer, 41.4 statute miles.

A yacht moving through the water should have its speed noted constantly for it's subject to variations of wind, current, tides, and inaccuracies of steering. This checking up of the speed may be accomplished in one of three ways: first, by bearings on recognizable objects on land; second, by the use of a patent log; and third, by engine revolutions.

The taffrail, or patent log is a device for measuring the distance run through the water. It consists of a rotator with spiral blades, a braided line from 30 to 100 fathoms in length for towing the rotator, and a mechanical recording device that registers the revolutions of the rotator and shows, on a dial, the distance run. To prevent erroneous readings, care should be taken to insure that the blades are not bent or fouled with seaweed. Dependent upon speed of the vessel, the rotator line should be approximately 70 to 100 per cent of the vessel length when trailed. The rotator is towed astern. Spinning as it is drawn through the water, it rotates the line and records revolutions on the counter in nautical miles. To secure it after use, the line should be streamed out from counter end and coiled down, beginning with the rotator end.

Because of the difficulty in handling patent logs, most yachtsmen compute the ratio of the average revolutions per minute (r.p.m.) of the propeller to "knots" or nautical miles per hour. Thus if an engine is rated at 450 revolutions per minute to drive the boat ten nautical miles per hour, we have only to look at the tachometer, or instrument measuring the r.p.m., to ascertain the speed. In this case if the tachometer reads 990 r.p.m. the speed will be 22 nautical miles per hour $\left(\dfrac{990}{450} \times 10 = 22 \right)$.

On many inland bodies of water and sheltered bays and sounds on the coast mariners have marked off measured miles where yachtsmen may take their craft and test the engines for various speeds. That is the simplest way to determine how fast your boat will go with the engine turning over at any selected number of revolutions. To calculate the speed of boat, the following table can be used on either type of measured mile—nautical or statute. Let's suppose you cover the measured mile at 4 minutes and 20 seconds. Look under the column headed "4 Min." and read down to opposite the figure "20" (in the column headed "Secs." at the extreme left). You'll see that your yacht is traveling at 13.84 miles an hour.

MEASURED MILE SPEED TABLES
(For use with either Nautical or Statute Miles)

Sec.	1 Min.	2 Min.	3 Min.	4 Min.	5 Min.	6 Min.	7 Min.	8 Min.	9 Min.	10 Min.	11 Min.
0	60.00	30.00	20.00	15.00	12.00	10.00	8.57	7.50	6.66	6.00	5.45
2	58.06	29.50	19.78	14.87	11.92	9.94	8.53	7.46	6.64	5.98	5.43
4	56.25	29.03	19.56	14.75	11.84	9.89	8.49	7.43	6.61	5.96	5.42
6	54.54	28.57	19.35	14.63	11.76	9.83	8.45	7.40	6.59	5.94	5.40
8	52.94	28.12	19.14	14.51	11.68	9.78	8.41	7.37	6.56	5.92	5.38
10	51.42	27.69	18.94	14.40	11.61	9.73	8.37	7.34	6.54	5.90	5.37
12	50.00	27.27	18.75	14.28	11.53	9.67	8.33	7.31	6.52	5.88	5.35
14	48.64	26.86	18.55	14.17	11.46	9.62	8.29	7.28	6.49	5.86	5.34
16	47.36	26.47	18.36	14.06	11.39	9.57	8.26	7.25	6.47	5.84	5.32
18	46.15	26.08	18.18	13.95	11.32	9.52	8.22	7.22	6.45	5.82	5.30
20	45.00	25.71	18.00	13.84	11.25	9.47	8.18	7.20	6.42	5.80	5.29
22	43.90	25.35	17.82	13.74	11.18	9.42	8.14	7.17	6.40	5.78	5.27
24	42.85	25.00	17.64	13.63	11.11	9.37	8.11	7.14	6.38	5.76	5.26
26	41.86	24.65	17.47	13.53	11.04	9.32	8.07	7.11	6.36	5.75	5.24
28	40.90	24.32	17.30	13.43	10.97	9.27	8.03	7.09	6.33	5.73	5.23
30	40.00	24.00	17.14	13.33	10.90	9.23	8.00	7.05	6.31	5.71	5.21
32	39.13	23.68	16.98	13.23	10.84	9.18	7.96	7.03	6.29	5.69	5.20
34	38.29	23.37	16.82	13.13	10.77	9.13	7.93	7.00	6.27	5.67	5.18
36	37.50	23.07	16.66	13.04	10.71	9.09	7.89	6.97	6.25	5.66	5.17
38	36.73	22.78	16.51	12.95	10.65	9.04	7.86	6.95	6.22	5.64	5.15
40	36.00	22.50	16.36	12.85	10.58	9.00	7.83	6.92	6.20	5.62	5.14
42	35.29	22.22	16.21	12.76	10.52	8.95	7.79	6.89	6.18	5.60	5.12
44	34.61	21.95	16.07	12.67	10.46	8.91	7.76	6.87	6.16	5.59	5.11
46	33.96	21.68	15.92	12.58	10.40	8.86	7.72	6.84	6.14	5.57	5.09
48	33.33	21.42	15.78	12.50	10.34	8.82	7.69	6.81	6.12	5.55	5.08
50	32.72	21.17	15.65	12.41	10.28	8.78	7.66	6.79	6.10	5.53	5.07
52	32.14	20.93	15.51	12.32	10.22	8.73	7.63	6.76	6.08	5.51	5.05
54	31.57	20.69	15.38	12.24	10.16	8.69	7.59	6.74	6.06	5.50	5.04
56	31.03	20.45	15.25	12.16	10.11	8.65	7.56	6.71	6.04	5.48	5.02
58	30.50	20.22	15.12	12.08	10.05	8.61	7.53	6.69	6.02	5.47	5.01
	30.00	20.00	15.00	12.00	10.00	8.57	7.50	6.66	6.00	5.45	5.00
	3 Min.	4 Min.	5 Min.	6 Min.	7 Min.	8 Min.	9 Min.	10 Min.	11 Min.	12 min.	

Before you run a measured mile course choose two structures aboard boat—a stay and a stanchion perhaps—which are approximately in line and along which you can sight to line up your boat with the starting marker. When the three structures—two aboard boat and one on shore—are in line, begin your timing (we suggest a stop-watch for real accuracy). Similarly, at the conclusion of the measured mile use exactly the same arrangement for sighting the finish marker. In that way you'll have an accurate measurement of your boat's time for the distance—even if the sighting structures are on a bit of an angle to each marker (since the sighting method was exactly the same at the start and finish, the distance has to be a measured mile). Then you refer to the Measured Mile Speed Tables to determine your boat's speed.

Make your trial runs at one-quarter, half, three-quarter, and full throttle. Obtain your engine revolutions for these known speeds by reading your tachometer, and once the r.p.m.'s are known, a graph can be plotted to indicate the speed of your cruiser at various throttle settings. By making a table or chart comparing your r.p.m. and the speed over the measured distance, you'll have some indication of your speed by a glance at the r.p.m. gauge or tachometer. This information will also be very helpful in figuring the time a trip may take, and by comparing it with fuel records, you'll be able to figure out your optimum or efficient speed.

In all speed checks, however, keep in mind that various elements will affect your cruiser's speed, such as wind, current, running into a heavy head sea, or before a following. (Experience will give you some indication of how much these factors will influence your boat's performance.) Other items might affect your graph, such as tachometer error, atmospheric conditions, etc., but let's not labor the point. If you're as accurate as possible in your figures and prepare your runs carefully, you won't be off by too many r.p.m. Also, keep in mind that a normal loss of speed can be expected after the cruiser has been in the water for some time. This is due to the possibility of marine growth, bilge water, changes in gear and/or passenger loads, or damaged underwater equipment. A periodic check of r.p.m. and speed is essential to good navigation.

TAKING SOUNDINGS

The hand lead line is a device for determining the depth of water. It consists of a suitably marked line and a shaped lead weight. The weight of the lead and length of the line vary on different vessels. A 25-fathom hand lead line with a 5- to 14-pound weight is generally sufficient.

Marking the Line. The line is marked as shown below to provide a quick method of reading any coastal depth within the range of the length of the line.

Fathoms	Mark
2	2 strips of leather
3	3 strips of leather
5	White rag
7	Red rag
10	Leather strip with hole
13	3 strips of leather
15	White rag
17	Red rag
20	Cord with 2 knots
25	Cord with 1 knot

Using the Line. The bottom of the lead is hollowed out to allow it to be armed. Arming the lead consists of packing grease or tallow in this hollow. When the lead strikes the bottom, it picks up particles which may be compared with data on the chart showing the nature of the bottom. An excellent check of the boat's position is often secured in this manner. In taking a sounding, the lead is cast well forward so that it will strike the bottom directly below the leadsman as the boat moves slowly through the water. The soundings are reported by the leadsman by calling the fathom points that are marked on the line as marks and the fathom points between as deeps. Depths between marks are estimated.

The following are examples of typical reports and corresponding depths.

Report	Depth (in fathoms)
By the mark five	5
And a quarter five	5¼
And a half five	5½
A quarter less six	5¾
By the deep six	6
And a quarter six	6¼
And a half six	6½
A quarter less seven	6¾
By the mark seven	7

Using Sounding to Pilot. A line of soundings may be the only way left to the navigator to determine the yacht's position, especially in fog. A series of soundings is taken at regular intervals throughout a portion of a run while the boat maintains a steady course. These soundings are plotted on a piece of transparent paper and the course line passing through them is labeled. The paper is then moved about on the chart until the sounded depths agree with the charted depth and the course line is properly oriented.

The depth sounder, or depth finder as it is sometimes called, is another way of determining water depths and its method of operation is fully described in the next chapter.

THE PELORUS AND ITS USE

The pelorus is a dummy compass fitted with sight vanes for taking bearings of celestial or terrestrial objects. It is generally made of brass. It is without magnets and wholly non-magnetic. The dial, or card, has a compass rose painted or engraved upon it and is divided into 360°. The card and the sight vanes revolve, independently of each other, upon a pivot. Two clamps, one above the other on the top of the pivot, permit the card and the sight vanes to be set in any desired position. One clamp is used to set the card, the other to set the sight vanes.

A bearing is taken on an object by first alining the pelorus card with the compass card and clamping it in position. The lubber's line must be alined with the boat's keel. The sighting vanes of the pelorus are then alined on the object of the bearing and are clamped in position. The bearing is read from the pelorus dial. For the bearing to be accurate, the yacht must be kept exactly on the course on which the pelorus dial is clamped.

The bearing thus taken from a pelorus is a compass bearing and must be corrected in the same manner as a compass reading. The pelorus is also used to obtain relative bearings. In obtaining a bearing of this kind the pelorus dial is clamped in position with 000 on the lubber's line. After the lubber's line is alined with the vessel's keel, a bearing can be taken, the sighting vanes clamped in position, and the bearing read. This bearing is relative to the yacht's heading at the time the bearing was taken and must be added to the ship's heading to obtain compass bearing of the object.

PILOTING TECHNIQUES

There are several different piloting methods for finding a yacht's position, depending upon the number of objects in sight, their bearing relative to the heading of the craft, and the character of the sailing area.

In order that the information plotted on a chart may be of value to the navigator and to other people who are required to interpret correctly what has been drawn, a system of marking or labeling is required. All lines of position (bearings) and courses should be true (referring to direction). The alternate and intermingling use of magnetic bearings and true bearings can result in costly errors. Lines of position and course lines are each drawn distinctly. Care should be taken not to draw heavy lines on the chart which may damage the chart or mislead the navigator when the chart is used again. Course lines should be labeled on the upper side of the line by writing C (course) followed by the true course in three figures. On the lower side of the line, under the course label, S (speed) and numerals indicating the speed in knots should be written.

Over the lines of position (bearing lines) the time of observation should be written in four figures; the three figures denoting the true bearing should be written beneath the time figure. The label now contains both a time notation and an abbreviation for the type of point identified. Identification points are normally written to one side of the points they identify and at an angle to the course line or the lines of position on which they lie.

The Cross Bearing

To get a cross bearing, take bearings with your pelorus or compass sight vanes on two or more charted objects: buoys, lighthouses, lightships, church steeples, etc. Apply error and convert to magnetic or true bearings, then lay them on the chart by using a course protractor or by extending the bearing from the compass rose on the chart with your parallel rules. Your "fix" is where the lines converge.

The cross bearing method of obtaining a fix affords a high degree of accuracy, especially when three bearings can be used for lines of position. The most accurate fixes are those obtained from lines of position that are at a 60° to 90° angle from each other and are made from established navigational marks. It is well to remember that whenever possible the navigational mark should be a landmark or a lightship. Buoys may shift position and are relatively hard to locate and identify from small boats. It is most important to be sure that the mark being used for a bearing has been properly identified.

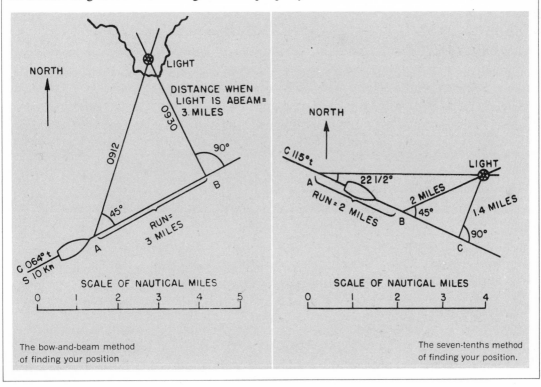

The bow-and-beam method of finding your position

The seven-tenths method of finding your position.

85

The Bow-and-Beam Method

In coastwise navigation it isn't always possible to see more than one established navigational mark at a time. Therefore, some means must be found for obtaining a fix from one visible object. The most commonly practiced method of doing this is known as the bow-and-beam, or four-point bearing, method. It is used to determine position by taking a bearing and computing the distance over the ground which the yacht has made. Currents and other factors must be considered when estimating distances run. The bearings used in this method of obtaining a fix are relative bearings. The term means that the bearing is in relation to the centerline or keel of the ship. The bow of the vessel, therefore, is considered as being 000°, whereas the stern is considered as being 180°. Two relative bearings are used in this method, 45° and 90°. It makes no difference whether these bearings are taken to the left or right of the bow. The vessel in the illustration has noted the exact time the light bore 45° to port. The time is again noted when the light bears exactly abeam, or 90°, as at B. The run between points A and B is estimated from taffrail log revolutions during this time, or by other means available to the navigator. This estimated distance run is equal to the distance the vessel is off the light when the vessel reaches point B. This holds true only if the vessel maintains the same course throughout the run. A fix can be plotted on the chart from this method by noting that the ship's heading during the run was 064° true. At B, the angle of the bearing was 090°. The line of position then, from B to the light must be 064° less 090°. In this case, 090° cannot be subtracted from 064°, therefore, add 360° to 064° and then subtract, giving a true bearing from the ship to the light of 334° true. This line of position is drawn on the chart, then, with a pair of dividers, the distance run along this line is measured from the light to the ship, and a fix is obtained.

The Seven-tenths Rule

The seven-tenths rule makes use of two angles, 22½° and 45°. Here, the time is first noted when the navigational mark bears 22½° off the bow. The time is again noted when the mark bears 45° off the bow. Again, the distance off is equal to the run between bearings. If the yacht maintains course until the mark is directly abeam, the distance off will be seven-tenths the distance run between the first and second bearings. The seven-tenths rule and bow-and-beam bearings are two of the most valuable methods of determining position that are available to the yachtsman in coastwise navigation. If your craft doesn't have a pelorus aboard, satisfactory results can be obtained if the 22½°, 45°, and 90° points are marked in some manner, both port and starboard. Thumb tacks in the railing, precisely placed, can be used. It's not absolutely necessary to plot the estimated positions.

Doubling the Angle on the Bow

Study of the two preceding methods reveals that in each one the angle on the bow of the second bearing was twice that of the first angle. This principle can be used by the navigator at any convenient time regardless of the angle of the first bearing. For example, a bearing is taken of a mark that bears 34° off the bow and the time is noted. Doubling the angle equals 68°; therefore, the time is noted again when the mark bears 68°—the yacht's course and speed being unchanged. The distance run is equal to the distance off the mark at the time of the second bearing.

The Seven-eighths Rule

This rule can be applied when the yachtsman has missed the 22½° bearing necessary when using the seven-tenths rule. He substitutes 30° for the first bearing, 60° for the second bearing, and uses seven-eighths of the distance run as the distance off the mark when it passes abeam. The importance of these two rules is apparent when it is realized that they enable the navigator to know in advance how far off the vessel will be when passing a navigational mark. This knowledge permits a vessel to change course promptly if the distance off would be unsafe.

The bearings in the following table have such a relationship to each other that the distance of the run between them is always equal to the distance off when the navigational mark is passed abeam. The use of these angles when navigating eliminates the necessity of applying either the seven-tenths or the seven-eighths rule. Using these bearings, the navigator may take his first bearing at any bearing between 20° and 45°.

SPECIAL BEARINGS

First bearing	Second bearing	First bearing	Second bearing
°	°	°	°
20	30	33	61½
21	32	34	64½
22	34	35	67
23	37	36	69½
24	39	36½	71
25	41	37	72
26	43½	38	74
26½	45	39	77
27	46	40	79
28	48½	41	81
29	51	42	83½
30	53½	43	86
31	56	44	88
32	59	45	90

Danger Bearing

The danger angle is used to avoid sunken rocks or shoals or other dangers marked on the chart. As shown, the desired course line is CD. A and B are two prominent objects shown on the chart and S and S′ are the danger points through which the ship wishes to pass. Describe a circle around the danger nearest the beach, well clear of the danger. From E,

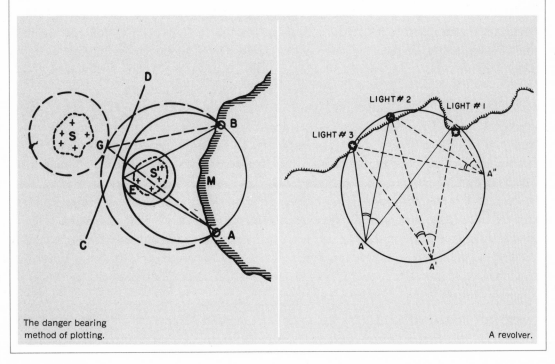

The danger bearing method of plotting.

A revolver.

the outermost tangent of this circle, draw a line AE and BE to the objects ashore. The angle AEB is the greatest angle which can safely be reached in making the pass. Describe a similar circle around the outlying shoal. Lines GB and GA are joined, forming the angle AGB which becomes the minimum angle that can be attained to safely pass the outlying shoal or danger.

The Three-Point Method

The procedure in the three-point method is to choose three objects on shore that are clearly marked on the chart. Measurement of the angles between points 1 and 2 and points 2 and 3 constitute the fix as shown here. The measuring of the two angles should be made as nearly simultaneous as possible to avoid error. One man may accomplish this by measuring 1 and 2, 2 and 3, and then repeating 1 and 2. The mean of the two angles measured between points 1 and 2 may be considered as being simultaneous with the angle between 2 and 3. It can be seen that compass deviation and variation don't enter into the method and that only angle differences are involved. A three-arm protractor is generally used to plot this type of fix on the chart in such a manner that the three lines intersect the three objects upon which the angles are measured. The vertex of the lines marks the fix. When using this method, the navigator must be wary of what is called a *revolver*. A study of the diagram below reveals that a revolver occurs when the ship is located on a circle drawn through the three objects—in this case, lights 1, 2, and 3. The same angles observed at A, would also serve for A′ and A″. In fact, the angles would serve to locate the ship anywhere on the circumference of the circle. Obviously, no fix can be obtained in this case. A revolver is easily avoided by remembering a simple rule—use the three-point method only when the middle object of the three is located nearer the vessel than the outer two. The navigator should, if possible, avoid near revolvers for even if the yacht isn't exactly on a circle, the fix from a near revolver is seldom completely accurate.

Dead Reckoning

Dead reckoning is the process of determining a ship's position by applying to the last well-determined position (fix or running fix) the run that has since been made, using only the true courses steered and the distance run as determined by log or engine revolutions, without considering current. By the process of dead reckoning, the position can also be run ahead to determine the predicted position at any desired time. If a yacht kept exactly to the predicted course and speed and there were no wind or current, dead reckoning would provide at all times a method of accurately determining the position of a boat. Since this is rarely the situation, a dead-reckoning position must be considered as only an approximation of the true position. This doesn't mean that dead reckoning is unimportant or may be neglected. On the contrary, it's highly important to know the approximate position, for this is a great aid in determining when to make turns, predicting the time of sighting lights and other aids to navigation, identifying landmarks, and evaluating information or the absence of expected information. To provide the necessary data for dead reckoning the navigator must keep a navigation logbook in which he records the time and all other data pertaining to changes in course and speed, time of getting under way and anchoring, and other useful data. Before charts became reliable, dead reckoning was done entirely by computation. In modern practice nearly all navigators do their dead reckoning graphically upon the chart of the locality into which they are cruising.

LOCKING THROUGH

Every year, more and more yachtsmen are enjoying new, extended cruising areas by making use of the systems of locks that are found on many of the nation's inland waterways. "Locking through" otherwise impassable sections of rivers and canals often brings together boats of all sizes; from seagoing commercial vessels and big luxury cruisers, to the smallest outboard runabouts.

It's easy to understand why certain precautions should be followed while locking when you consider how a typical lock operates. Let's say you are traveling upriver and come to a point where there is a waterfall twenty feet high. Off to one side of the falls, a channel has been constructed to bypass them and this channel includes a lock. This is an artificial basin with sidewalls extending upward at least twenty feet above the level of the water below the falls. Each end of the lock is equipped with gates and you enter through the downriver gate, which is the only one that is open. This gate then is closed and water is let into the lock. The rising water lifts your boat up until it is at the same level as the river above the falls. The upriver gate is now opened and you continue on upstream. If you were coming downstream, the operation would be reversed. The lock would be filled to start with, and then emptied of sufficient water to lower your boat to the level of the river below the falls.

When locking through, the U.S. Army Corps of Engineers, who operate the locks on the United States waterways, make the following suggestions:

1. Opening and closing locks creates a tremendous undertow. Therefore, it is to your best interests to stay at least 100 yards away from the lock and avoid these danger areas until you're ready to begin locking through. If the lock is equipped with a boat operator's signal, use it to notify the lock tender that you're ready to go through. (Some locks have a signaling device—usually electric push-button or pull-cord—on the downstream approach by which you may let the tender know of your presence. Otherwise, you may signal by horn blasts.)

2. Watch for and obey traffic signal lights. Special signals for boat operators have been installed at many locks. These are usually located about midpoint on the upper and lower guide walls to the locks. You notify the lock tender by pulling a chain connected to a signal located in his control room. Red, amber and green traffic lights will guide you at every lock. Look for them and be ready to act promptly when you receive the proper signals. (Because signaling systems for lockage vary somewhat from one river or canal to another, you should ascertain the method employed in the watercourse you are traveling.)

Red means "Stand clear—do not enter."
Amber means "Approach lock under full control."
Green means "Enter lock."

Some locks are also equipped with airhorns for signaling. Four different signals are used:
One long blast—Enter landward side of lock.
One short blast—Leave landward side of lock.
Two long blasts—Enter riverward side of lock.
Two short blasts—Leave riverward side of lock.

3. Carry at least 50 feet of line in order to hold your craft in position when the water is pumped into or out of the locks. After you have entered the lock at reduced speed, turn off your engine and make one end of the line fast. Appropriate signs, or the lockmaster, will tell you where and how. Obviously, boats can't be allowed to float free in lock basins. The resulting collisions caused by the turbulence of water being let in or out would be disastrous. So, a line generally is strung from the bow of the boat; around some fixture provided on the lock wall; and then back to a cleat on the stern of the boat. Depending upon whether your boat is being raised or lowered, the line is either taken in or let out while locking. If the lock operator permits, it is easy to keep a small boat under control in a lock by holding onto a lock

ladder by hand—shifting your grip upward or downward to different rungs, as the case may be. Also, it is common practice for small boats to be permitted to raft alongside bigger ones in many locks—which makes locking still easier.

4. To protect a yacht while locking, as many fenders as necessary should be used to keep the hull from coming into contact with the lock walls, which often are of rough concrete. Many boatmen also use fender boards. In many cases, lock walls are badly indented through constant use by heavy commercial craft. It is essential to keep any part of a boat from catching in such pockets, and so mops, boathooks and even human feet are used to keep the boat off from the walls.

5. Once the locking operation is completed and the lock gates are open, take in your mooring lines and move out of the lock area at a slow speed until you're free and clear. If the lock has an air horn, wait until you're given the proper signal (one or two short blasts) before you start your engine and proceed on your way.

6. For further instructions on different locking-through procedures, write to your local District Engineer office, or Office of the Chief of Engineers, U.S. Army Corps of Engineers, Building T-7, Washington 25, D.C. For various locks through the country, differences may exist on details such as pleasure boat regulations, hours of operation, and whether permits are required. For specific information, write to the individual State authority; usually the State Department of Commerce, or Department of Public Works.

ANCHORING AND DOCKING

Another art known to every yachtsman is anchoring and docking. While it takes special knowledge to get to the place where the yacht is to be anchored or docked, it is important to know about the procedure of anchoring or docking once your boat has reached that place.

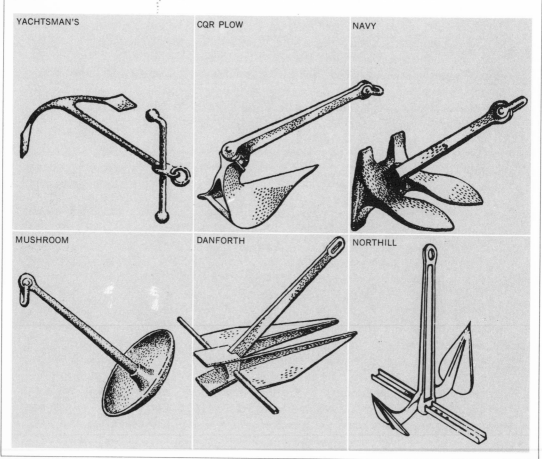

YACHTSMAN'S CQR PLOW NAVY

MUSHROOM DANFORTH NORTHILL

Types of Anchors

It is impossible to generalize about a particular type, size, or weight of anchor ideal for a particular boat. Experts agree that the choice depends on a number of considerations, including weight and shape of the hull, type of water bed generally encountered, usual weather conditions, and the purpose for which the anchor is most often used. Of the seven most common anchors illustrated here, each has its specific uses and limitations. The *yachtsman's anchor,* or *kedge,* is for larger boats and is best in sheltered and currentless locations. It is very heavy and is often called a dead-weight type. The *twin fluke* (Danforth) has good holding power once dug in, but it tends to slide over the bottom in weedy areas. It is light in weight and is currently the most popular type on power boats not equipped with winches or other ground tackle to raise or lower the "hook."

SUGGESTED SIZES OF DANFORTH TYPE ANCHOR

Size of anchor for any boat depends upon harbor exposure, wind velocity, type of holding ground, scope, hull form, many other factors. Good seamanship requires that a storm anchor as well as a working anchor be carried. The table below assumes fair holding ground with winds up to 60 knots.

LENGTH	BEAM		STANDARD Sizes			HI-TENSILE Sizes	
	Sail	Power	Working	Storm	Lunch Hook	Working	Storm
10	4	4	2½	4	—	5	5
15	5	5	4	8	—	5	5
20	6	6	8	13	—	5	12
25	6½	7	8	13	5	12	12
30	7	9	13	22	5	12	18
35	8	10	22	22	5	18	18
40	9	11	22	40	5	18	28
50	11	13	40	65	12	28	60
60	12	14	65	85	12	60	90

The *mushroom* type is good for permanent moorings in soft and yielding bottoms. In the lighter weight sizes, it makes a good temporary anchor for small fishing boats. The *CQR plow-type* anchor is used mostly on larger boats because of its heavy weight, and it is a good holder. The *Northill* is fine for all-round use, although it has its limitations in soft mud, and its free arm will sometimes foul the slack line. It is rather light weight. The *navy, stockless,* or *patent,* type has almost the same characteristics as the fluke type but is heavier in weight. Comparison of holding power of four major types of yacht anchors:

DANFORTH Lbs.	YACHTSMANS KEDGE Lbs.	STOCKLESS Lbs.	MUSHROOM Lbs.
2½	22	60	75
4	35	70	100
8	60	100	180
13	140	210	400
22	225	340	650
40	270	400	800

Whatever the type of anchor, the secret of successful anchoring rests on two things: making the length (scope) of anchorline (rode) as long as possible, and keeping the anchor on its side so that its flukes can penetrate the bottom. Rope is generally preferred for anchoring boats up to 50 feet in length with chain or cable used for the larger boats. (Six to ten feet of chain is recommended as part of any anchor rode. The chain leader helps keep the line on bottom and avoids chafing.) Following are the tables of recommended anchor lines:

RECOMMENDED ANCHOR LINES FOR POWER CRAFT

Over-All Length of Boat	Anchor Used	Length of Anchor Lines	Manila Rope Dia.	Nylon Rope Dia.
Under 20'	Light	100'	½"	⅜"
	Heavy			
20'-25'	Light	100'	½"	⅜"
	Heavy	150'	⅝"	½"
25'-30'	Light	100'	⅝"	½"
	Heavy	180'	¾"	⁹⁄₁₆"
30'-40'	Light	125'	¾"	⁹⁄₁₆"
	Heavy	200'	1"	¾"
40'-50'	Light	150'	1"	¾"
	Heavy	250'	1⅜"	1"
50'-65'	Light	180'	1¼"	⅞"
	Heavy	300'	1½"	1⅛"

RECOMMENDED ANCHOR LINES FOR SAIL CRAFT

Over-All Length of Boat	Anchor Used	Length of Anchor Lines	Manila Rope Dia.	Nylon Rope Dia.
Under 20'	Light	100'	½"	⅜"
	Heavy			
20'-25'	Light	125'	½"	⅜"
	Heavy	200'	⅝"	½"
25'-30'	Light	150'	¾"	⁹⁄₁₆"
	Heavy	200'	¾"	⁹⁄₁₆"
30'-40'	Light	150'	1"	¾"
	Heavy	250'	1⅛"	¹³⁄₁₆"
40'-50'	Light	200'	1¼"	⅞"
	Heavy	300'	1½"	1⅛"
50'-65'	Light	200'	1⅜"	1"
	Heavy	300'	1⅝"	1⅛"

Rules for Anchoring

The following points on anchoring are well worthwhile:

1. Know the type of bottom. Hard sand holds anchors best; soft sand, next; then soft mud, coral and rock. Charts usually show bottom conditions you may encounter. If not, heave a lead with tallow on it to pick up bottom specimen. Also don't pick an anchoring spot so shallow that you may be aground at low tide; or one that's a hundred feet deep when there is one 20 feet deep a little further away. A chart or lead-line will give you the answer, too.

2. Come up to your planned anchorage into the wind or current, whichever is the stronger. Don't pick a spot too close to other boats. You may swing down onto them if the wind shifts or the tide turns. Actually, shelter from wind is an important consideration. The wind often changes in the night, so make sure you have enough room to swing in a full circle without knocking into other boats, piers, or the beach. Avoid anchoring in or near busy channels where the traffic and the wash from other boats might keep you awake all night.

3. Never drop an anchor from the bow while the boat has headway, except for the purpose of preventing her going ashore or into something. Have your yacht reversing slowly when you drop—*not throw*—the anchor. This will avoid fouling the line and will help "set" the anchor. Never, under any conditions, should you toss out the anchor like a shot-putter trying for an Olympic record. If you don't end up in the drink with the anchor you'll be lucky, and a stumble can cause the anchor to gouge the bow or break the windshield. Also, feed the anchor line out by hand so it doesn't touch the side of your yacht.

4. When the anchor is down, be sure to let out enough line. This is the most important single factor in safe anchoring. The amount should never be less than five times the depth of the water, and as much as ten times may be proper depending upon conditions of weather, exposure of location, velocity of current, etc. In extremely rough weather, increase the length of the anchor line even more. In other words the longer your anchor line the better your anchor will hold. The effectiveness of an anchor at different scopes is as follows:

2 to 1—13%	5 to 1—65%	8 to 1—77%
3 to 1—46%	6 to 1—72%	9 to 1—82%
4 to 1—54%	7 to 1—75%	10 to 1—85%

5. Your boat will be most secure if the "pull" on the anchor is as nearly horizontal as possible. This way the stock can position the flukes properly so anchor can "dig in." Should you want to make certain how much line you are putting out, paint the anchor line every ten feet, or tie on markers of light line that you can see by day and feel by dark. Count these markers as the anchor settles straight down and strikes bottom.

6. If the anchor line is too short or if you must anchor in a confined area (such as close to other boats) to allow enough scope to hold the boat in heavy seas, add a second anchor to the line, tied about one-third to one-half the distance from the terminal anchor. The second anchor doesn't need to be as heavy as the lower one. This will increase the scope of the lower end of the anchor line from 50 to 90 per cent, by decreasing the lift of the line. In other words, the line between the two anchors will remain nearly horizontal, depending upon the weight of the upper anchor and the size of the waves lifting the boat. This will cause the lower anchor to bite deeper into the bottom instead of lifting or dragging. The upper anchor has almost no bite into the bottom and acts as a shock absorber. Instead of the boat coming up short against the heavy anchor, the boat will have to lift the upper anchor before it can pull against the lower one. This will eliminate any sudden jerks against the mooring bitt.

7. In crowded areas, it may be necessary to use a stern anchor to prevent your yacht from swinging into a nearby boat. But, this should be done only where there is very little likelihood of strong cross currents or winds, since a strong push from the side would exert tremendous pull on the two anchors, possibly causing one or both of them to drag.

8. If you know you're anchoring in rocky or snag-strewn waters, attach the end of your line to the anchor's crown, then lead it past but not through the ring. Bind the line to the ring with two turns of twine. Then run the line to the boat. When you anchor, the hook will act the same as if it were conventionally fastened to the line. But should your anchor foul under a rock or snag and refuse to break out, haul up on the line until it is straight up-and-down. Jerk repeatedly as you run your boat slowly ahead until the binding breaks and the pull is transferred to the anchor's crown. It should then back out from whatever has fouled it.

9. With the anchor and line set, it may be desirable, particularly during heavy weather, to install chafing gear to protect the anchor line. The chafing gear might be split hose or canvas wrapped around the anchor cable where it would rub.

10. Don't shut off the engine until you're sure the anchor is holding. Then, make a note of the position of other boats or landmarks in relation to your yacht. In this way, you can tell if your anchor breaks loose and the boat starts to drift. Always examine the gear before leaving your boat or turning in. When anchoring overnight, be sure to display the anchor light.

Similarly, there are several precautions to follow when you plan to pull your anchor and leave:

1. Start the engine and run slowly up to the anchor, having a member of your crew haul in the line as you go.

2. If the anchor doesn't let go easily, move up until the line is as short as possible and have it fastened to the cleat or bitt in the bow of the boat. Then, move ahead over the anchor at slow speed. As soon as the anchor breaks loose from the bottom, stop the boat and have the anchor brought aboard.

3. After pulling up the anchor, make it fast in its proper place and, if possible, put the line where it can dry out before stowing it away. But don't leave it loose where it can go overboard and foul the propeller.

Docking Procedures

Tying up at a dock usually depends on the strength and direction of wind or current. First, however, there are a few other things to consider. For one thing—again unlike a car—a boat has no brakes. True, a good reverse gear is helpful but remember that, depending upon its speed and weight, a boat may require a run of considerable distance before losing headway when thrown into reverse. Therefore, always plan to make a landing at a dock by coming in just fast enough to keep your boat under control. Plan ahead, too, by having all the lines you will need ready for use. And, remember, the time to protect the hull with fenders is before tying up, not after. Keeping the following points in mind:

1. With wind or current behind when approaching a dock, if possible always make a turn to bring the bow into the wind or current before you come alongside. Start reversing just before the boat is parallel to the dock. And again remember what happens with a single inboard-engine boat that has a right-hand propeller: When reversing, the stern tends to swing to the left no matter which way the wheel is turned. Therefore, try to come in with the *left hand* (port) *side* of the boat facing the dock so that when you check forward speed by reversing, this will also swing the stern alongside. Otherwise, reversing will swing the stern out and *away* from the dock.

2. If you come in with the bow facing into the wind or current, secure the *bow* line first. The stern then will drift in against the dock.

3. If you *must* come in with the stern facing the current or wind, first be sure to kill your boat's headway by giving it sufficient reverse in time. Then, secure the *stern* line first and the bow will drift in alongside the dock.

4. Sometimes you get the break of landing with the current or wind carrying you toward the dock. Here, you simply bring your boat parallel to the dock while several yards out from it. Then, let it drift in alongside and tie up.

Leaving a dock usually calls for one of two procedures, depending upon the directional effect of the wind or current, whichever is stronger:

1. If the directional effect of the wind or current is away from where you are tied up, the procedure is simple: Just cast off all lines and let the boat drift out far enough from the dock to give you clearance for going ahead or turning, as you wish.

2. If the effect of the wind or current is toward the dock or toward the bow of your boat, cast off all lines—turn the wheel hard over toward the dock—then go ahead slowly for a few revolutions in forward gear. This should kick the stern well out and away from the dock. Have someone stationed forward with a fender to cushion the bow if it hits the dock. Next, reverse far enough to get the boat clear of the dock so that you can go ahead. Remember that the wind or current will be trying to push you back toward the dock, so be sure to swing the stern out far enough to make allowance for this.

TOWING

Your dinghy may be more than your tender, it may prove your life boat, so safety requires a good boat, not a cockleshell with barely enough freeboard to float two people in a mill pond. If you employ a tender on a cruise, the best place to "tow" your dinghy is on deck; but if you haven't the room or facilities to stow it on deck, nor davits to swing it, it has to be towed. The following rules should be applied to towing a tender behind your cruiser:

1. The towline (the painter) should be as substantial as a quarter- or half-inch anchor line and free from chafing. (In heavy weather, bend on an extra line.) It should be secured to a hefty cleat bolted through the deck or to two cleats using a bridle. Cork floats on your painter will prevent it from fouling your propeller.

2. Your dinghy will tow best when the painter is made fast to the stern just above the waterline.

3. Always lash your oars and rowlocks in the boat before towing.

4. Pay out the painter to get the dinghy riding on the down side of the second following stern wave. Hold the line in your hand and adjust its length until you feel the least amount of strain. Remember that a too-close tow may sleigh ride down the first wave into the towboat's transom. If a light dinghy yaws or "walks" over the wake, add weight in its stern to bring the bow up. A small boat towed incorrectly will reduce your speed a good deal.

5. Another way of making your towed dinghy behave in a following sea is with a sea anchor towed astern of it and keep a shorter tripline attached. This keeps the dinghy from charging up on your transom.

6. Shorten your dinghy painter on entering a harbor, for greater ease in maneuvering and to minimize possibility of fouling propeller.

7. Shift your tender to outside your boat when going alongside a dock.

8. See that your painter is renewed now and then and is in good shape for towing.

Besides towing a tender, it's sometimes necessary to tow another boat or possibly be towed yourself. Remember that it's part of the tradition of the sea to offer such aid whenever it is required, and both the aiding craft and the one needing the assistance should know the techniques involved so as to make the operation successful. In calm waters, there is no real problem to towing another boat. The boats get as close as possible to each other, and a line is tossed aboard the disabled craft. But in rough weather, this maneuver is a little more difficult. (If the water is rough, use a long tow line.) It's usually best for the towing boat to pass the line whenever possible, because there is much less chance of fouling the line with the propeller. Once the towline is secured aboard the disabled craft, the towing boat starts off in the direction to be towed, having secured its end of the line to the strongest cleat on the boat. Whenever possible, this should be secured amidships, and somewhat forward of the rudder, so that the towing craft can steer properly. It is imperative that the towing boat keep a very close watch on its tow, both to make sure that it doesn't break free and to insure that it's not in any further difficulties. Adjust the length of the line so that the boat being towed rides on the crest of a wave, not in the trough. Towing speed should be adjusted to the capabilities of the two boats and to the weather they are encountering, and it shouldn't in any case be excessive, because the towing process imposes rather serious strains on both craft.

MARLINSPIKE SEAMANSHIP

Some of the greatest uses of rope today are in the pleasure boating field. Rope hoists the sails on sailing dinghies, catboats, sloops, ketches, yawls, and schooners. Rope helps to anchor these craft and their motor-powered sisters, and hold them snugly at the dock. Yet despite this widespread use of rope on and around the water, many pleasure-boat owners—with an accent on newcomers—are practically unacquainted with that very valuable bit of mariners' lore known as marlinspike seamanship. In the broad sense, marlinspike seamanship concerns itself with the care, handling, and uses of rope. It becomes involved when a new coil of line is opened, then goes on to dictate how it may be put to best service, an item which includes such details as knots and splices.

Types of Rope

In the days of the square-riggers, rope used aboard ship was almost invariably hemp or manila. Today, with synthetics supplementing natural fibers, it's different. Properties of the various fibers differ. One may be superior in tensile strength, another in elasticity, a third in resistance to abrasion, still another in its soft, smooth handling qualities.

Manila rope will function satisfactorily in virtually any use as a line—provided it is top quality manila. But you may need larger, heavier manila than would be required if a synthetic line were used.

Nylon rope is more than twice as strong as manila, size for size, permitting use of smaller, lighter lines that are smoother and easier to handle. It is also quite elastic. This quality is fine in mooring and anchor lines where shock absorption is desirable.

Dacron rope is nearly as strong as nylon, but has less stretch in it. This makes dacron suitable for sheets and halyards, or other places where strength is desirable, but strechiness would be a disadvantage.

Polyethylene rope is made in different grades, the strongest being about the same as dacron. Its main quality is that it floats, making it an ideal line for sky towing, heaving, and for the dinghy painter.

Here are representative strengths in pounds of different yacht ropes:

Dia.	Manila	Filament Nylon	Spun Nylon	Filament Dacron	Spun Dacron	Polyethylene (High Tenac)
¼"	600	1,320	1,120	1,070	960	1,100
½"	2,650	5,180	4,400	4,450	4,000	3,700
1"	9,000	19,800	16,800	17,400	15,700	12,000

Knots and Their Uses

Hundreds of knots, simple and complex, have come to us down through the decades. All have served well in one chore or another. Some have outlived their usefulness; many continue to serve. Among the latter there are certain basic fastenings which persist as the work horses among knots and which should be mastered by every yachtsman.

The ideal knot, bend or hitch is one that is quickly and easily tied, has great strength with no tendency to slip, and can be readily untied even when wet or after being subjected to a heavy strain. This last attribute is one the average amateur either ignores or forgets. There are times when a rope must be cast off in a hurry, and any delay can have serious consequences. The knots illustrated here will adequately handle all the jobs that are required on the yacht. Practice each one assiduously, until you can tie it in the dark, and above all, learn to use each one correctly—for the specific use it was designed to serve. You can then rest assured that you've taken an important step toward avoiding trouble.

A good step toward mastery of knots is familiarization with terms used in tying. So that's where we'll begin, with a little glossary of knot-tying terms. A piece of rope, regardless of length, used in knot tying has sections, each with a specific name. When you make a bend in a length of rope it becomes divided into three parts. The area of the bend becomes a *bight*. The shorter free part of the rope becomes its *end*. And the longer section becomes its *standing part*. All knots are tied by using these components—end, bight, standing part.

Bight and Loop

Like the earthworm, a rope has two indistinguishable Ends. Everything in between is the Standing Part. The simplest maneuver is a change of direction, called a Bight. A cross over or under is called a Loop. The end left hanging is called the Bitter End, a term you'll consider appropriate before you master all the following knots.

Figure-Of-Eight

Less complicated than the knot you put in your shoelaces, the Figure-Of-Eight is an ideal basic knot for use at the end of a line to prevent a sheet or line from slipping through a block. Make an underhand loop, then bring the free end over the standing part and bring it under and through the loop.

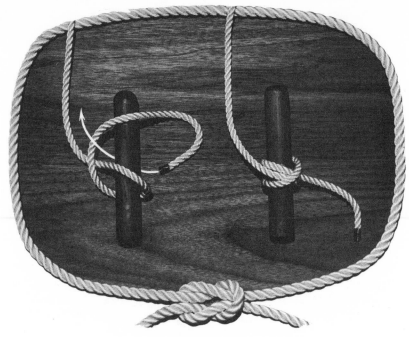

Clove Hitch

When a line has to be made fast to a pile or a spar quickly, the Clove Hitch is the simple, speedy answer. A simple loop around the pile, followed by a second, with the free end crossed under and pulled tight, results in a hitch that gets even tighter as tension increases on the standing part.

Bowline

For a simple running loop, the Bowline is the sailor's best friend. Begin with a small overhand loop, make a larger loop and bring the free end through the first loop, as shown at left. Now form a bight by bringing the free end under and over the standing part, then back through the loop. This won't slip or snarl under strain, yet unties easily with one tug on the bight.

Fisherman's Bend or Anchor Bend

The two loops that swivel freely make the Anchor Bend perfect for making fast a line to an anchor, buoy or spar. Take two turns through the ring, followed by an underhand loop, then thread the bitter end through the turns and pull tight. You should give the bitter end an extra hitch around the standing part for greater strength.

Rolling Hitch

Here's something similar to the Anchor Bend. The Rolling Hitch is especially useful when there's a strain on the line—you can tie it with one hand while holding the line taut. Take two turns through the ring or around the post, then finish up with a clove hitch over the standing part. Keep this one set snug.

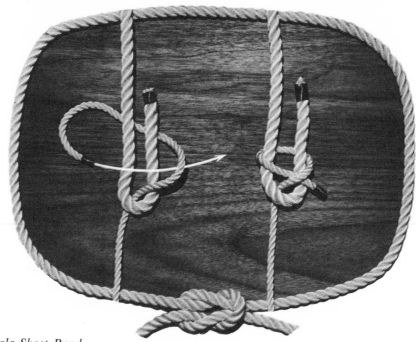

Single Sheet Bend

The Sheet Bend, used to tie two ropes together, is at its best when things are complicated by ropes of unequal size. Form a bight in the larger line. Thread smaller line bitter end through the bight, around it, back through under itself, and out over on the same side as the large line's bitter end.

Double Sheet Bend

When the strain on the two ropes you are joining is particularly great, tie the Single Sheet Bend, as above, leaving enough length in the small line bitter end for another loop around, under itself inside the bight and out over again. To prevent slipping and jamming, always make sure that both bitter ends are on the same side of the knot.

Belaying

Endlessly winding rope around a cleat is not Belaying. Loop the line around the base, under the arms of the cleat, then bring it up and over diagonally, around and under one arm, then over, around and under the other, in a continuous figure-8, securing the bitter end by tucking it under the last crossover.

Tug Boat Hitch

Ready for the final exam? The Tug Boat Hitch is ideal for heavy towing, yet can be released under great strain when necessary. Take one or two turns around the towing post, cross bight under, then drop bight over top. Now loop bight back around the standing part, drop bight over the top with half twist, and pull taut. Congratulations.

How to Make Fast. Many methods of making fast are used but the correct one is usually the easiest. One easy but effective method is illustrated here and is accomplished as follows:

    1. Loop the running part around the cleat's far side, away from the direction of the strain.

    2. Then take a turn around the stem with the running part and up and over the center (additional turn would jam the line).

    3. Add several more figure eights or slip a half-hitch over a horn of the cleat immediately if there is little strain.

    4. Your line is now made fast, yet ready for prompt cast off with no part under tension binding loops. This method makes it easy to cast off without having to take up the slack in the standing part and ensures against accidents that occur when lines couldn't be freed quickly.

Whipping. A whipping is a binding on the end of a line to prevent unraveling. When employing fiber ropes, the common or plain whipping is used and this is how it's done: Use a fine yarn, spunyarn, marline or sail twine. Lay the yarn, with a loop, alongside the rope (or strand) as shown. Then wind the yarn tightly around both loop and rope (or strand) for a distance equal approximately to the diameter of the rope (or strand) being whipped. Finish by putting the winding end through the loop, then pull the end (on left in illustration) tight until the loop is drawn back out of sight. Snip the ends close to the whipping and it is done.

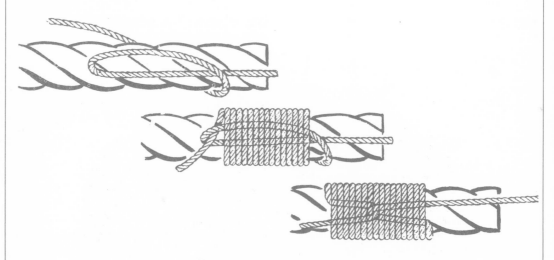

With nylon, dacron, or polyethylene ropes, the best rope end is obtained after whipping by cutting with a hot knife. However, great care must be taken that the hot knife doesn't come in contact with the rope at any place but at the point of cut. The knife should be very sharp and hot so that, when it is drawn quickly through the rope, the filaments will be fused together at the point of cut. If a cold knife must be used, a somewhat ragged end results. It may be evened by heating the fiber ends in a match flame sufficiently to fuse them together. Again, this must be done carefully, and the match flame kept away from the whipping itself. A waterproof tape is sometimes employed to complete the job.

Heaving a Line. To throw a line to another vessel or to a shore installation, make up the heaving line into two coils—about two-thirds of the rope held in the left hand, about one-third in the right hand for throwing, and the whole ready to run out easily. The end of the left-hand coil should be made fast. The right-hand coil is thrown by swinging the arm and body.

Splicing Rope. When a yachtsman wishes to secure two ropes together permanently he does what is known as splicing. While the long splice is the smoothest and neatest of splices, and necessary where the rope must pass through a block, the short splice is the one commonly used. To know it is to know also the eye and back splice, as these are but slight variations of the short splice. The illustration here shows how these splices are made.

The Short Splice:

1. Lash rope about twelve diameters from each end (A). Unlay the strands up to the lashings. Whip strands to prevent untwisting and put together as in diagram above, alternating the strands from each end. Pull up taut.

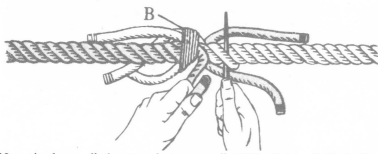

2. Now tie down all the strands temporarily (B). Take off the lashing from one side of the rope and raise one strand on this side, using a fid. Take the middle strand of the opposite side. Tuck it over one strand and under the raised strand. Pull it up taut.

Every time you tuck a strand, let out a little of the turn. And be sure to keep some tension on the raised strand under which you are tucking. The prevents strand kinking.

3. Tuck against the twist or "lay" of rope. What happens is that the tuck goes over one strand, under the second, and out between the second and third.

4. Roll the rope toward you. Pick up the second strand. Repeat the some operation. Then do it again with the third strand. You have now made one full tuck.

To tape the splice, first make one more tuck like the first one. Then make the third tuck the same way, but first cut off ⅓ of the yarns from the strands. For the fourth tuck, cut off ½ the remaining yarn.

For the untapered short splice, you do not cut the strands. You just make three more tucks, exactly like the first one.

5. Take both lashings (which were applied in No. 1 and No. 2) off the other side of the rope. Repeat above operations.

6. To finish, cut off ends of strands, leaving about one or two inches protruding.
To Splice Nylon Rope—The above procedure applies to splicing of nylon and other synthetic ropes except that one additional full tuck should be used.

The Long Splice:

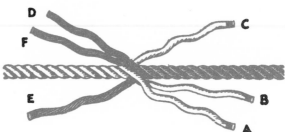

1. Unlay the end of each rope about 15 turns and place the ropes together, alternating the strands from each end, as shown above.

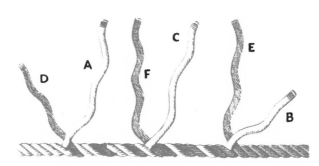

2. Start with any opposite pair, unlay one strand and replace it with strand from the other part. Repeat operation with another pair of strands in the opposite direction as shown above.

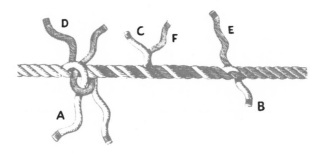

3. Now tie each pair of opposing strands, as B and E above, with an overhand knot, tuck each strand twice (see Figure 4), as in the Short Splice, and then twice more as for the Tapered Splice—see page 30. Or, halve each strand (see A and D), and tie with an overhand knot before tucking. By this latter method a smaller splice results—but at a considerable sacrifice of strength.

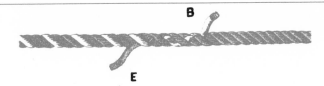

4. Roll and pound well before cutting strands off close to rope.

The Eye Splice:

Used in the end of a rope for mooring, the Eye Splice is the strongest, most permanent rope loop. It's made exactly like the Short Splice, except that it is made with one rope. The end, after being unlaid, is bent around to form the eye, and is spliced into its own strands of the standing part.

Care of Lines

Another part of your becoming a seasoned yachtsman, wise in the ways of marlinspike seamanship, is to know the proper care of your lines. You will:

1. *Avoid kinks*. Kinks cause overstress at the sharp bend, weakening fibers inside the strands. Because of this, always coil a line when you have finished using it. The correct method is to coil a line with the sun, that is clockwise, or to the right. This is because of the twist imparted to the rope in manufacture. However, if the rope tends to kink when coiling this way, it's because a reverse twist has been imparted to the rope in use and to take out this twist, the line must be coiled counter-clockwise.

2. *Keep your lines clean*. To clean, drape in loops over rail and hose down gently, with fresh water if possible. A high pressure stream will only force grit and grime deeper into a rope's fibers.

3. *Stow carefully*. Dry lines thoroughly before stowing. Rot fungus and mildew will grow on a stored wet line and destroy it in short order. If possible, stow by hanging from pegs rather than on deck so air will circulate around it. Never use a line that has been frozen without allowing it to thaw out and dry.

4. *Prevent chafe and abrasion*. Never allow line to rub on sharp edges, or one rope chafe against another. When riding at anchor for long periods, it is well to 'freshen the nip' by playing out the line slightly so wear isn't centralized on one spot.

5. *Don't lubricate the line itself*. Manufacturers treat rope with an oil or solution which preserves and lubricates internal fibers. Users are cautioned against trying to improve on the manufacturer's protection.

6. *Beware of chemicals*. Acids and alkalis attack rope. They burn the fibers and make them brittle. Be careful when using hydrometers for testing batteries as the acid in them will burn rope badly. Rust, too, is bad for rope. Spots of discoloration are a danger sign showing when fibers have broken down.

7. *Never overload*. The safety factor allowed in determining the load on a rope is commonly taken as 5 to 1. That is, if a rope must lift 500 pounds, select one of sufficient tensile strength to handle 2,500 pounds. If the load ever exceeds 75 per cent of the rope's breaking strength, chances are it will be permanently injured.

8. *Check lines during yachting season*. To make sure the line is serviceable during a season's usage, it should be inspected inside and out. On the outside, you should look for signs of abrasion and broken fibers. The fibers should also have a certain luster to them without any signs of brittleness or limpness.

CHAPTER FOUR: ELECTRONIC YACHTING

You're tooling down the highway when your car konks. Maybe the gas tank is dry or the coil has shorted. No sweat! You lift the hood and wait for help or, at the worst, trudge to the nearest telephone. But when a boat quits running, what do you do? You can't "get out and under" when you're off-shore. And, just as with automobiles, things sometimes happen that are beyond your ability to fix. You don't just sit in the boat and stew. You turn on the radiotelephone and call your mechanic or some other boat nearby; or (if there is no other possibility) the Coast Guard. Help arrives, and you get home without having to paddle. "Ah, electronics," you'll say. "It's wonderful!"

Another time, you're off on an overnight cruise . . . getting away from it all, letting the world spin by itself. But, having one cell of your brain on the job even while relaxing, you turn on your radio receiver and get the weather forecast. "A low pressure system to the west has picked up speed," the man inside the box says, "and a sharp frontal squall line, with thundershowers and high winds, is expected to hit the area this afternoon . . ." You turn off the radio and announce: "Get ready to haul anchor. If we start for home now, we can miss the storm." Or, you may be more experienced and know where to find a safe berth. So, you head in and drop that "spare" anchor. By the time you are safe at your mooring, the first black clouds are in sight. But you get home in good shape. Ah, electronics!

Then, there's the day of the fog. First the distant landmarks fade out. Soon, you're sitting under an inverted gray bowl. Maybe you haven't kept track of your navigation too well; now, where in the world are you? And where are those shoals and rocks that show on the chart? Ill-equipped skippers might panic. But you simply drop anchor, turn on your radio direction finder, "take a cut" on a couple of radio stations, and mark your position on the chart. Knowing where you are, it is a simple matter to follow a compass course to where you want to go, considering tide and wind. You turn on the depth sounder to make sure you won't hit bottom, use the proper sound signals with your horn to warn other boats of your presence, and go on your way at proper speed. Electronics!

What kind of equipment should you have? If yours is a large boat and you have currency stacked around like old newspapers, there is no problem. March to the nearest marine electronics dealer and get the works. You'll have use for all of it sooner or later, and it will make your boat look as salty as a North Sea herring trawler. However, most pleasure boats can do very well with just a few items of electronic equipment. The ones to choose and how much they will cost depend upon your own particular boat and cruising waters, and the kind of activity you enjoy.

RADIOTELEPHONE

Do you navigate the high seas or offshore waters? If so, a standard marine radiotelephone is the Number One item. With it, you can talk directly with other boats, shore stations, and vessels of the U.S. Coast Guard, and through commercial telephone facilities (paying a small toll charge) to your home, office, shipyard, or any other party on land. Use is restricted to water craft, so you aren't competing with taxicabs or oil trucks for air time. Intership channels are reserved for safety, operational, and "ship's-business" conversations. There is also a special distress frequency, monitored by other boats and the Coast Guard.

Built-in electronic console features,
top row left to right:
Radar, depth sounder,
citizens band two-way radio.
Bottom row: Radio direction finder,
marine radiotelephone.

Marine radiotelephones come in a sufficient number of shapes, sizes, operating ranges and prices to meet all requirements. To begin with there are three types of two-way marine radiotelephones in use today. The first, and most commonly used range is the Marine Radiotelephone, Medium Frequency Band. Its channels include the following:

2182 Kcs—International Calling and Safety in all areas. The law requires that it be guarded, and the Coast Guard guards it.

2670 Kcs—Common working frequency with Coast Guard.

2638 Kcs—Ship to ship in all areas.

2738 Kcs—Ship to ship in all areas *except* the Great Lakes and the Gulf of Mexico.

2003 Kcs—Ship to ship in the Great Lakes only.

2830 Kcs—Ship to ship in the Gulf of Mexico only.

Note. A radiotelephone set will always have 2182 as one channel. It may in addition have 2638, 2738, etc. The above system is known as Simplex—the same channel is used to send and receive. In addition to the above, the set will have one or more of the below channels, depending on the area in which the boat will be operated. Most of the below channels are Duplex—one frequency is used ship to shore, and another from shore to ship.

The second type of radiotelephone is called the Citizen's Radio Service (CRS), or more commonly, Citizen's Band (CB). Recently, the FCC has authorized the use of 22 channels in the Class D, 27-megacycle Citizen's Radio Band. This is a sincere effort to ease the traffic problem in the 2- to 3-megacycle band, and to supply a much needed medium of communication for use between boats working or cruising together or between a shore station and a station afloat. This is not marine radiotelephony. You don't have the common calling frequency of 2182 kc, nor do you have the range available in the 2- to 3-megacycle band. You do, however, have at hand reliable line-of-sight, relatively short-range radio communication between stations equipped with similar equipment. Overwater range of the citizens band radio has been in the neighborhood of 25 miles, but here again, land configuration must be taken into consideration when using the equipment for shore-to-boat communication. The high CB frequencies act like rays of light. They can't bend over the horizon and tend to "skip" or bounce off the ionosphere to more distant areas. However, some of this tendency is avoided by the FCC requirement limiting power to 5 watts in the sets.

You can't call the Coast Guard on Class D citizens band. Nor is there a common calling and distress frequency, as there is in the 2-3 mc marine band. Of the 22 channels available on this short range radiotelephone, it is generally accepted that channel 9 should be used ashore as a monitored frequency for the H.E.L.P. (Highway Emergency Locating Plan) recently initiated by the Automobile Manufacturers' Association. The manufacturers of citizens band equipment for the marine industry have recommended the use of channel 13 or a monitored frequency for use afloat. Regatta control, yacht club launch calling and dispatching, commercial team-fishing operations, short range communications between cruising boats, and the use of CB for a home-car-office-boat communication line are just a few of the duties to which CB has already contributed immeasurably.

The third type of radiotelephone equipment is in the VHF-FM maritime mobile band (152 to 174 mcs.). Because of interference, static, the increase in the number of radios in use, and the tendency to buy "power" to blast through the jumble of unnecessary traffic on the 2-3 mc marine band, there was a definite need for a solution to the problems.

VHF-FM is rapidly coming into its own as a solution to the problem since it offers a safety and calling channel 16 or 156.8 mc, multi-channel selection, static-free land-line connection, and bridge communications when within range (usually up to 35 miles) of shore station or ship. Although at present there is a shortage of land based facilities, many more are rapidly being built. The Coast Guard is installing this equipment at over 240 of its shore stations and on all of its search and rescue vessels. Marine telephone operators in many areas provide service in this band. Since this is a relatively new and uncluttered band for the mariner, and the longer range ship to shore radiotelephone band is quite congested, its use seems quite attractive. Its channels include the following:

156.8 Mcs —International Calling and Safety. Similar to 2182 Kcs.

156.6 Mcs —Ship to shore.

156.3 Mcs—Ship to ship in all areas. There are several other frequencies available for ship to ship, and ship to shore use.

Note. The FCC has authorized one frequency in this band for use in communicating with government operated locks and bridges.

Compact Marine Citizens Band
two-way radio
that operates from
boat's regular
12-volt batteries
drawing less current
than an ordinary running light.

License Information

Every radio broadcasting station of every type and every frequency must be licensed by the Federal Communications Commission, and all personnel using these broadcasting units must be licensed. In the case of the Medium Frequency Band and VHF-FM Mobile Band (which the FCC calls the "Marine" bands) the set *and* the operator have separate licenses. In the case of the Citizen's Band (CRS), the Station's License and the Operator's Authority are one and the same document. Details are:

For the Individual. For the Medium Frequency and VHF-FM Marine Mobile Band: This is applied for at the nearest office of the FCC by filling out Form FCC 753-1 (no knowledge of code required). A Restricted Radiotelephone Operator's Permit is then issued, good for life. Calls may be made by anyone on board, but the set is in the charge of the licensed operator.

For the Radiotelephone Set. For the Medium Frequency Band Set and VHF-FM Mobile Band Set: This is applied for at the nearest office of the FCC on Form FCC 501-A. An Interim License is then issued and, in time, Washington issues a license good for four years.

For CRS. The "Citizen's Radio License" is good for five years and is authority for both the set and the operator.

Procedure for Handling an Emergency Call

All distress and emergency calls are made on 2182 Kcs. To make a distress call, repeat the MAYDAY* three times, followed by "This is" the call letters and name of your yacht.** Repeat call three times, then slowly and clearly, give the following information:

"(Coast Guard station being called), this is (your boat's name and radio call letters). I am (nature of distress—grounded, disabled, on fire, sinking, etc.) in position (latitude, and longitude or bearing—true or magnetic—and distance from some prominent point of land). I have (number) of persons aboard. I am in (no immediate or immediate danger). My boat is (length and type, type of rig, color of hull, and color of superstructure). I request (source of aid, Coast or commercial) assistance. I will stand by (radio frequency). Over."

Note: *Two other priority calls—PAN and SECURITY—are used for urgent messages concerning safety of vessel or her crew (PAN) and for meteorological or hydrographic warnings (SECURITY). The signature "MEDICO" is sometimes used to precede an appeal for immediate medical advice or aid. These words are repeated three times before transmission of such messages.

**The Radiotelephone Alarm Signal (if available) should be transmitted prior to the Distress Call for approximately one minute. The Radiotelephone Alarm Signal consists of two audio tones, of different pitch, transmitted alternately. Its purpose is to attract the attention of persons on watch and shall only be used to announce that a distress call or message is about to follow.

After sending the distress message, listen on 2182 Kcs. for a reply. Allow time for stations hearing the distress message to reply. If there is no reply, repeat the distress call and distress message. Once a reply is heard, you may elect to continue handling the distress traffic or conversations, or you may transfer such control to another station if you are needed away from the radiotelephone to cope with the emergency.

When replying to a distress message, the following procedure should be followed:

1. Do not answer a distress call until the distress message has been heard (unless no message is transmitted).

2. Do not reply to the distress message immediately unless you are in the vicinity of the ship in distress. Someone may be closer who could render immediate aid.

3. Do not, under any circumstances, continue with normal radiotelephone use after you have heard a distress call or message. Continue listening on the frequency where the distress call or message is heard. Do not make any transmissions that might possibly interfere with distress traffic.

4. When replying, use the distress frequency and say: *(Name of vessel in distress, repeated three times),* this is *(your radio call sign and ship's name, repeated three times).* Your MAYDAY and distress message received. We are *(distance and bearing, true or magnetic, from a prominent point of land; or longitude and latitude),* approximately *(distance)* from your position on a course to you of *(your course).* Our speed is .... knots. We should reach you in .... minutes. Over."

5. If the station in distress requests that you handle additional distress traffic, do so. There may come a time when you will need such assistance.

It should be remembered that MAYDAY should *not* be used unless immediate assistance is required. You may be depriving a fellow boatman of help who really needs it. As previously stated, distress calls have priority over all other traffic, and any boat hearing one should go off the air immediately and listen on the frequency used for sending distress calls. If the distress call is from a boat in your vicinity, answer it immediately. If the distressed boat definitely isn't in your vicinity, allow a short interval of time before acknowledging receipt of the message in order to permit those nearer to answer without interference. For the duration of distress traffic, it is forbidden for all but those taking part in the traffic to transmit on the frequencies being used.

Note: The International signal for an aircraft that wants to direct a surface craft to a distress is: Circling the surface craft, opening and closing the throttle or changing propeller pitch (noticeable by change in sound) while crossing ahead of the surface craft, and proceeding in the direction of the distress. If you receive such a signal, you should follow the aircraft. If you can't do so, try to inform the aircraft by any available means. If your assistance is no longer needed, the aircraft will cross your wake, opening and closing the throttle or changing propeller pitch. If you are radio equipped, you should attempt to communicate with the aircraft on 2182 Kcs. when the aircraft makes the above signals or makes any obvious attempt to attract your attention. In the event that you can't communicate by radio, be alert for a message block dropped from the aircraft.

Procedure for Intership Calls

In making an intership call, do the following:

1. Listen on the calling frequency of 2182 Kcs.

2. If 2182 Kcs. is in use, wait until it is clear. If a distress call or message is heard on 2182 Kcs., continue listening, but do not proceed with your call.

3. When 2182 Kcs. is clear, operate your own transmitter and say: "*(station being called),* this is *(your radio call sign and ship's name).* Over."

4. During periods of good communication (most of the time), saying the call once is usually sufficient. The call may *not* be repeated more than three times.

5. Again listen on 2182 Kcs. If there is no reply, repeat the call after two minutes have elapsed. This may be repeated three times, then you must wait fifteen minutes before making another attempt. The time consumed in calling must not exceed 30 seconds.

6. If a contact is made, switch to the previously agreed upon intership frequency (2638 Kcs. or 2738 Kcs., for example) and proceed with conversation. Limit conversation to five minutes.

7. When conversation is finished, say: "This is *(radio call sign and ship's name)* signing off."

Replying to an intership call is done in the following manner:

1. Always maintain a listening watch on 2182 Kcs. If you hear your call sign and/or ship's name, operate your transmitter on 2182 Kcs. and say: "This is *(your radio call sign and ship's name)*."

2. After making your reply: switch to the previously agreed intership frequency and proceed.

3. When the conversation is over, say: "This is *(your radio call sign and ship's name)* signing off."

Procedure for Ship-to-Shore Calls

The following are the recommended steps for making a ship-to-shore call:

1. Listen to make sure the working channel you wish to use is not busy. If it is free put your transmitter on the air and say:

2. "This is *(call sign and name of your yacht)* calling the *(coast or commercial station desired)* Marine Operator." Listen for a reply. If no contact is made, repeat after a short interval.

3. When the Marine Operator answers say: "This is *(your radio call sign and yacht's name)*.

When you hear the name of your yacht called, or the bell associated with your selective signalling device rings, put your transmitter on the air and say:

1. "This is *(your radio call sign and yacht's name)*."

2. After conversation is completed say: "This is *(your radio call sign and yacht's name)* signing off."

Procedure for Making a Test Transmission

When making a test transmission, do the following:

1. When making a test transmission, take every precaution not to interfere with normal traffic on the channel being tested.

2. Listen on the frequency of the channel being tested.

3. If the frequency is in use, wait until it is clear. When it is clear say: "This is *(your radio call sign—test)*." Listen for an appropriate interval; if the word "wait" is heard suspend testing. After an appropriate interval of time the announcement is repeated and if no response is observed, and careful listening indicates that harmful interference should not be caused, the operator shall announce "testing" followed by:

    a. 1, 2, 3, 4, ——etc. OR

    b. Test phrase sentences not in conflict with normal operating signals. Test signals shall not exceed ten seconds.

4. At the conclusion of testing say: "This is *(your radio call sign and ship's name, and general location of ship)*." This test transmission shall not be repeated until at least one minute has elapsed.

5. You may wish to make a radio check prior to sailing to ensure proper operation. It is recommended that this be done by viewing a specially installed meter, measuring the output with an RF (radio frequency) meter or holding a neon bulb close to the antenna lead-in wire. Should you wish to contact another station as part of this test, use the appropriate intership or ship-to-shore calling procedure. You must remember, however, that the calling frequency, 2182 Kcs., is also the distress frequency. It is imperative that unnecessary calls on this frequency be eliminated so that distress calls may be heard. When you desire a radio check, make it with some-

one in your vicinity, preferably one who has just been transmittng, and not with the Coast Guard. The Coast Guard must be ready to handle distress cases and answering the ever growing demand for radio checks could reduce their ability to do so.

Note. The spelling or phonetic alphabet is to be used to identify letters when spelling out words, names, abbreviations, and call signs in voice communications. There have been many changes made in this alphabet since its inception. Many yachtsmen are familiar with the World War II alphabet, "Able," "Baker," "Charlie," etc. This is now changed and the new one is as follows:

Letters to Be Iden-tified	Identifying Word	*Spoken as:	Letters to Be Iden-tified	Identifying Word	*Spoken as:
A	Alfa	*AL* FAH	N	November	NO *VEM* BER
B	Bravo	*BRAH* VOH	O	Oscar	*OSS* CAH
C	Charlie	*CHAR* LEE (or *SHAR* LEE)	P	Papa	PAH *PAH*
			Q	Quebec	KEH *BECK*
D	Delta	*DELL* TAH	R	Romeo	*ROW* ME OH
E	Echo	*ECK* OH	S	Sierra	SEE *AIR* RAH
F	Foxtrot	*FOKS* TROT	T	Tango	*TANG* GO
G	Golf	GOLF	U	Uniform	*YOU* NEE FORM (or *OO* NEE FORM)
H	Hotel	*HOH* TELL			
I	India	*IN* DEE AH	V	Victor	*VIK* TAH
J	Juliett	*JEW* LEE *ETT*	W	Whiskey	*WISS* KEY
K	Kilo	*KEY* LOH	X	X-ray	*ECKS* RAY
L	Lima	*LEE* MAH	Y	Yankee	*YANG* KEY
M	Mike	MIKE	Z	Zulu	*ZOO* LOO

*The syllables to be emphasized are in italic type.

Station Log

An accurate radio station log must be kept. Each sheet of the log shall be numbered in sequence and shall include the name of the boat, the official call sign of the station, and the signature of the licensed operator who is responsible for the operation of the station. The required log entries are: Log every transmission, call, reply, or test. Log all distress traffic, made or received. Include all pertinent data. Log all service and maintenance data. Any change made in the installation must be entered in the logbook. Keep logbook for one year. Logbooks containing distress traffic must be kept for three years. Keep all service and maintenance data until the next time the installation is checked by a properly licensed technician.

Rules to Remember

Your radio can mean your safe arrival; use it with respect. The following are ten points which have been abstracted from the FCC's "Rules Governing Stations on Shipboard in the Maritime Services—Part 8." (Part 8 covers all the rules applicable to these services. It is now one section of Vol. IV of the FCC's "Rules." Available from the Superintendent of Documents, U.S. Government Printing Office, Washington 25, D.C., for $2.50.) It is suggested by the FCC that the following rules be posted as a reminder near your set.

1.	Maintain your watch	Listen to 2182 Kcs. when not in communication with another station (Rule 8.223)
2.	Listen before you talk	Avoid interference with calls in progress. (Rule 8.181)
3.	Identify your vessel	Give your call sign and vessel's name at beginning and end of each communication. (Rule 8.364)

4. Make calls correctly	Call other vessels on 2182 Kcs. then switch to intership channel. (Rule 8.366) Call Commercial Shore stations on an appropriate working channel. (Rule 8.366)
5. Use channels properly	2182 Kcs. for emergencies and brief calls and replies. (Rule 8.353) Intership for safety, navigation or operational and business needs of vessels. (Rule 8.358)
6. Watch your language	Use of profane or obscene language is a criminal offense.
7. Be brief all the time	Limit calls to 30 seconds; conversation to 5 minutes. (Rule 8.366)
8. Keep an accurate log	Enter all transmissions made and distress calls heard. (Rule 8.368)
9. Have documents handy	Ship Station license; Operator license or permit; Part 8 of the FCC Rules; Log Book. (Rule 8.367)
10. Have equipment checked	Periodic checks insure safety and good operation.

RADIO DIRECTION FINDER

When you are in sight of landmarks you navigate by taking bearings on known objects and plotting them on your chart. However, when landmarks are not in sight, because of poor visibility or distance, you must rely on a form of navigation called "DR" for "Dead Reckoning." This is a chart record of where you think you are, based on your course, time and speed and last known accurate position. A radio direction finder (RDF) will remove the guesswork and ascertain your actual position.

There are several classes of radio stations that can be used in conjunction with RDF, and they are listed here in their order of general preference:

Marine Radio Beacons. A description of the characteristics and operating procedures of the U.S. Coast Guard Radio Beacon System operating in the marine radio frequency band of 285 to 325 Kcs. and Consolan are outlined in Hydrographic Office publication, *Radio Aids to Navigation H.O. 117 A* and *H.O. 117 B*. In addition, beacon characteristics are listed in the *Light Lists and Coast Pilots*. The location of the beacons, for piloting purposes, can be obtained from the U.S.C. & G.S. navigation chart on which radio beacons are identified by the abbreviation *R Bn*. In general, the basic characteristics of the system are as follows:

1. All beacons operate 24 hours a day regardless of the weather conditions. For identification, the radio frequency takes the place of the light's color, and audible dots and dashes take the place of the light's flashing or occulting.

2. The characteristic radio signal used to identify the particular beacon consists of a series of a simple combination of dots and dashes. This signal will consist of the characteristic identifier transmitted for 50 seconds followed by a 10 second dash. Special exceptions to this rule are noted in the official publications.

3. The characteristic identifier is superimposed on a continuous carrier when they are transmitting to facilitate use by navigators using Automatic Direction Finders.

4. Normally up to six radio beacons will be sequenced on a single frequency and will transmit for one minute in consecutive rotation. The order of rotation will

be according to the assigned sequence number which is indicated by a Roman numeral one (I) through six (VI).

    5. Certain stations will continue to be equipped with synchronized equipment for Distance Finding as detailed later.

    6. Special calibration stations transmit on a frequency in the marine band and on 480 kc to allow for the calibration of direction finders.

    7. A most useful function of many RDFs is the reception of Consolan signals. Consolan is a long range navigational aid and the signals are a series of dots and dashes transmitted on a continuous wave so the BFO (Beat Frequency Oscillator—an electronic circuit that some RDFs contain) must be used to receive them. At the present time there are only three stations in operation (other stations are now in the planning stage): Nantucket, TUK, 194 Kcs., position 41—15.6 N, 70—09.3 W; San Francisco, SFI, 192 Kcs., position 38—12.2 N, 122—34.1 W; Miami, MMF, 190 Kcs., position 35—36.16 N, 80—34.16 W.

This system is completely described in Hydrographic Office publication *No. 117*. With the "Ranger II" and the tables contained in *H.O. 117,* you can get accurate lines of position at long range, up to as much as 1,000 miles from the Consolan station. These signals radiate like the spokes of a wheel—24 spokes or sectors that reach out more than a thousand miles from the station. The sectors are alternately coded as dot and dash sectors. These stations transmit 24 hours a day. They send out and constantly repeat a 30-second keying cycle. When you tune in, listen for the station's identification in Morse code. Then you will hear the 30-second keying cycle of dots and dashes; there will be a total of 60. If you hear dots first, you are in a dot sector; dashes, a dash sector.

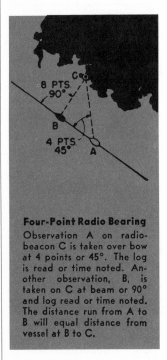

Four-Point Radio Bearing
Observation A on radiobeacon C is taken over bow at 4 points or 45°. The log is read or time noted. Another observation, B, is taken on C at beam or 90° and log read or time noted. The distance run from A to B will equal distance from vessel at B to C.

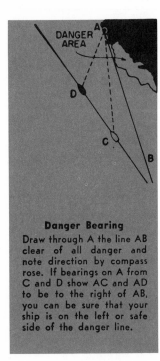

Danger Bearing
Draw through A the line AB clear of all danger and note direction by compass rose. If bearings on A from C and D show AC and AD to be to the right of AB, you can be sure that your ship is on the left or safe side of the danger line.

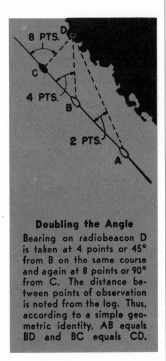

Doubling the Angle
Bearing on radiobeacon D is taken at 4 points or 45° from B on the same course and again at 8 points or 90° from C. The distance between points of observation is noted from the log. Thus, according to a simple geometric identity, AB equals BD and BC equals CD.

Standard Broadcast Stations. Standard broadcast stations that are located close to the coastline are suitable for radio navigation. You can receive these radio transmissions on a band covering 540 to 1600 kilocycles. Bearings taken on inland stations are not recommended for direction finding, because they're subject to refraction (bending of a radio signal as it travels over land), and that can cause serious errors in plotting your position from the station's antenna and transmitter location and not the studio location, which may be many miles away. Some manufacturers of direction finders publish lists of suitable radio stations, with the location of the transmitting towers given in latitude and longitude. Stations having towers of navigational value are usually marked on the large-scale navigation charts. If they are not, you may learn the antenna location by contacting the station manager or engineer. It's helpful to mark the location of such stations on your chart.

Aircraft Beacons. Airway beacons operate in the 200- to 415-kilocycle band, and they can be identified by their code signal "AN," which sounds like "dit dah, dah dit." However, because the antenna is often located far from the airfield with which the beacon is associated, you shouldn't rely on bearings taken from these signals unless previous experience has proved their dependability.

Operation of RDF

Bearing taken with an RDF may be *relative, magnetic,* or *true.* Which you elect to use will depend on which is most desirable for your particular situation. Whether you read relative, magnetic or true bearings will depend on how you set the azimuth scale on the RDF. The azimuth scale is the plastic ring on top of the unit immediately beneath the antenna. It is calibrated from 0 to 360 degrees and is rotatable so that you may set your own boat's course opposite the lubberline.

First the RDF should be so positioned that the two lubberlines are lined up parallel with the ship's keel. To take relative bearings, set the azimuth scale with zero opposite the forward lubberline. Read the bearing opposite the line on the end of the antenna. One end of the antenna will indicate bearing to the station, the other end will indicate bearing away from the station. These bearings are *relative* to your own ship's heading.

To take magnetic bearings, set your ship's compass course opposite the forward lubberline. If your ship's compass has deviation on the particular heading, add or subtract the correction and set the corrected magnetic bearing on the azimuth scale. Read the indicated bearing from the mark on the end of the antenna for relative bearings described above. The indicated bearing will be *magnetic,* and can be plotted directly on the chart using the magnetic compass rose on the chart.

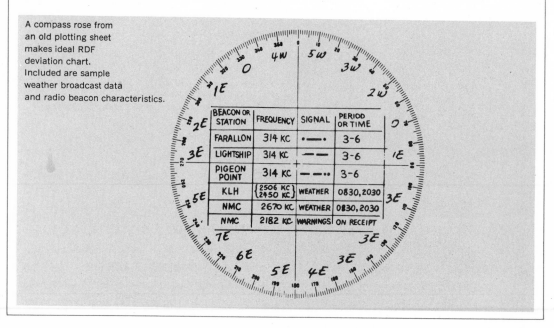

A compass rose from an old plotting sheet makes ideal RDF deviation chart. Included are sample weather broadcast data and radio beacon characteristics.

BEACON OR STATION	FREQUENCY	SIGNAL	PERIOD OR TIME
FARALLON	314 KC	•▬•	3-6
LIGHTSHIP	314 KC	▬ ▬	3-6
PIGEON POINT	314 KC	▬ ▬ ••	3-6
KLH	2506 KC 2450 KC	WEATHER	0830, 2030
NMC	2670 KC	WEATHER	0830, 2030
NMC	2182 KC	WARNINGS	ON RECEIPT

To take true bearings, proceed the same as for magnetic bearings except correct the compass course for deviation and variation, and set your true course on the azimuth scale. Bearings read opposite the end of the antenna will be *true* and can be plotted directly on the true bearing compass rose found on all navigation charts. Regardless of whether you take relative, true, or magnetic bearings with your set, bearings on the navigational chart must be plotted in true or in magnetic. Also, the bearings that you take are the bearings of the station *from* you and must be reversed to be plotted. Finally, all bearings must be corrected for the error of the compass on the ship's heading on which the bearing is taken. Personally, your editor likes to use relative bearings, but this merely is a matter of choice. At any rate, exercise care in correcting, regardless of the method used. This is most important.

A radio direction finder can be used in much the same way a pelorus is used for taking cross-bearings. Just like the visual line of position obtained with the pelorus, the radio bearing obtained with the direction finder is plotted on the chart and, when crossed with a second radio bearing, will give a radio fix. The sequencing of Coast Guard radio beacons should be very helpful when taking cross-bearings. Very often two beacons which lend themselves to cross-bearings will both be found on the same frequency. When possible it is always better to take bearings on three stations. All three lines won't always cross at a point, but will form a small triangle. The center of the triangle should be assumed to be your probable position.

Radio direction finders may also be used in connection with such visual piloting techniques as bow-and-beam bearings, doubling the angle on the bow, danger bearings, etc. The data may be determined by radio rather than eye, but the navigational procedures are the same.

An extremely valuable part of radio navigation is homing, whereby the boat's head is swung so that the null point of a beacon is just over the bow. If the craft wanders off course, the radio signal will pick up in strength, and the boat must be turned to restore the signal to the null point. By repeating the bearing every time the beacon is transmitting it's easy to run up the beam to the beacon. Actually this system is so accurate that lightships with beacon-transmitting equipment on board have been rammed by vessels homing on them.

A radio beacon signal travels a great circle track and a correction must be applied when 50 miles or more from the station. A table for correcting these bearings is found in H. O. #117, *Radio Aids to Navigation*, and in the *Coast Pilot Books*. Sunrise-sunset effect is the distortion of a radio signal caused by the rising or lowering of the Heaviside layer in the atmosphere at this time. This causes the intensity of the signal to vary from time to time and will upset a null.

Before relying on RDF bearings for navigation during poor visibility, it's recommended you practice with it under conditions of good visibility. It's also recommended you make up a calibration curve or table showing deviation for each heading. This can be done very simply by taking visual bearings on a known transmitting tower and at the same time taking radio bearings on the station. Bearing should be taken with boat's heading on various courses from zero to 360 degrees at about 20 degree intervals. The results should be tabulated for future reference. The deviation should be marked plus if it has to be added to the radio bearing to agree with visual bearing, and minus if it has to be sub-

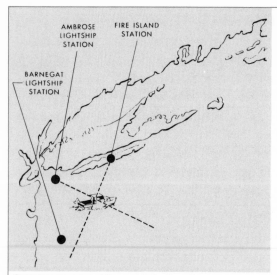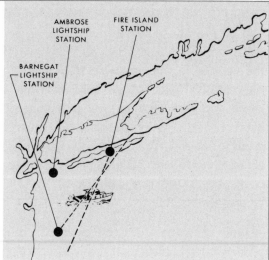

Cross-bearings are of the greatest value when
the angle is nearly 90 degrees as possible (left).
This would apply to any set of bearings, of course,
as bearings separated by a small angle are worthless (right).

tracted from the radio bearing to agree with the visual bearing. As you become familiar with your set you may use any of the equally valuable visual methods to obtain a "fix." Cross your beacon bearing with a visual bearing, or with a sounding from your depth sounder. Or, if the beacon station has synchronized signals for distance finding, take your stop watch and measure the time interval in seconds between the radio and sound signals and divide by five to find your distance off in nautical miles. In short, use all your navigational aids for the purpose for which they were designed and in an intelligent and efficient manner for your own safety and protection.

LORAN

The traditional method of navigation offshore is to put your eye to a sextant, and measure the altitude of the sun, moon, stars, or planets. The main trouble with this (aside from the mathematics involved) is that you can sail days without seeing either heavenly bodies or the horizon. Consequently, many skippers turn to Loran as a supplementary navigational aid.

Government-operated Loran stations spread a grid of radio lines of position over the face of the earth. With a Loran receiver you can pick up and identify these lines, fair weather or foul. You twist a few knobs, line up a pair of "pips" on a cathode-ray scope tube, read a number from a dial and look in a table or on a Loran chart to find the Loran line you are sitting on. By getting two crossed lines of position, you can obtain an accurate "fix." The size and electrical power consumption are practical for boats large enough to need Loran. Although no license is required, it is a good idea to have the equipment put in and checked out by a genius of at least junior grade.

RADAR

Radar is the glamour puss in the electronic family. It paints a living chart of your surroundings (out to several miles distant) on a small TV-like "scope" tube, in spite of fog, rain or darkness. Other boats, as well as prominent buoys, beacons, and land objects are shown as lighted areas on the scope. When a skipper is properly trained in its use, radar is the happiest sight for sore-eyed harbor navigators ever invented. The word radar

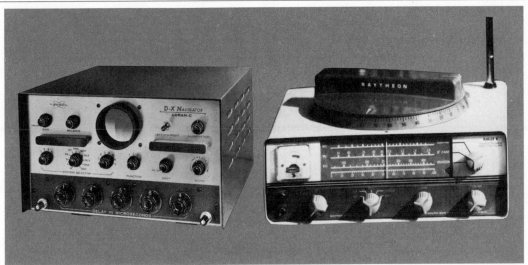

A typical Loran unit.

A typical radio direction finder

is an acronym derived from the phrase "*RA*dio *D*etection *A*nd *R*anging."

Essentially a marine radar consists of (1) high frequency radio signals generated in a particular form called microwaves; (2) sending these out over the water in a narrow beam from a rotating antenna; (3) receiving the echoes returned from any "target" in the area surrounding the ship; (4) measuring the time taken for an echo to return; and (5) displaying the echo visually on a tube so that the bearing and range of each target from the ship are evident. The main components of radar, then, are a transmitter, an antenna, a receiver and an indicating unit.

To find your position by radar, refer to the navigation chart for the area in which you are operating. Although you may be familiar with the area, review it again as the radar sees it. It can't see shoals or submerged reefs and it will have difficulty in reporting a shoreline that rises gradually from a flat, sandy beach. Look for rocky shorelines, lighthouses, bridges, prominent peninsulas and high ground even if it's not right at the water's edge. Examine the contour lines on the chart. Where they are close together the land rises abruptly and will show up prominently on the radar scope.

With this chart familiarization completed, refer to the scope and orient yourself. Your craft will always be at the center, of course. (Some new-type true motion radars are now being introduced on board ocean-going vessels. These picture own ship moving across a space-stabilized chart presentation. This rather costly and space consuming equipment is not designed for yacht use and will not be considered in this discussion.) Identify as many points as you can remember from your chart study. Note the ranges of three or four points, preferably at least 30 degrees apart, and record them on a piece of paper along with the time of the observation.

Radar is more accurate in range than in bearing. This is because of own vessel's motion, accuracy of the steering compass, and the inherent properties of the radar beams, which are about two degrees wide. If only one landmark is available on the radar you could, of course, plot the range and bearing and consider it a fix. For such a range-and-bearing fix simply note this information given by the radar. If your boat has a gyro compass and

The skipper of this radar-equipped cruiser heading west on Long Island Sound takes a round of ranges from easily identified landmarks on the scope (above), sets drafting compasses to the observed ranges, and strikes arcs to obtain a radar fix on chart (below). Ranges taken from scope (on 4-mile scale) are: "A" Execution Rocks, 2.0 miles; "B" Prospect Point, 1.5 miles; "C" Mott Point, 2.3 miles; "D" Weeks Point, 2.1 miles; "E" Matinicock Point, 3.0 miles. Small pips near center of scope represent other boats in vicinity. White line extending from center is own cruiser's heading.

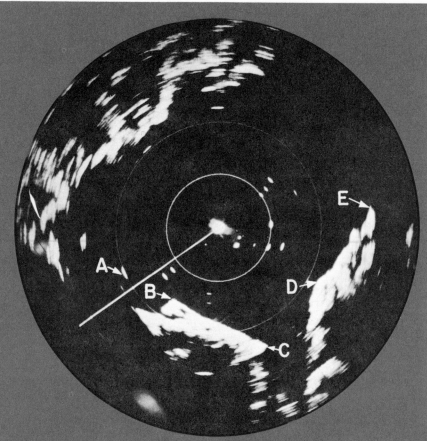

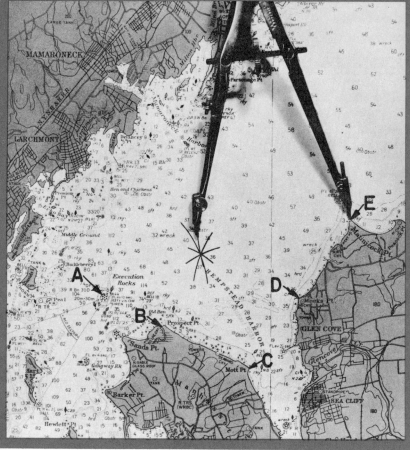

your radar is synchronized for true bearings, your observation is complete. However, most pleasure boat installations employ relative bearing so it will be necessary to note the heading of the steering compass when the observation is made. Correct this for deviation and variation to find the true heading, then add the relative bearing from the radar and you'll have the true bearing of the landmark ready to lay down on the chart.

It's easier and more accurate to work with multiple ranges if they're available. Let's go aboard a cabin cruiser underway in Long Island Sound a few miles east of Execution Rocks and get a radar fix. Referring to the accompanying photograph of an actual radar scope, we can identify the contours of Hempstead Harbor and can take a round of ranges quite readily. This radar, on the four-mile scale, indicates the following ranges:

A.	Execution Rocks	2.0 miles
B.	Prospect Point	1.5 miles
C.	Mott Point	2.3 miles
D.	Weeks Point	2.1 miles
E.	Matinicock Point	3.0 miles

Taking drafting compasses and extending them to two miles we strike an arc two miles east of Execution Rocks. Resetting the compasses to 1.5 miles and placing the pointed end on Prospect Point we can strike a second arc that crosses the first. Repeating the process for the other three radar landmarks the pencil arcs converge on our position.

Develop your radar navigating techniques in good weather when you can check your observations against good visual bearings and you'll gain confidence for the day when the fog closes in suddenly and your radar becomes your best shipmate. Try checking your position with your depth sounder as well, to see if it confirms your fix.

Buoys marking a channel present the same reassuring pattern on the radar scope as they do when viewed on the chart. In many key areas the U.S. Coast Guard has installed radar reflectors on sea buoys and buoys marking fairways in wide channels, turns or unusual obstructions. These metal reflectors resembling crumpled top hats are mounted on top of the buoys and return extra strong echoes when bombarded by radar beams. Consequently, radar reflector buoys, marked "Ra Ref" on the chart, will appear on the scope at longer ranges and will stand out among the other buoys in a channel so that they are easily identified.

Care should be exercised in relying solely on radar for navigation, for as we mentioned earlier it cannot see things beneath the water's surface and a new course arrived at solely by radar observation could be an unwise one. The navigation chart should be consulted frequently. In laying down a new course, check carefully the depth of water.

While concentrating on the position-finding properties of radar keep an eye out for other traffic, too. It's easy to become so fascinated with the geographical plot that you neglect the smaller pips between you and your destination. These pips won't stand still while you practice your navigation. Here we have an opportunity to use radar in its other application as an aid to preventing collisions.

Nautical Rules of the Road emphasize the need for taking frequent bearings of all ships sighted. This same responsibility extends to radar users. A single radar observation gives only the range and bearing—adequate information for navigating but insufficient data, in itself, to avoid risk of collision. To utilize effectively radar's capabilities as an anti-collision device it is essential that all objects reported by the radar be plotted progressively to establish their relative motion with respect to you. Relative motion has been used by mariners for centuries who have called it the "seaman's eye." After all, everything we see in our everyday lives appears to us with respect to our own motion. If you walk down a sidewalk and remain the same distance behind a person walking in front of you the relative speed of the person ahead of you is zero. If you are opening or closing the distance between you the relative speed is the difference between your true rates of speed.

The Rules of the Road still apply. Radar has simply acted as an extension of your powers of observation. Radar has told you that "risk of collision" exists and from here on out you must take the proper action, according to the Rules. A change of course, promptly and dramatically, is usually preferred to a change of speed, for your course change will be noticed, visually or on the other vessel's radar, much more positively than a speed variation. If you're in fog or reduced visibility be sure that you're sounding your fog signals.

The characteristics of the radar pip are often deceiving. Don't be misled into thinking that you can read another ship's heading from a pip. While a very large ship will produce a substantial pip in almost any attitude, other ships may not. A small wooden-hulled pleasure boat or fisherman may present virtually no pip when heading towards you, while his beam view could return a target suggesting a much larger vessel. But, before making your change of course you should complete the plotting sufficiently to determine what the other vessel's actual course is. The relative motion plot simply told you whether you were closing or opening the range and in which direction. It can't tell you, for example, whether you are overtaking a vessel ahead or whether you are, in fact, in a meeting situation.

To sum up, radar is an extremely valuable aid to navigation and an important tool to help prevent collisions. It will do its best to protect the owner's investment if he learns how to interpret correctly all the information that this electronic wizardry makes available to him.

DEPTH SOUNDERS

Next time you're out in your boat, look around. Where's the nearest land? Over there? Wrong. The nearest land is straight down, and if you get too close, you're in trouble. As described in Chapter 3, you can use the old-fashioned lead line to feel for the bottom. But it's a lot faster and more efficient to have a depth sounder, or depth finder as it is sometimes called. By continuously indicating the depth of the water underneath, it gives instant warning if you wander out of a channel or slip toward a shoal or rocks. Sometimes you get a bonus—it may spot fish for you, as well as the bottom.

All depth or echo sounders work in the same manner and consist of the same basic parts —transmitter, transducer, and receiver. They vary in the presentation of the information which may either be by a flashing red light or a recorded trace on a special graph paper or a direct-reading meter. They may further vary according to their application in shoal, moderately deep or deep water, the frequency of the sound pulse, number of soundings per minute, voltage, power requirements, and type of transducer.

As explained to us by experts at Raytheon Company, who invented the Fathometer depth sounder 40 years ago, the portion of the device which sends out the impulse is a crystal, called a transducer, which is installed in the bottom of the boat. When an electric

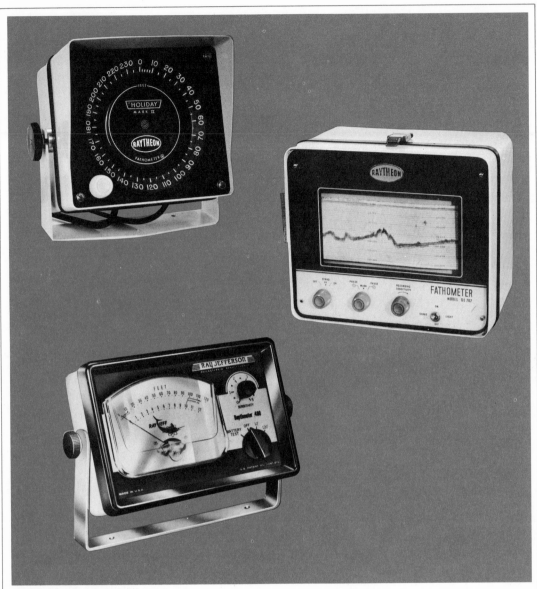

Three types of depth sounders:
flashing (top), recording (center),
and direct-reading (bottom)

current is applied to the crystal it flexes, compressing the water and sending the sound wave to the bottom. The returning echo reverses the process, exerting pressure against the crystal which then produces a trickle of electrical energy. This is instantaneously amplified and sent back to the indicator. The elapsed time is measured against a constant speed motor and recorded as a flashing light on a dial, a line on a graph, or a meter reading, depending on the device preferred.

The echo returning from a hard, flat bottom is sharp and precise. A rocky bottom deflects the sound waves so that in addition to a well-defined bottom signal, subsequent echoes bounce back as the sound waves ricochet from rock to rock and back up to the surface. A muddy bottom tends to absorb some of the sound and give a diffused echo.

Fish appear on the flashing light unit as secondary flashes above the main bottom flash,

Because the bottom of the sea is composed of varied substances (stones, gravel, sand, mud, etc.) and never level, it reflects varying echoes. Generally, the bottom of the sea will give fewer strong and useful echoes as it inclines from the horizontal. However, due to its large area in relation to other sound reflective objects, the bottom echo usually predominates and is easily distinguishable as a relatively steady reading.

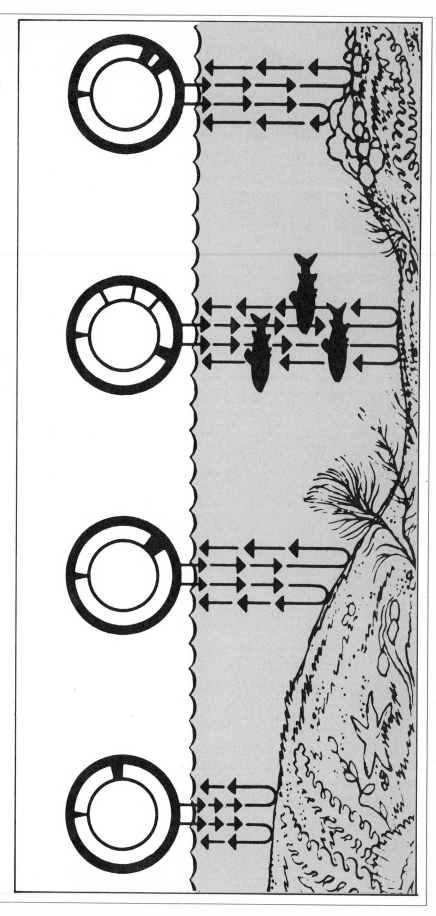

and on the graph as fine lines above the heavy continuous line of the bottom. A large school of fish, densely packed, will produce a strong echo. Smaller schools of fish produce varying echoes. This is caused by some of the transmitted pulses being reflected off the fish and others continuing between them to the bottom. Generally, the more dense a school is, the stronger is its echo. The movement of fish through the water produces echo indications which are constantly changing, and are easily distinguished from the bottom echo which is relatively stable. Deep holes or reefs that show up are also prime fishing spots. Knowing your course and speed will enable you to return to the same place next time, and the depth finder will tell you when you are Johnny-on-the-spot. (More on fishing with a depth sounder can be found in Chapter 6.)

In navigating with a depth sounder, it is well to remember that exact agreement with the chart is rarely found. Such things as the state of the tide, weather conditions, accuracy of the survey of the chart, and the depth of the transducer below the water must be taken into consideration. Every attempt should be made to get a visual bearing or radio direction finder bearing when running a "chain of soundings" in navigating. This provides you with a "fix" from which you may take your next departure. In addition, knowledge of the depth of the water beneath the boat enables the yachtsman to follow known channels between two points. If, for instance, you plan a trip from one marina to another, and you know that there is a 20 foot channel between these two points, then by checking the depth indication on your depth finder while under way, it becomes relatively easy to stay on course. Any reading on your recorder of less than 20 feet would indicate that you are sailing away from the channel and course correction is required. When charts are available, the yachtsman can often utilize the depth sounder readings to aid in ascertaining his boat's position by comparison with the depths printed on the navigation charts. Regardless of whether one uses a depth sounder for a navigational aid on a commercial vessel or a pleasure vessel, off-shore cruising or racing, fishing or just gunk-holing, it is valuable equipment, one with which you should be familiar, and one in which you should have confidence.

AUTOMATIC PILOT

There are two ways to free yourself from a constant wheel watch when you're under way: you can sign on a quartermaster or two—or you can be practical about the whole thing and install an automatic pilot. There isn't a helmsman in the trade who can beat one of these electronic watchkeepers in keeping a good course. The automatic will also cut down on running time and fuel bills, and make your boating a whole lot safer and more fun.

The automatic pilot works on a simple principle: In the binnacle unit is a magnetic compass; instead of degrees and quarter points, this compass has a semicircular aperture. Through this two exciter lamps are beamed at two photoelectric cells. When the vessel swings, the balance of light becomes unequal and the binnacle unit signals the relay unit. This component in turn telegraphs "right rudder" or "left rudder" to the power drive unit—the "muscles" of your automatic pilot...a control console by the wheel and a remote control capsule—located anywhere on the boat—give you instant command of the steering system.

To set your course on a typical automatic pilot, you steady on the desired compass heading for about 30 seconds with your hand steering gear; then press the *Clutch In* switch on your control console for three seconds. Your sensitivity switch is set to *High*.

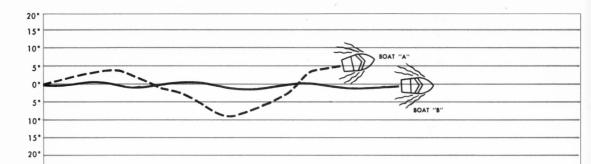

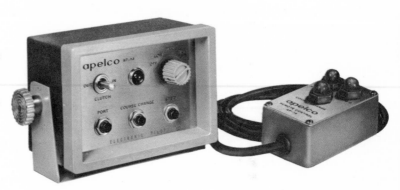

A typical electronic automatic pilot is shown at the right. As shown above, yacht "B" with an automatic pilot, can average this much better course and distance made good than yacht "A", with hand steering gear. Identical speed, running time and sea conditions.

A lazy sailor makes the best helmsman—using the least amount of rudder to keep his course true. That's what the sensitivity switch is for. Reduce sensitivity till the vessel remains on course with the least amount of action by the power drive unit. In quiet water you can tune the automatic pilot to within one degree of the course; in a following sea you can let her yaw five degrees on either side of your heading before any rudder action is applied.

Suppose a floating log looms ahead. Faster than you can say "Hard over!" you can push the *Port* or *Starboard* button on your console and swing clear of trouble. Release the button and the automatic pilot takes you back on course—even if you've swung up to 170 degrees . . . Perhaps you want to maneuver for a few minutes without disengaging the automatic pilot completely. Set your control to *Electric Steering* and use the *Port* and *Starboard* buttons for pushbutton steering. With the Remote Control Capsule you can steer, dodge or change course from any place on the boat—handy if you spend any time forward, fishing or tending gear.

With an automatic pilot you'll have a degree of freedom—and safety—you've never enjoyed before. One thing to remember: with the automatic pilot on watch, the ship no longer needs your hands on the wheel, or your eyes continually on the compass card. But there's still no substitute for keeping a sharp lookout.

Electronic Yachting Aids of the Future
The increase in the use of electronic aids in the pleasure boating field today is not a passing fad. It has strong roots in the education programs of various groups and in individual desires for safer and more pleasant times afloat. Continued expansion of this market should keep pace with the growth of the boating industry itself. There is an old saying that "There are no two boats alike." We can add "Neither are they used alike, nor by the same people." It is under these circumstances that electronic equipment is being used and these are the conditions for which it should be designed—the result being flexibility, compactness, ruggedness, and dependability.

Esquire's staff asked Dr. Allen B. DuMont to design for us a perfect control panel for power cruisers that would combine all the electronic miracles available to today's yachtsman. Dr. DuMont has often been called "Mr. Television," for it was he, as much as any other man, who made television possible. As early as 1930, at age twenty-nine, as Chief Engineer of the De Forest Radio Company, he insisted that the way to practical television was through development of the cathode-ray tube, then a short-lived, expensive laboratory curiosity manufactured for the most part in Germany. His career has been based on the continuing improvement of this tube, finding new uses for it and adapting it for further uses. In 1931 he founded his own company, competing eventually with the giants of two industries; in television manufacturing against G.E., Westinghouse, and R.C.A.; and in television broadcasting against C.B.S., A.B.C., and N.B.C. The whole multibillion-dollar industry depended, originally, on his insistence on development of the cathode-ray tubes. But Dr. DuMont is also a yachtsman and in summer enters his fifty-four-foot motor yacht in the series of predicted log races that take place on the East Coast. In a predicted log race the emphasis is not on speed but on accuracy of navigation. The skipper files in advance a list of the times he expects to pass by certain markers, buoys or lighthouses. All chronometers (clocks and watches) are then removed from the boat and the course is run, so to speak, "blind"—at least as to time. The skipper who most accurately follows his outlined schedule wins the race.

It was logically to Dr. DuMont that *Esquire* would turn with a request for a comprehensive, workable layout for all the new equipment available to the yachtsman. Instead, what he devised for us was a whole new machine, utilizing several new developments of the cathode-ray tube, and many other *available* electric and electronic devices never used in boat navigation before. Altogether, this is an extraordinary device, which will revolutionize navigational methods. There are in it a number of unusual features (the night-and-haze electron telescope and the direct view storage tube used on the radar are two examples), but the most significant innovation is the overall one; the idea of making simultaneous use of all the information-gathering methods—such simultaneous use multiplying the effectiveness and utility of each individual instrument.

In the drawing on the next page, the view, is of course, forward from within the pilothouse of a motor yacht. Overhead, near the cabin light, are such standard items of equipment as the wind gauge, chronometer, barometer and thermometer. The panel itself is divided in three parts: on the right and on the left are similar information and controls for the starboard engine and the port engine, with many of the standard engine dials. An innovation is showing the revolutions-per-minute of the engine in a digital read-out form, more convenient and accurate than the conventional tachometer. The throttles are an original feature, too. Where the conventional throttle operates either mechanically or hydraulically and is subject to change by vibration, etc., these are adjusted by means of an open-loop servo system, a method which is extremely accurate and is used on rockets.

Instead of a clutch lever, three buttons (similar to those used on some cars) shift the gears electrically in the engine room. Instead of a wheel, a rudder-control handle is provided, just under the center panel, which can be pulled out as needed. As the boat will be on automatic pilot most of the time, the steering handle is mainly used in docking and in congested waters. It power-controls the rudder faster than any wheel, and its position indicates the position of the rudder.

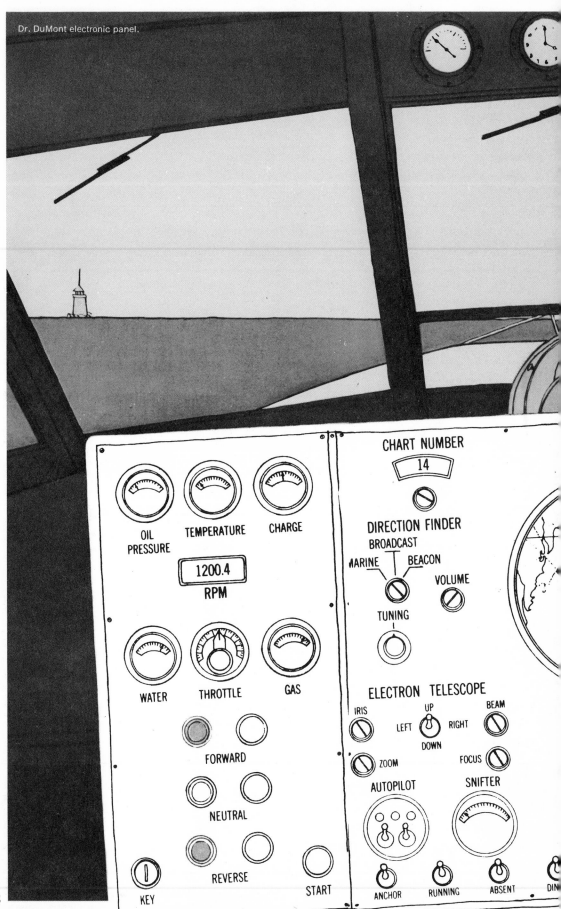

Dr. DuMont electronic panel.

128

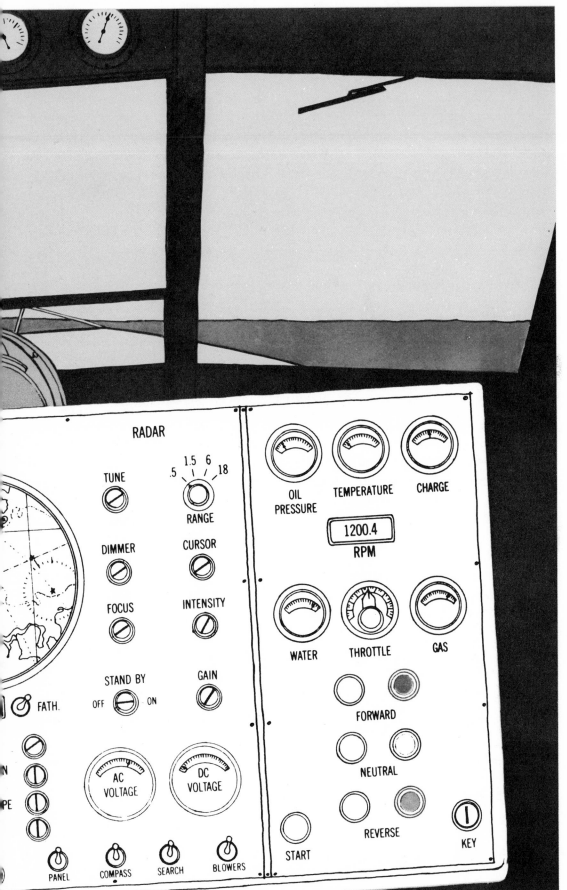

RADAR

TUNE

1.5 6
.5 18
RANGE

DIMMER

CURSOR

FOCUS

INTENSITY

FATH.

STAND BY   GAIN

OFF   ON

AC
VOLTAGE

DC
VOLTAGE

PE

PANEL   COMPASS   SEARCH   BLOWERS

OIL
PRESSURE   TEMPERATURE   CHARGE

1200.4
RPM

WATER   THROTTLE   GAS

FORWARD

NEUTRAL

START   REVERSE   KEY

The central feature of the center panel is a new sort of television tube, called a direct view storage tube, with a number of advantages over the conventional cathode-ray tube, a brightness twenty times that of the usual radar screen, no need for a hood for daylight viewing, and no flicker to cause eyestrain. Charts are photographed, put onto a rotary projector containing eighty 35-millimeter slides, then fed by an inexpensive pickup camera to the viewing tube. Slides are selected by a remote-control switch similar to the channel selector on a TV set, the controls for which are in the upper-left-hand corner of the center panel. The conventional radar controls are to the right. Under the viewing tube are switches and intensity controls for the devices that appear on the tube. The radio direction finder is to the left, a selector knob allowing the navigator to choose from the marine, regular commercial stations, or beacon signals. Indications from the RDF show up as lines on the chart on the viewing tube pointing in the direction of the station being received. The chart and the radar and the RDF can all be on the viewing tube at the same time, making possible an unprecedented degree of accuracy in determining position. The charts can be changed in size and moved around so as to correspond with the radar pattern and be superimposed in register on it, thus locating the vessel on the chart at the exact center of the viewing tube. And because the viewing screen is a direct view *storage* tube, it stores the blips that register on the screen, making it easier to interpret the radar pattern. Thus, as the previously registered blips accumulate on the screen, the course of an oncoming boat is actually plotted out drawn upon the screen. The stored pattern can be instantly removed or the tube adjusted to act without the storage feature.

Below the RDF is the most extraordinary instrument of all: the electron telescope. It appears on the same viewing screen, but of course not at the same time, because it shows actuality—like looking through a pair of binoculars. This telescope is actually a low-light television camera, so sensitive that excellent pictures can be obtained under starlight conditions; if used within twenty-five miles of a large city, the glow in the sky is sufficient light. It is the first electron telescope to be devised which will "see" in *both* night and haze simultaneously. An ultra-sensitive material is used in the pickup tube, plus a high-gain amplifier. The camera itself is mounted on the cabin top on a platform kept stable by gyroscopes and is remotely controlled by the so-called "joy-stick" (the center control marked "Up," "Right," "Down" and "Left"). The zoom lens has a gain of twenty, where normal binoculars have a gain of only eight.

Directly beneath the viewing tube is another new feature: the depth sounder in digital read out, for more accurate readings, and beneath the electron-telescope controls is the automatic pilot, which keeps the vessel on a predetermined course, and the "snifter" gauge indicating gasoline fumes in the bilges. Along the bottom of the center panel are a number of light switches, in the middle of which is the button for the horn, for use in the unlikely event that anything should still be in the way.

Dr. DuMont says that the whole outfit takes less electricity than the items would separately and emphasizes that all of the equipment incorporated in this device is available in one form or another. This system, which could revolutionize the whole method of navigation, in the Navy and elsewhere, is not a dream device of the future; it is possible to put together any time.

NON-ELECTRONIC COMMUNICATION AT SEA

While the radiotelephone is the most highly refined and far-reaching method of communicating at sea, there are several other ways it can be accomplished. They include signal flags, flashing lights, and sound (horns, whistles, and bells). The good yachtsman will learn these communication methods, too, as well as the radiotelephone.

Signal Flags

In all too many yachting circles, the International Code flags are mainly employed as a decoration for yachts when they dress ship at regattas, on holidays, and so on. While they are certainly attractive for these purposes, they are a great deal more valuable for their basic intent—that of conveying messages from one vessel to another.

While many yachtsmen don't carry a set of International Code signal flags aboard their craft, it is important that "Urgent and Important" flag hoists are understood when they appear. (Every yacht should carry a "T" flag since this is the easiest method of requesting tender to go ashore when at a yacht club.) The Code comprises 40 flags: 26 alphabetic flags, ten numeral pennants, one code pennant, and three repeaters. The purpose of the repeaters is to enable the sender to transmit the same letter or number more than once in the same message. The code or answering pennant is used by the receiving vessel to indicate recognition and compliance with the message transmitted. Each flag has a meaning in itself which should be known to everyone who may come in contact with this method of communication. For complete information on all the various hoists, we suggest that you purchase a copy of *International Code of Signals, Vol. I, Visual, H. O. Number 87* from U.S. Government Printing Office. While it is a very good idea to have this aboard, here are the hoists that are important to the average yachtsman:

Single Flag Hoist Meanings

    (Only those marked with an asterisk should be used by flashing.)

A: I am undergoing a speed trial.

B: I am taking in or discharging explosives.

C: Yes (affirmative).

D: Keep clear of me. I am maneuvering with difficulty.

E: I am directing my course to starboard.

*F: I am disabled. Communicate with me.

G: I require a pilot.

H: I have a pilot on board.

I: I am directing my course to port.

J: I am going to send a message by semaphore.

*K: You should stop your vessel instantly.

*L: You should stop. I have something important to communicate.

M: I have a doctor aboard.

N: No (negative).

*O: Man overboard.

*P: In harbor—All persons are to repair on board as the vessel is about to proceed to sea. (Note: to be hoisted at the foremost head.) At sea— Your lights are out, or burning badly.

Q: My vessel is healthy and I request free pratique.

*R: The way is off my ship: you may feel your way past me.

S: My engines are going full speed astern.

T: Do not pass ahead of me. (At yacht club, please send a tender.)

U: You are standing in danger.

V: I require assistance.

W: I require medical assistance.

X: Stop carrying out your intentions and watch for my signals.

Y: I am carrying mail.

*Z: To be used to address or call shore stations.

Two Flag Signals—Urgent and Important

A D: I must abandon my vessel.

L T: I am dragging my anchor.

A M:	Accident has occurred. I require a doctor.	L V:	I am in distress for want of fuel.
A P:	I am aground.	M J:	Have you a doctor?
A T:	I am aground and require immediate assistance.	N C:	I am in distress and require immediate assistance.
C U:	Anchorage is dangerous.	P C:	I am not in correct position. (Used by lightship.)
D N:	I am coming to your assistance.		
D O:	I am drifting and require immediate assistance.	P Q:	I have sprung a leak and require immediate assistance.
D Q:	I am on fire and require immediate assistance.	P T:	I require a pilot.
		Q W:	I have mail for you.
D U:	I have parted towing hawser; can you assist me?	R G:	I have telegram for you.
		R H:	Message has been received.
D V:	I have sprung a leak.	R J:	Have you a message for me?
D Z:	I require immediate assistance.	R S:	Is all well with you?
E J:	Do you require any further assistance?	R V:	Where are you bound?
		R W:	Where are you from?
E U:	Bar is dangerous.	S D:	I am short of lubricating oil. Can you supply?
E X:	Bar is impassible.		
F R:	I require a boat. Man overboard.	S E:	I am short of gasoline. Can you supply?
F U:	I require a water boat.		
F V:	It is impossible to land.	S T:	I require a police boat.
H P:	Submarines are exercising; navigate with caution.	T H:	I have lost my propellor.
		T K:	I require provisions urgently.
J D:	You are standing into danger.	T Z:	My radio is not working.
J T:	You should follow me or vessel indicated.	U W:	I cannot distinguish flags.
		V C:	Your distress signal understood. Assistance coming.
J Z:	I have damaged rudder. I cannot steer.	V B:	Signal is not understood though flags are distinguished.
L I:	I am disabled.		
L J:	I am disabled. Will you tow me in or into place indicated?	W U:	What course should I steer to make nearest land?
		X Y:	Can you take me in tow?
L O:	My engines are disabled.	X Z:	Shall I take you in tow?
L P:	My steering is disabled.	Y J:	I require water immediately.

The flags are hoisted, the first letter above the second on the same halyard where they will be most visible. As a general rule, only one hoist should be shown at a time, but each hoist or hoists, should be flown until answered. In answering a flag signal, hoist your answering pennant half way up as soon as you see the signal, then all the way up when the signal is understood.

Flashing Lights

Flashing lights, employing combinations of dots and dashes that constitute the International Morse Code, are often used to send messages. Although receiving blinker signals takes practice, it is impossible in an emergency at night to slowly spell out a message from a Morse Code chart and send it by flashlight, spotlight, or white range light. In determining the duration of dot and dash signals, the dot is taken as a unit; a dash equals three dots, and the time between any two elements of a symbol is equal to one dot. Between two complete signals, the interval is three dots; between two words or groups, five dots. This spacing of the letters, words, etc., is an important element of successful signalling.

International Morse Code

A . —	N — .	1 . — — — —	A (German) . — . —
B — . . .	O — — —	2 . . — — — .	A or A (Spanish and Scandinavian) . . — — . —
C — . — .	P . — — .	3 . . . — —	CH (German-Spanish) — — — —
D — . .	Q — — . —	4 . . . . —	E (French) . . — . .
E .	R . — .	5	N (Spanish) — — . — —
F . . — .	S . . .	6 —	O (German) — — — .
G — — .	T —	7 — — . . .	U (German) . . — —
H	U . . —	8 — — — . .	
I . .	V . . . —	9 — — — — .	
J . — — —	W . — —	0 — — — — —	
K — . —	X — . . —		
L . — . .	Y — . — —		
M — —	Z — — . .		

Period . — . — . —	Interrogation . . — — . .	Parenthesis — . — — . —
Semicolon — . — . — .	Exclamation — — . . — —	Underline . . — — . —
Comma — — . . — —	Apostrophe . — — — — .	Double Dash — . . . —
Colon — — — . . .	Hyphen — . . . . —	Distress . . . — — — . . .
From — . . .	Wait . — . . .	Understand . . . — .
Error	Received (OK) . — .	Inverted Commas . — . . — .

Bar Indicating Fraction — . . — .
Attention Call, To Precede Every Transmission — . — . —
General Inquiry Call And General Call To All Stations (CQ) — . — . — — . —
Invitation To Transmit — . —
Warning——High Power — — . . — —
Question (Please Repeat After) . . . . .   Interrupting Long Messages . . — — . .
Break (BK) (Double Dash) — . . . —
Position Report (To Precede All Position Messages) — . — .
End of Each Message (Cross) . — . — .
Transmission Finished (End of Work) (Conclusion Of Correspondence) . . . — . —

Sound

Most primitive, but still good under certain circumstances, are sound signals. A power "bull horn" or electronic hailer is a useful item to assist in speaking to a person on shore or on board another vessel. Amplification of the human voice will permit hailing at greater distances, and in some cases makes it possible where it would otherwise be drowned out by the sounds of a storm or the noises of the boat's engines. Some models of radio-telephone equipment have a connection for a loudhailing speaker. In these instances the regular radio microphone and a portion of the radio set are tuned to pick up and amplify the person's voice. An external weatherproof speaker is all that is additionally required.

In an emergency situation, the universally recognized aural method sounding the fog signal should give the desired results. While voice commands may be misunderstood, a continuous or prolonged sounding of your ship's whistle, horn, or bell should indicate just one thing to anyone within hearing distance: a serious effort to attract attention to which all yachtsmen should respond. As detailed elsewhere whistle signals also play a necessary role in the carry out of the Rules of Road, as well as in fog operations.

CHAPTER
FIVE:
THE ART OF
CRUISING

We knew a man once who was, by the most generous definition, a hurricane-hunter. By less genteel standards he was slightly erratic mentally, but nontheless his hobby consisted of going looking for hurricanes to flirt with in his 65-foot yacht. We don't know him any more simply because he finally found a hurricane to play with. To him, hurricanes were fun. He wasn't happy unless he and his really marvelous boat were battling waves as high as the pilothouse. In short, he was a nut, but he *was* doing what he most wanted to do in his boat.

Essentially, that is the very foundation of boating pleasure—*doing what one most wants to do*. In this regard the bachelor-boat-owner has any number of jim-dandy roads open to him since he is the only one who has to be considered. But, because the world of "distaffless" boaters needs no advice on the subject of fun in any form, we will leave them to their own devices and concentrate on the "boating family;" the unit that makes up the majority of the boating public today and cruising is the favorite of all yachting activities.

A WIFE AS A CREW MEMBER

Let's face it. The girls are here to stay and the more we men get them interested in the things *we* want to do, the more fun the whole family will have. And, incidentally, let's not make any mistake about it: They're just as smart as we are. They can be of tremendous help aboard a boat, and have a lot of fun, too.

One of the old bugaboos for girls going to sea was the fact that they tended to wind up as galley slaves. Needless to say, if that's the way the deal works out, Mom—or the girl friend—won't be too keen about a return engagement aboard the boat. If the lady goes with the boat, certainly one or two departments can be turned over to her for management. And it will be better management than we men could provide.

But, be fair about galley arrangements. She didn't come aboard to cook. When you tie up for the evening, occasionally leave the boat and eat ashore—at a restaurant, not a picnic table. If you are going to be at sea for more than a day, take turns in the galley. You may even turn out a better meal than she can. Teach her about your yacht and how the boat is handled. If the girl is bright (and she must be if she married you), encourage her all you can. Send her to U.S. Power Squadron or Coast Guard Auxiliary courses. Let her read this book from cover to cover, and point out yachting magazine features. If she is never going to have a clue about boat-handling, steering, or navigation, at least you've tried. Concentrate on helping her to enjoy boating and don't belittle her. Strive to enlist the little woman's enthusiasm, sharpen her desire to be part of the activity and keep her in the midst of all yachting action from shopping to purchase to maintenance to planning to fun. You can figure you've won your case when you note that "the boat" and "the galley" becomes "our boat" and "my galley." On the day you overhear your "first mate" discussing "my yacht" you can pretty well lean back comfortably in the knowledge that you'll probably die with a deck under your feet and your hand on a wheel.

To the Ladies. When you're invited out in the boat, a few common sense precautions on your part will help. In the first place, don't wear high heels. They can be dangerous for you because they slip. And they can be harmful for the boat because they dent and scratch the deck. Ordinary sneakers or the very comfortable "Topsiders" will get you around a lot better. Don't wear frilly clothes that blow in the wind. Slacks or culottes will be much more comfortable. And when it begins to rain and perhaps the wind begins to blow a little, a foul-weather suit will keep you dry, warm and attractive.

On any boat, the lady will find that she can be of great help in letting go the lines when getting under way, and helping to anchor or pick up a mooring. If the skipper sends you up to the bow and asks you to give him a hand at anchoring, you will find that you can do the job successfully with very little practice. And the fact that you do will rate a bow from your man.

The young children will most likely fall under command. It's wise to remember, however, that sometimes they can grow restless on board a boat; just as when they are ashore. And the same answer applies—extra toys, crayons, games or what have you, to keep them occupied. And don't let the skipper "cruise" them too long at a time. Send them ashore every couple of hours and let them run, swim, play and explore.

Sooner or later, the yacht will be used for entertainment and one or more guests will be invited aboard. Then, of course, you become hostess. This is no world-shattering event and your guests do not expect canapés on a silver tray before the "happy hour." If you make a federal project out of hospitality, you soon will find that there is no fun in boating for you, your husband, or your guests either. More details on entertaining afloat can be found later in this chapter.

A word about your own comfort. Some girls are more susceptible to the sun than others and have their own personal remedies. Whatever your favorite suntan oil or lotion is, be sure to keep some on board, and as a general rule remember to bring a hat and dark glasses. We have read of the most remarkable cruises, where a man and his wife and several children make a thousand mile cruise in a 16 foot boat; outstanding examples of "togetherness." Whether you and your family ever sail that far or not, just a day spent on the water or a vacation spent on a boat will give all of you a tremendous amount of fun, a lot of good, outdoor health, and some wonderful memories.

PLANNING A CRUISE

A lot of things go into making any cruise a happy and memorable experience for everybody aboard. None is more important than first deciding on the right answers to some basic questions, such as:

    1. What time of year will we go? This can make a big difference. For instance, in some sections of the country long-distance cruises should be made in early sum-

mer rather than late summer when there is greater likelihood of foggy weather.

2. How much time is available? From a sheer mileage standpoint, how far you can get on a cruise depends upon the cruising speed and range of your boat in relation to the amount of time you have. But no matter what the case may be, don't figure on eating up distance by running continuously from breakfast to dinner time. Everybody will be much happier if you stop several times each day . . . for a swim . . . for exploring and sightseeing . . . for just plain leg-stretching. Also leave time to change your plans somewhat to conform to items of interest that arise and other factors, including weather and water conditions.

3. What kind of boat will you use? Water conditions can vary considerably in different parts of the country. Obviously, a small, light runabout is apt to be wetter and less comfortable than a heavy cruiser when waves kick up on a large, open body of water.

4. What's the objective? Naturally, if you are out for rest and relaxation, you would pick a very different kind of cruise than if fishing were your chief objective . . . or exploration . . . or sightseeing.

5. What about supplies en route? In picking a cruising route, you will want to be sure of sufficient marinas—in the right locations—to get gas, food and other supplies.

6. What about accommodations? You will also want to be sure the route selected has the right kind of accommodations for you and your family: Places where you can sleep on board . . . or rent a motel, or "boatel," if you prefer the comforts of home.

7. What about entertainment? Having a good time is the primary objective of everybody on a cruise. What will that mean in your case? Quiet anchorages to "get away from it all?" Visiting lively boating centers where something is always going on? Visiting waterfront towns where there are movies to see and other things to do? Do you want to visit friends or relatives along the way? It's not difficult to plot a cruise that will include any one or several such forms of entertainment.

CRUISING GEAR

A good deal of the success of any cruise depends upon having the proper equipment on board. For instance, if you're prepared for it, rough or rainy weather will be part of the adventure. If you're not prepared, the first cold, rainy day can easily douse the spirit of your crew. For this reason, we don't fully subscribe to the old theory of "traveling light." Actually, we believe there's more danger that you'll take too little than too much. There's more likelihood that you'll neglect your comfort than be over-thoughtful of it. But because every pleasure craft has its limitations for gear storage, the experienced yachtsman knows that what to leave behind is just as important as what to take. The newcomer to cruising should make an inventory of all items he would like to take and should then go over the list several times, eliminating those items not wholly essential to the safety, comfort, and pleasure of those taking the cruise. The gear required by law and for safety was mentioned in Chapter 2, while the navigating equipment was fully discussed in Chapter 3. Galley gear and supplies are described later in this chapter.

One place most yachtsmen can travel light is in their cruising clothes. It's not necessary to have a full wardrobe aboat for every member of your crew. The growth of automatic laundries along popular cruise routes has been little short of phenomenal lately, and this will allow you to keep clean with a minimum of clothing.

All members of your crew—and this includes the children—should have a suit of foul-weather gear on board. But, when selecting the suits, consider the type of cruising you're going to do and the locale. In general, fabrics used in the better foul-weather suits are light to wear, pliable in varying degrees, don't crack or peel in sun or salt, don't stiffen in cold climates; are odorless; and are impervious to the effects of fuels and most chemicals. The zipper and other fittings on a good suit are made of either noncorroding metal or plastic. In spite of long-wearing qualities of the fabric in the suit you select, the foul-weather gear deserves to be properly dried after use and the salt rinsed off before prolonged storage.

While the present-day cruiser offers two to three times more clothing storage space than one designed even ten years ago, it still requires that wardrobes be limited by common sense. But there are several things that may be done to get more clothes in less space. For instance, the triple-deck, plastic hanger, having a shoulder piece and three bars, will hold a jacket or shirt and three pairs of slacks. There are also six-tier blouse hangers that allow you to put six blouses or shirts in the hanger space usually taken by one. Another suggestion in the case of an extra-deep hanging locker is to install an extension rod (you've seen them in apparel shops). Such a rod should run athwartship, to the very back of the locker, but arranged so that it will pull out into the cabin to make the clothes at the back more easily accessible. If such a rod isn't possible, use rods going in two directions. A long rod is run the depth of the locker, and you use the back of the locker to store the dress shore clothes or seldom-used clothes in plastic zipper bags. A shorter rod is placed at right angles to this, across the opening and just inside, for your other clothes. The clothes in the back are hard to get at, but the arrangement does save crowding in the front.

Here's an idea that may solve some of your clothes storage problems. Additional unused space, which is excellent for certain types of storage, is under the bunk mattresses. Here, for example, you can stow skirts, shirts, trousers, linens and even some types of dresses. In the case of trousers, for instance, the under mattress location will keep them pressed. It's a good idea to place each garment in a plastic bag.

All washable clothes are usually stowed in bunk lockers, foot lockers, drawers, or duffel bags. These are folded, slipped into plastic envelopes or bags, and stowed. (The plastic bags not only keep out dampness, but help keep clothing clean.) It is wise, however, to check folded clothing every two or three days for dampness, and all such stowage should be removed at the end of each cruise. Towels and personal belongings (shaving cream, toothpaste, make-up, and so forth) are part of your cabin gear and are usually packed with your clothes. In drawers and lockers where clean clothes, bedding, etc., are stowed, never store oilskins, greasy work clothes, soiled clothing, or wet bathing suits. In a tight cabin, these give off a very unpleasant odor that lingers on and on, even after the clothing has been removed and the cabin aired. In addition, such clothing constitutes a possible fire hazard (through spontaneous combustion) when confined in an unventilated locker. They should be hung loosely in a well-aired place of their own.

Before leaving the subject of clothing, remember that rigid suitcases are awkward to store aboard a boat, and, in addition, good luggage may also be damaged by the dampness. Save weight and space by packing all clothing gear in sea (duffel) bags or the new foldaway suitcases. An extra sea bag or two will be handy for storing soiled clothing and will serve to lug groceries or carry laundry to laundromats.

Just like an airline pilot before take off, plan to run through a simple check-off list like the following:

    1. Check the weather . . . if possible, at least a day before you plan a cruise. Get to know signs of the weather changes by cloud formations, the sun and moon. Check radio reports and the newspapers for storm warnings. Keep your weather eye peeled at all times.

    2. Tell where you're going . . . just as a pilot benefits by filing a flight plan, you add an extra margin of safety to every cruise if, before you go, you leave with a responsible friend or relative, or your local yacht club, a description of your boat, your cruising plans and destination. Then should something happen and you are overdue this person can make an accurate report to the Coast Guard or local rescue agency so help can reach you without delay. For years the Coast Guard has urged boatmen to follow a procedure of this kind. Below you'll find a "float plan" form designed by the Marine Office of America and free pads of this form are available from their offices at 123 William Street, New York, New York 10038.

    3. Check fuel supply . . . fill the tanks and make sure that you've your refuel location picked out. Also be certain that there are no fuel vapor odors, no spills, no leaks. And if you have an outboard, remember to take along a few quarts of oil. You'll have to mix it with the emergency gas if your regular supply runs out.

    4. Carry life preservers for all hands . . . this is not only good sense, but mandatory in all areas. Be sure yours are Coast Guard approved. Also make certain that all required gear is on board. *All* gear should be properly stowed.

    5. The proper U. S. C. & G. S. navigational charts . . . lay out your course beforehand on updated charts.

    6. If it's vital that you receive mail, check in advance for the names of major marinas or yacht clubs along your cruise route and have mail addressed to you care of these locations. Ask senders to mark envelopes "Please hold for arrival." Also, a number of the major gasoline companies offer mail port service to the cruising yachtsmen. Contact the marine division of the firm whose products you generally use, and ask for a list of their marine service stations on your cruise route. Be sure to inform those writing you to include a return address and the number of days the letter should be held pending your arrival. Yachtsmen expecting mail after their departure from a mailing location may leave their estimated arrival dates at points ahead and the mail port operator will usually be glad to forward letters to meet them.

FLOAT PLAN

of _____
(name of boat owner)

{ **IF TROUBLE OCCURS** while you're cruising on your boat, help will come faster if the Coast Guard or other rescue agencies know *where to look for you*. For your safety and your family's peace of mind complete this form— leave it with a responsible person whom you can depend upon to notify authorities if you're overdue. }

IF OVERDUE, CONTACT _____
(name, phone number of nearest Coast Guard Rescue Coordination Center or other rescue agency)

BOAT: Name of vessel_____ Length overall_____

       Registry number_____ Color of hull_____
(white hull, blue top, etc.)

       Power_____
(inboard, outboard, sail)

       Radio aboard { _____ (transmit frequency)

NUMBER OF PERSONS ABOARD_____ _____ (receive frequency)

DEPARTURE FROM_____ DATE & TIME DEPART_____

DESTINATION_____ DATE & EST. TIME RETURN_____

ROUTE OR CRUISING PLANS_____

* * *

One of the most essential things on any cruise is that the work of your vessel shouldn't be neglected, and it is the lack of the day-by-day boatkeeping and care of the craft that can quickly negate all the enjoyment of cruising. There is no question about the fact that cruising offers a splendid opportunity for long, lazy hours of sheer relaxation and physical comfort, but when the lazy hours dominate and the care of your boat is neglected, you make more work for yourself in the end. The easiest way to keep up with the task of boatkeeping, as well as the other duties about the boat, is to conform to an exacting routine. This routine will make the work seem easy and makes the boat much more livable. Thus, before starting out on any cruise, set a routine for yourself and your crew (this includes the children). This will make the voyage easier, smoother in operation, less demanding, and safer. Assignment of shipboard duties—anchoring, cooking, boatkeeping, and the like—beforehand gives each crew member time to understand his particular job and prepare for it.

For the average family vacation cruise the routine may be divided into two general departments: navigating and steward's. The navigating department, under the command of the skipper, is responsible for operation of the craft while under way; speed and course; handling of sails and helm; operation of engine; and anchorage. The steward's department duties, usually under the command of the first mate, should include maintaining sufficient food supplies; preparation of meals; obtaining fresh food, ice, smoker's supplies, and liquid refreshments; boatkeeping below deck; making-up of berths; replacement of galley and cabin gear; laundry or laundry service; stove maintenance; and ship's mail.

Boatkeeping Afloat

It is essential that the boat be kept clean and shipshape at all times. This means not just the living quarters but the entire boat. The first rule of good shipboard housekeeping is to have a place for everything and have everything in its place. To make the most of the room available, there are several things you can do. For instance, a shelf can often be near the ceiling, under the deck, along the inside of each sleeping berth. This shelf should have a good high rail and, if space permits, should be wide enough to hold spare clothing, oilskins, and other miscellaneous articles. If impracticable to fit a shelf, pullman-berth hammocks make an excellent substitute.

A well-kept craft calls for a regular daily boatkeeping routine. But, the actual cleaning aboard ship is the same as at home and generally requires the same techniques. The tools are the same, too. While attending to daily boatkeeping routine, you should also make a maintenance check. While cleaning, carefully inspect the plumbing, electrical appliances, stoves, etc., and take immediate steps to repair any faulty items.

To make your (or your first mate's) boatkeeping tasks simpler, you and your crew should develop good habits while afloat. Make certain to clean up messes as they occur, and you'll never be faced with accumulated work, which can spoil the entire voyage. Jack Owens, former president of the Owens Yacht Company, offers the following boatkeeping tips in his book, *Cruising Fun for the Family:*

> 1. Use a detergent rather than soap because it will generally clean better in salt water. Also avoid foamy, sudsy cleaners in the galley or around the boat. Fresh rinse water is seldom plentiful aboard little ships; suds do little cleaning and demand lots of rinse. Cleansers high in trisodium phosphate do an excellent job and don't froth too much.

2. Keep two large sponges handy—one for topside cleanups and one for below.

3. Wet bathing suits should be dried or taken off before the wearer enters the sleeping quarters of your floating home. Nothing gives a cabin or bunk a more miserably moist smell than salt water dampness impregnated in bed clothing.

4. The best way to clean glass windows on shipboard is to wash first with vinegar and water solution. Use paper tissue rather than a cloth. Clean plastic windshields and windows most gingerly. These plastics are soft. Hard rubbing on plastic window surfaces will cause scratching and reduce transparency. Lots of fresh-water and very gentle washing with soft cloth or sponge is best, or use one of the special cleansers made for this purpose and follow the manufacturer's instructions. Hard rubbing and abrasive cleaners are *verboten*.

5. Sanitation requires ventilation of the bilge. A foul bilge is unhealthy. Although an electric bilge blower helps a great deal, the bilge should be kept clean by scrubbing it occasionally. (This is definitely the skipper's job.) After all, the boat is only a big tub; everything not washed or brushed away winds up in the bilge. Never allow oil, grease, or gasoline to float around beneath your floor; a drip pan under the engine or engines will help prevent this. An occasional purging with a bilge cleanser or solvent—available from boating supply dealers—will sweeten the bilge and make the entire boat smell nicer. To give a little more freshness, use a few drops of essence of spearmint or pine in the bilge.

6. Ventilate lockers, drawers, head, and cabin as much as possible. Leave doors and drawers open when you are away from the boat. Lots of light and fresh air reduce rot, mildew, and that smell of dampness. Linens, clothes, and towels are subject to more dampness on the boat than at home. Air them frequently.

7. Keep refrigerator or icebox spotless. If it gets sour and moldy, it will smell up all the food stored inside. Wash the refrigerator interior frequently with soda, ammonia, or bleach solution. When the box is out of operation, keep it wide open; give it plenty of light and air to help it stay sweet. To reduce odors in an icebox, use sheets of transparent plastic (the self-sealing kind) for wrapping melons, cut onions, cheese, and so forth.

8. Use only metal polish meant for boat work, and sold at yacht supply dealers.

9. Sprinkle dry asbestos cement over oil spots. It will rapidly absorb the oil. Then sweep up. Grease can be removed from linoleum and similar floor coverings by using carbon tetrachloride.

10. To whiten enamel toilet bowls, sinks, etc., fill with water and pour in a little laundry bleach. After a few hours of soaking, even the most stubborn stain will come off.

11. Use a tank type vacuum cleaner at dockside to clean the entire boat, particularly the cabin. There is nothing like the vacuum cleaner to suck up dust, sand, dead flies, lint, and all the rest. If the bilge is bone dry, the vacuum cleaner can be used to remove chips, sawdust, and dirt from between frames. Never dip the suction end of vacuum hose in water; a slug of water will ruin the machine's innards.

12. Bait, live, dead, or doubtful, should be kept in the bait tank. Nothing, but nothing, can make a boat smell like an abandoned fish market quicker than a few slivers of ripe bait in deck seams or between frames in the bilge. Fish-cleaning hygiene rules should be the same as for bait. Every single scale must go overboard if the cruiser is to remain livable.

13. All crew members should be urged to eat snacks of such things as cookies, toast, crackers, and chips outside the cabin. It is easier to brush or hose crumbs and chips from the cockpit deck than from the deep recesses of the cabin floor and crevices in the bilge.

14. Check fabrics (upholstery, rugs, curtains) occasionally for stains. Most fabrics used on modern cruisers, even the most luxurious-looking ones, lend themselves nicely to vigorous soap-and-water cleaning.

15. Use ammonia as a grease cutter rather than the stronger household preparations. Coffee grounds in a greasy frying pan will absorb most of the grease, making it easy to wash. Take heavy cleaning jobs home when possible. It's lots easier, for example, to boil out and scour a greasy, charred frying pan in the cool convenience of your home kitchen than in the limited quarters of the boat's galley.

16. Shun washing in and around the cabin interior with salt water. The water evaporates, leaving a salt film; the salt attracts dampness and makes things feel clammy.

17. Wash varnished work with plain, clean, fresh water or weak soap solution. Varnish may lose gloss if scrubbed with gritty cleansers or strong detergent. Mahogany can be cleaned with lemon oil. A few drops will suffice to clean the varnished surface.

18. Clean rags and waste should be stored in plastic containers. Other such material soaked with oil, paint, or any combustible matter should be gotten rid of promptly.

19. Lines that are lying around loose make a deck a potential booby trap. Furthermore, letting them lie around in sloppy fashion is almost as sure a sign of the novice yachtsman as calling them ropes. To avoid being classed as a poor seaman, keep them coiled and secured—and to make the job of coiling them less of a job, try winding them around the back of a deck chair.

20. Folding metal-wire shopping carts, used by city housewives who walk to and from the supermarket, are wonderful gadgets for boat-wives who have to do likewise or carry a load of bundles down a long pier. If you can't spare boat room to store one, even folded flat, look for (or makeshift) an enormous canvas or plastic shopping bag with wheels at the base. You'll bless it the next time you go ashore for canned foods or beer. Remember that all hands should pitch in to help while loading food, duffel, and gear. Many hands make light work of this task.

21. Toy cleaning implements (brooms, carpet sweepers, and the like) stow more easily than the large household ones and are sometimes even more efficient because they will fit into impossible angles.

22. Stow an electric iron for use on extended cruises, if dock current is available. Use it not for real ironing, but for important small jobs like collars and cuffs on nylon and seersucker, crushed skirts, etc. A sheet on a bunk makes the ironing board. Also useful for freshening up mussed slip covers, bedspread, upholstery.

23. While attending to the daily chores, you should also make a maintenance check. While cleaning, carefully inspect the plumbing, electrical appliances, stoves, steering gear, etc., and take immediate steps to repair any faulty items.

24. Make everything fast before going out into open water. This means lamps, ashtrays, bottles (full or empty), pots, clock, radio—everything that isn't a part of the boat.

Cleaning aboard a cruiser is the same as at home and generally requires the same techniques. The tools are the same. Have plenty of rags, paper toweling, cleaning compounds, wax, polishes, ammonia, copper or bronze wool, and a supply of cotton waste. Metal buckets and tin dishpans should be avoided when possible. Collapsible canvas pails are excellent on shipboard.

A WORD TO THE GALLEY DETAIL

On board your yacht, the food you provide can make or break your weekend or cruise, or even just a day's sail. Fine weather afloat can't make up for poor meals, but when the weather closes in to keep you at anchor, tasty food cradled in good conversation around the cabin table can make you forget a lot of rain on the deck. It takes a great deal of forethought and no little physical effort to produce tempting fare for four or five, on a two-burner stove and with a minimum of working area. It you don't understand the job, or don't like it, turn it over to someone who does. It can be a lot of fun, and on the water the results of your labors will be fully appreciated by appetites whetted on fresh air.

Laying in Supplies

The art of cooking on board is mainly a matter of adroit planning ahead. For instance, many factors enter into your initial grocery list:

1. How many persons are to be served how many meals?
2. How long between ports where you can get fresh supplies?
3. What storage areas do you have, and how much perishable food can be put in your icebox along with the minimum ice you want to carry—allowing plenty for cold drinks?
4. What size and type of stove do you have, and can you plan on oven-cooking?
5. What utensils do you have—if you plan a mess of crabs or fresh corn do you have the pot to cook them in?
6. Finally, what are the food preferences of your crew?

With these ideas in mind, you can devise a series of menus which will include simple, appetizing food, and plenty of it. As a guide in figuring quantities, a table of the approximate needs per man per day which was used successfully on several long passages is as follows:

	Oz. per man per day
Meats, poultry, fish	14.5
Beverages (not milk)	4.0
Dairy Products (incl. milk)	22.0
Cereals and Bread	13.0
Fruits	8.0
Vegetables	11.0
Soups	3.0
Sweets (sugar, syrup, chocolate, jam)	12.5
	88.0 oz.

or 5½ lbs. per man per day

Meat. Since the foregoing table says that you should plan almost a pound of meat a day per man, it will be the mainstay of at least one meal and probably more, so order generously. A roast of beef, lamb, or veal can be brought aboard cooked and ready to slice for sandwiches, or to have as cold cuts with gravy, or a special sauce, poured over.

It will keep well while you have a quick-cook meat the next night—chops or fried chicken —and will probably end up as sandwich filling or in stew ladled over stale bread. A baked ham, especially the boned and rolled variety which gives more meat per pound, keeps several days, can be served in numerous ways for lunch and dinner, and is a welcome replacement for bacon for breakfast. Nothing smells quite as delicious as bacon in the morning, but its grease is treacherous in a galley. When you do cook it, have a large empty can standing in the sink to receive the grease, which should never go down the drain. If you toss it overboard, see that it won't float along the boottop of your own or a neighboring boat.

Before buying a thick, juicy porterhouse steak with which to dazzle your crew, be sure that your marine stove will do it justice. Many a luscious piece of meat has stewed to tastelessness over a too-faint flame.

For the unexpected—when guests come aboard for a drink and stay for dinner, or when the weather prevents making your next supply port on schedule, keep the larder stocked with tasty canned meats. Whole chickens, chicken fricassee, beef stew, canned hamburgers, franks, bacon, ham, and your favorite meat-heavy brand of stew or corned beef hash provide hearty, quickly-prepared dishes. Such popular fare as Swedish meat balls, in their own gravy, a meaty spaghetti sauce, and other seasoned dishes whose flavor improves if left standing a day while the seasonings go to work, can be prepared at home and are better than ever when you get around to serving them on board. Of course, with a pressure cooker you can always do a fresh roast with which to start the hot-cold-sandwiches-hash sequence all over again. Also plan to make plenty of use of both canned and dehydrated soups. Both are available in many varieties.

In addition to canned meats, there are also the so-called "freeze-dry" meats. These packaged foods are light in weight and so small they are convenient to store and require no refrigeration. In complete meals you can get swiss steak dinner, pork chop dinner, and ranch style breakfast. You can also get beef steaks, pork chops, scrambled eggs, and gravy and sliced beef. And, for a one dish meal, there are many kinds of stews: vegetable and beef, chicken, rice and chicken dinner, chili with beans, and shrimp creole.

Of course, there's a gimmick to pulling a complete roast beef dinner out of a seagoing hat, so to speak. The legerdemain really has its beginning at home. Roasts, turkey, and such are prepared in the shoreside kitchen. But the skilled galley wife need never confess the truth. Her day-old roast can be presented with a tantalizing, fresh-out-of-the-oven look, thanks to that modern culinary aid, sheet aluminum foil.

On your editor's cruiser, *Alpha-Nan*, we learned long ago that moisture-repelling, heat-conducting aluminum foil is the best thing that ever happened to the seagoing cook. The shiny stuff makes a disposable liner for the frying pan, eliminating one hard-to-wash item. Left-overs can be sealed in it and stored much more readily than in a bowl. But this wide, heavy-duty foil comes into its own as a restorative for a day-old roast: Into a large sheet of foil goes the cold roast or pre-cooked, dismembered turkey. The meat is wrapped steam-tight. Then it's lowered into a generous-size spaghetti pot, which, incidentally, is itself a vital bit of galley gear. (Where else could one steam fresh-caught blue-claw crabs?) The foil-covered meat is supported in the pot by the perforated coffee grounds holder, borrowed from the percolator. An inch or two of water is added. Steam thoroughly heats the meat without cooking it.

Take along plenty of eggs, whether you're off for a weekend, a month or a week. They'll stay fresh in a locker (save icebox storage), and will serve in a variety of ways for any meal. But remember though that eggs need careful handling. While the new plastic egg-containers are fairly good, it's best in rough going to open the eggs and put them in a glass jar with a screw-top, which should then be kept on ice.

Don't overdo any one meat at a stretch just because you have it aboard. Wrap it in foil after a couple of meals and stow it while you serve alternates. You might even end up taking it home after the weekend, to get your money's worth, but your menus won't have become tiresome.

Vegetables. According to the quantity table, each person requires about ¾ pound of vegetables a day, and there's such a wide selection available, your chief concern need only be what best complements the meats you plan to serve. For weekend cruising you can count on the time-saving frozen variety. But for longer cruises when supply ports are scarce, frozen vegetables take up valuable icebox space and soon thaw to where they must be used anyhow. Fresh vegetables—potatoes, asparagus, beets, spinach, the gritty ones especially—should be washed before being taken aboard—or washed before stowing, particularly items which will be put on ice. If the lettuce is leafed, carrots are scraped, asparagus cropped, and cauliflower denuded, you'll have that much more time in the cockpit during the cocktail hour.

Canned vegetables should be stowed in a semblance of order so you can find what you want when you want it. A list of what and how many cans you bring aboard, checked off as they are used, will help you to know what you have left, without having to take inventory. If there's even a remote chance that labels may come off, mark the contents on the up-end of the can with a grease pencil. Any cans stowed in the bilge should certainly be marked this way.

You can use your ingenuity in dove-tailing cooking processes in a number of ways. If you must use the pressure cooker for asparagus, save time and use a quick-cooking rice, instead of potatoes, for a starch. The rice must cook and then stand for 10 minutes before being served. Incidentally, using consommé as the liquid in cooking rice, instead of water, gives an unusual taste lift. If you plan to cook two vegetables together in a sectioned pot, use two which won't impart their respective tastes or colors to each other. On the other hand, you can mix some new partners together in the same undivided pot, to good effect. Peeled onions and peas or string beans—sliced onions in stewed tomatoes—and peas with mushrooms, are tempting companions. Whatever your vegetable purchases are, be sure there is enough variety to add color and interest to your meals.

You can do yourself a service by cooking more than enough at one meal for use the next. Do extra potatoes to serve hash-browned in the morning. Extra bacon goes on sandwiches, left-over string beans go in salad, or can be creamed, for example.

Salad ingredients don't last too long on board; first, because they're eagerly devoured and secondly, because they lose their crispness fast. However, after you've been cruising for a few days and eating out of cans, the sudden appearance of a cool, fresh vegetable salad, born of a recent trip to town, hits the spot with everyone, even the big meat and potato specialists. Incidentally, a tablespoon of sugar added to any tossed salad adds a nice flavor, and be sure to take a good basic dressing which can be doctored with blue cheese, orégano, etc., to individual tastes.

Desserts. Dessert is often a problem afloat. It's often passed up after you've gone to work and prepared one, but if you don't provide it there's sure to be a howl from some quarter. However, you can get away with the usual run of bakery products. But you'll really make a hit if you bake a cake for the occasion. A moist fruit or spice cake won't dry out—if it lasts that long—and can sit securely in its own pan until served. Layer cakes don't stow as happily—in fact, they're adept at upsetting and ending up as pudding. Canned fruit and cookies top off a cruising meal nicely and, of course, if you have an oven and enjoy baking in it, anything you produce will be sensational, especially after the crew has been primed by the homey aroma from the oven.

Whether you have dessert or not, some allowance for sweets should be made in the form of candy, syrup, jellies, etc. Our quantity chart says a little more than ¾ pound per man per day. Other enjoyable nibbles include raisins, dried prunes and apricots, nuts, crackers and cheese or peanut butter, apples and oranges.

Bread and Cereal. If you carry a bun-warmer you can heat old bread to a delicious warmth and freshness (wrap it in foil first), putting this on a burner as the plates are served, and it will be ready just as everyone gets settled. Breakfast buns, doughnuts, coffee cake and loaf bread all respond favorably to this treatment. There are also some especially good canned breads on the market, besides date-nut and brown breads, and you'll never be without if you stow some of these in the dry locker.

As for cereals, you'll find people eating them afloat who never do ashore, and hot cereal makes the heartiest one-dish breakfast you can have, particularly in rough weather, when your crew needs a hot and filling meal and you feel least like producing one.

Sandwiches. For sandwiches, if you can get around to preparing fillings at home and bringing them aboard in mason jars, you'll be able to produce greater variety and save yourself more time for fun. Otherwise the first half day of your cruise finds you in the galley. You surface for a breath of air only to find the skipper and crew yelling for lunch, and down you go again. Salad mixes—egg, tuna, chicken, ham, keep for a long while on ice. Any sandwiches should be hearty. Few men will smack their lips over a cream cheese and jelly sandwich after a morning of rigorous crew work in the fresh air.

Beverages. Don't dismiss your liquid supplies with "a pot of coffee will do." Fruit juices are more popular than ever as eye-openers, and, while the frozen juices are fine for short hauls, be sure to stow plenty of cans of orange, grapefruit, pineapple and apple juice, too. The flavor of canned juices improves a great deal if you aerate them just before serving. Most juices also blend wonderfully with vodka, too.

Milk is important aboard boats—especially those with children on board—but without refrigeration it sours very quickly. Most of the many varieties of powdered milk are excellent substitutes. Small portions can be made as needed, which win the milk battle before it has begun. If you do use fresh milk and will be without ice for a short while, put a half teaspoon of salt in each quart of milk. This will preserve its freshness. A half teaspoon of baking soda in a cup of *slightly* sour milk will make it palatable for cooking purposes.

Coffee, tea, and soup alternate with each other for cool weather sailing; orangeade or lemonade, for hot weather sailing, and you'll always have some on tap if you make a thermos full in the morning for anyone to help himself as he pleases. As in other foods, variety in liquids, including beer, will be appreciated, and even the inveterate coffee drinker may sidle up to tea or cocoa for a welcome change. (Spirits are not galley supplies and are under the full control of the skipper.)

Suggested Menus
The following is a sample list of menus for a week's cruise for four persons, and a list of the groceries necessary to provide them. One midweek supply stop is allowed for.

Saturday

NOON
Tomato Soup
Egg Salad Sandwiches
(Eggs prepared at home beforehand)
Cupcakes   Milk

DINNER
Sliced Ham (baked at home)
Boiled Sweet Potatoes
Succotash   Salad
Tea   Bananas & Cream

Sunday

BREAKFAST
Pineapple Juice   Dry Cereal
Bacon & Eggs
(cook extra bacon to use at noon)
Corn Muffins (packaged, heated)
Coffee   Jam

NOON
Tomato Juice
Peanut Butter & Bacon Sandwiches
Egg Salad Sandwiches
(if some remains from previous day)
Cake   Milk

DINNER
Spaghetti with vegetable-meat sauce made at home
(or canned sauce with some spices
and hamburg added)
Salad   Italian Bread
Elberta Peaches   Cookies   Beverage

Monday

BREAKFAST
Prunes   Dry Cereal
French Toast   Syrup
Bacon   Coffee

NOON
Vegetable Soup
Ham & Cheese Sandwiches
Tea   Cookies

DINNER
Fried Chicken
Candied Sweet Potatoes
(made from leftovers from Saturday dinner)
Canned Asparagus   Warm Bread
Tea   Coffee   Milk
Fruit Salad   Cookies

Tuesday

BREAKFAST
Fruit Salad
Dry Cereal (Canned Milk)
Ham and Eggs
Warmed Doughnuts, Coffee Cake
(warmed to restore freshness)
Coffee

NOON
Tomato Juice
Spaghetti   Beer
Cheese & Crackers

DINNER
Ham & Corned Beef Hash
(or ham and canned stew mixed)
Lima Beans   Boiled potatoes
Pilot Crackers & Canned Butter
(if fresh supply gone)
Tea   Coffee   Milk
Vanilla Pudding, Canned Raspberry Sauce

Wednesday (shopping trip in the morning)

BREAKFAST
Apple Juice
Cereal & Bananas (Canned Milk)
Coffee
Datenut Bread (Canned Butter)

NOON
Hamburgers on Rolls
Potato Chips
Cake   Tea   Coffee   Milk

DINNER
Roast Beef (cooked in pressure cooker)
Potatoes   Peas
Sliced Tomatoes
Blueberries & Cream
Cake   Tea   Coffee   Milk

Thursday

BREAKFAST
Apple Sauce   Dry Cereal
Sausage & Eggs
Buns   Coffee

NOON
Vegetable Juice
Roast Beef Sandwiches
Cake
Tea   Coffee   Milk   Beer

DINNER
Pork Chops & Beans Grill
(Brown chops, add beans, sprinkle with
brown sugar, put covers on and finish
cooking—until chops are done and beans
very hot—over very low flame)
Brown Bread
Broccoli   Salad
Canned Berries on Pound Cake
Tea   Coffee   Milk

Friday

BREAKFAST
Prune Juice
Fried Potatoes & Eggs
(potatoes left over from Tuesday dinner)
Warmed Buns   Coffee

NOON
Tuna Salad or Cold Cuts Sandwiches
Tea   Coffee   Milk
Bananas   Cake

DINNER
Creamed Crabmeat on Rice with Pimiento
String Beans   Beets
Tea   Coffee   Milk
Fruit   Cookies

1st Supply List
Meat and Fish

10-12 lb. Ham (boned and rolled)	1 large can Crabmeat
3 lbs. Bacon	4 cans Stew
1 frying Chicken	4 cans Hash
2 cans Tuna Fish	4 cans Fricassee

Vegetables and Soup

2 lbs. Sweet Potatoes	5 fresh Tomatoes
5 lbs. White Potatoes	2 head Lettuce
2 #2 cans Succotash	Carrots
4 #2 cans Asparagus	6 Onions
2 #2 cans Lima Beans	2 Green Peppers
2 #2 cans String Beans	Celery
1 large can Beets	Pkg. Minute Rice, Spaghetti,
2 cans Baked Beans	Macaroni
1 can Pimiento	4 cans Tomato Soup
2 cans Spanish Rice	4 cans Vegetable Soup

Bread and Cereal

Pkg. of assorted Cereals	Cookies—Assortment ⎫ (1 box
Corn Muffins (pkgd.)	Orange ⎬ each
4 loaves Bread	Toll House ⎭ kind)
Loaf Cake	1 doz. Doughnuts
½ doz. Cupcakes	2 cans Datenut Bread
Saltines	2 cans Brown Bread
Crackers	1 can of Bread

Beverages

Tea Bags (or liquid tea)	Soft Drinks—1½ doz. or more
Pineapple Juice (2 #2 cans)	Apple Juice (4 #2 cans)
Coffee (1 large, 1 small	Vegetable Juice—(4 #2 cans)
Instant brand)	Prune Juice (2 #2 cans)
Tomato Juice (2 #2 cans)	Beer—1½ doz. cans or more

Dairy

2 lbs. Butter	5 qts. Milk
2 pints Cream	1½ lbs. Cheese
3 doz. Eggs	Canned Milk, Canned Butter

Dry Staples

Sugar, brown & white	Oil
1 pkg. Flour	Syrup
1 pkg. Oatmeal (or other hot cereal)	Ketchup
Salt & Pepper	Onion Salt, Garlic Salt, Celery Salt
Mustard	Meat Tenderizer
Jam	Pint of Mayonnaise
Peanut Butter	Nutmeg
Salad Dressing	Cloves

Fruit

Bananas—6	Raspberries—2 cans
Elberta Peaches—large can	Applesauce—2 cans
Prunes—large can	Figs—2 cans
Fruit Salad—4 #2 cans	Oranges—1 doz.

Other items which could be included:

Peanuts	Candy
Dried Apricots, Prunes	Cheese Spreads

2nd Supply List (For midweek shopping day)
Meat

8 Pork Chops	1 lb. Bacon
6 lb. Roast of Beef	2 lbs. Ground Steak
1 lb. Sausage	

149

Vegetables

	Frozen Peas (2 pkgs.)	Broccoli—bunch fresh
	Tomatoes—3 fresh	Celery
	Lettuce—large head	

Bread

	Hamburger Rolls—8	Cakes
	Buns	Coffee Cake
	3 loaves Bread	

Dairy

	Butter	5 qts. Milk
	2 pts. Cream	Eggs

Fruit

	Blueberries—1 qt.	Melon—green when purchased
	Grapefruit	

Stowing of Food

Stowing your food aboard shouldn't be a hit-or-miss operation. All like items should be placed together as you unpack the carry-all, and then the group stowed in icebox, locker, or cabinet all at once. If you can pre-cool your icebox, after a thorough scrubbing and airing, by filling with ice and leaving it a day or two before you bring food aboard, your ice will last longer and foods stay colder. You're also more fortunate in this respect if your box is of the top-opening type rather than side-opening, as the latter dumps a certain amount of the settled cold air every time you open the door. Wash the ice before putting it in and wipe off all containers and milk bottles. Stow things with a semblance of order so you know just where to find what you want without losing valuable cold air.

Fresh meats should be taken out of their store paper, rinsed and wrapped in waxed paper —it's the juice around the meat that deteriorates first, and might give the idea that the meat itself is bad when it really is not. Vegetables should be washed and made ready for use before stowing, and special attention should be given to placing the milk so that it won't upset with the motion of the boat. Incidentally, waxed milk cartons sometimes give way after being soaked and squeezed in the icebox, so check yours to be sure all is well, or transfer the milk to your own plastic or bottle containers. Have on hand plenty of the latter for stowing left-overs and dry staples.

To prevent butter from absorbing other food odors, and to keep the icebox generally sweet, a container of charcoal or charcoal derivative placed in the box will help a lot.

In stowing dry goods, place the most-used containers where they're handiest, and keep a roll of scotch tape handy to tape opened boxes when there's a possibility of spilling. Crackers, cookies, nuts and other foods which get stale when soggy can be kept in a dehumidifying can, which has a dehydrating unit in the lid to absorb moisture from the can's contents. Sugar, salt and flour are best kept in jars with screw tops, particularly if left aboard from weekend to weekend.

Clean-up detail, when the weekend, or cruise, is over, is also preparation for the following trip, and requires a thorough job if you want to enjoy yourself the next time you come aboard. The icebox should be cleared of food and washed out, the remaining ice tossed overboard, and the lid left off when you depart. Unused perishables should all go in the homebound duffle and, as a finale, take the last bag of garbage ashore and put in the cans your club provides for this purpose.

Galley Gear

When assembling galley equipment, don't make the mistake of saying, "it's only for the boat, I'll get a cheap pot." The cheap pot may not last through the season; it will be the devil to clean, will dent and not sit squarely on the burners, will not have an insulated handle, will tip unless half full, and won't give an even heat to its contents. In a good grade of cooking ware, an adequate complement of utensils could include: 10-inch frying pan; one or two 4-quart pots; a 6-quart pot (or a several-utensils-in-one unit); pressure cooker, bun-warmer, coffee pot, tea kettle and some flat pans. If you have an oven, include a casserole dish, baking square and muffin tins. A large roasting pan with a 2-inch lip serves many purposes, from serving as a dish drainboard to holding condiments, silver, napkins, bread and butter and other accessories for passing to the cockpit or around the cabin in one easy motion.

By the simple addition of a few wires and electrical outlets, any cruiser can be equipped to plug into dockside electric-power lines. It is equally true that many models come already equipped for dock power. Either way you may wish to go, there is an arm-long list of electrical cooking accessories that can be used aboard boats and which will astound guests —provided everybody stays out of the galley to give the cook swinging room. There are electric frying pans, coffee pots, griddles, ovens, stewing pots, deep-fryers and even electric bottle warmers for babies. If your tastes run to full course meals, and if your galley is equipped with electric appliances, you will quickly join us in our preference for that additional stowaway work table.

Icepick and its holder, bottle opener, beer can openers, and a special screw-top jar for matches are essentials, as are a strainer and sufficient sharp knives and mixing spoons, measuring cup, and tongs for grasping hot foods. A chopping board which doubles as a sink cover, thermos with pouring spigot are also helpful gear. Take into account the rust factor when selecting these small accessories for the galley.

Gourmet Cooking Afloat

While simplicity is the keynote of cooking afloat, there's no reason why the food needs to taste flat and uninteresting. The only truly expert galley cooks are those who have had the blind courage to push their luck to the limit with whatever galley facilities they have aboard their boats. What somebody else does, be it success or failure, has no real bearing on what you should or should not do in the way of "way-out" cooking afloat. Granting that the gastronomic well being of the skipper is important, the more experimenting the cook does, the more familiar he or she will become with the varying requirements of cooking aboard the boat. For example, a simple menu item like fried tomatoes can become an adventure if only a little imagination is used in preparing the flour or breadcrumb dip in which the slices of ripe tomatoes are placed before being put in the pan of hot cooking oil.

One of the easiest ways to add new flavors to simple foods afloat is to use wine. Even prepared mixes and other convenience foods take on your own individuality when you cook with wine. For example, use white dinner wine or sherry instead of half the liquid needed in a cake, cooky, pudding or pie filling mix. Favor gelatin desserts or salads by substituting wine for half the water in the recipe. (Choose red or white wines, depending on color of the gelatin.) Improve dry spaghetti sauce mix or dry salad dressing mix by substituting red or white wine for half the water specified on the package. Or you can give canned baked beans new interest by seasoning as follows: To 1 tall can (1-lb. 12-oz.) of beans, add ⅓ cup sherry, 2 tablespoons brown sugar, 1 teaspoon dry mustard, 1 teaspoon instant coffee powder. The sherry and coffee add a rich, nutty flavor that is impossible to identify, but very easy to enjoy.

Or for a show-off soup, serve your crew Chicken Soup Mongole. Mix 1 can each condensed tomato soup, pea soup and chicken-rice soup. Add 1 cup cream, ⅓ cup sherry. Heat piping hot; add dash of curry powder. A real taste-tempter.

No Fresher Fish

If boats are divided into types, certainly boat owners can be separated too. There are those who own boats simply for the pleasure of cruising, and there are those who own boats so they can fish. Whatever your class of boat owner, the joys of sea food are open to one and all. Since you get fun out of days on the water, why not get your food out of it as often as you can? Fresh fish are naturals for many tempting, delicious and easy-to-prepare sea food meals that a cook can whip up. By "fresh" we mean right out of the water, then under the cleaning knife and through the batter, and right into a hot skillet. For those who are not familiar with the steps in cleaning and dressing fish, here is the basic procedure:

1. Wash the fish in fresh water. Remove scales by scraping the fish *gently* from the tail to the head with the dull edge of a knife.

2. Remove the entrails after cutting the entire length of the belly from the vent to the head. Remove the head by cutting above the collarbone.

3. Break the backbone over the edge of the cutting board.

4. Remove the dorsal or large back fin by cutting the flesh along each side, and pulling the fin out. Never trim the fins off with shears or a knife because the bones at the base of the fin will be left in the fish.

5. Wash the fish thoroughly in cold fresh water. The fish is now dressed or pan dressed, depending on its size.

6. Large dressed fish may be cut crosswise into steaks, if desired. Cut steaks about ¾ of an inch thick.

7. *To fillet:* With a sharp knife, cut down the back of the fish from the tail to the head. Then cut down to the backbone just above the collarbone. Turn the knife flat and cut the fish along the backbone to the tail, allowing the knife to run over the rib bones. Lift off the entire side of the fish in one piece, freeing the fillet at the tail. Turn the fish over and cut the fillet from the other side.

8. If you wish, you may skin the fillets. Lay the fillet flat on the cutting board, skin side down. Hold the tail end with your fingers, and cut through the flesh to the skin. Flatten the knife on the skin and cut the flesh away from the skin by running the knife forward while holding the free end of the skin firmly between your fingers. When cleaning and dressing a fish while afloat, be very careful that you don't get any scales, entrails, etc., about your yacht.

If it can be accurately stated that there is a secret for cooking seafood to a pinnacle of taste and delicacy, that secret could only be—*do not overcook!* "Boiled" fish, like "boiled" chicken and "boiled" eggs, get tough if actually boiled; simmer is the better word. Cook fish gently. Fish may be simmered in plain old water, as any housewife can tell you, but the pros use instead what they call court bouillon. As you will notice, the consistent feature is cooking the liquid with the vegetables and seasonings for a while before adding the fish:

1. Simmer together 2 quarts water, 1 pint milk, a handful of salt, and the juice of ½ lemon. Simmer 20 minutes, then add fish and simmer until tender.

2. Simmer 2 quarts water with salt, vinegar, 2 sliced carrots, 2 diced onions, a bouquet garni, and peppercorns to taste. Simmer 30 minutes, then add fish and simmer until tender.

3. Simmer 2 quarts red or white wine with 1 quart water and all the ingredients mentioned in #2, above. Simmer for 30 minutes, then add fish. (Especially good when the court bouillon will be used for the fish sauce.)

4. Simmer for half an hour: 2 quarts water, salt, garlic, 1 carrot, 1 branch of celery, 1 onion, 1 clove, a bouquet garni. Strain, and add 1 quart milk. Bring to boiling point, then add fish and simmer until fish is tender. (Excellent for soups.)

When your fish is nothing but a pleasant memory, the liquid in which it is cooked can be made into a good soup. Add diced potatoes, sliced carrots, cut-up leeks, chopped water cress, and a bit of sweet cicely. Cook until vegetables are tender, add a glass of white wine, and season with salt and pepper. Finally, add a small piece of butter and pour it over small pieces of toast in the tureen.

Fish fumet or fish essence starts with the stock in which fish was cooked. (Water will do if you find yourself with no fish stock and a need for fumet.) Cook the bones, heads, and trimmings from 1 pound of fish in 2 cups dry white wine and 2 cups fish stock (or water) along with 1 chopped onion, a few sprigs of chopped parsley, 1 bay leaf, 1 whole clove, a little crushed thyme, a sprinkling of freshly ground black pepper, and the juice of 1 lemon. Simmer gently (with the lid off) until the liquid is reduced by one half, then strain through a fine sieve, pushing as much of the residue through the sieve as you can. Add salt to taste and store cold until needed.

Given a fish, a guest, and a dearth of ideas on how to put one before the other, you might find these standard methods helpful:

1. De-bone small pieces of fish, season them, roll them up, wrap a slice of bacon around each piece (fasten with toothpicks) and then broil the fish.

2. Cut the fish into slices. Place them, seasoned, in a pan with onions, carrots, peppercorn, and bay leaf. Pour in enough dry white wine to cover the pieces. Add the fish head, if you have it, wrapped in a cheesecloth bag for easy extraction later. Simmer gently, covered, until the fish is tender. Thicken the stock or not, as you like; there's a fish ragout.

3. Butter a pan and sprinkle it with flour. Place the fish in the pan, along with chopped shallots and parsley. Dot generously with butter on top. Bake for 20 minutes. A few minutes before the fish is tender, pour on a glass of dry white wine and the juice of half a lemon.

4. Fillet the fish and bread the fillets by dipping them first in beaten egg yolk, then in fine bread crumbs. Heat a heavy skillet in the oven; add a stick of butter and let the butter sizzle until it turns a rich brown (but not smoking black). Dip the fish into the butter to coat it on one side, then put the other side down in the butter. Bake 15-20 minutes, basting frequently with the butter in the pan. You won't have to turn it, and it will be done when it's nicely browned and the basting butter foams up on top of it.

Shellfish Afloat

While on a cruise, there are many opportunities to obtain shellfish—either from water-front markets, commercial fishermen, or by gathering them yourself.

Clams. When alive his shell will be closed tight. If it is slightly open, touch him and he'll close up immediately. If not, he's dead; throw him away.

To clean, wash clams thoroughly in water. Then put them in a pan with cold fresh water to cover and sprinkle a handful of corn meal over the top. Let them stand in this bath for two hours or more; the corn meal will prompt them to expel most of their sand and empty the black stuff out of their stomachs.

To open them, lift one out of the water, carefully but quickly, and stick a strong sharp knife between the slightly opened shells. Hold over a bowl, so you can catch the juices, and cut through the muscle to open the shell. You can escape this labor if you are going to steam them in their shells, of course; steaming opens them.

Small clams (littlenecks and cherrystones) may be served raw. Big ones are usually chopped up and cooked. The black skin around the neck is usually removed from soft-shell clams; ditto the hard part of hard-shell clams. These may be used if chopped or ground, but they're too tough to eat as is. When steaming clams, use half white dinner wine and half water with a tablespoon olive oil; when clams open, strain liquid through fine cheese cloth; add finely chopped parsley, green onion or fresh herbs to broth. Correct seasoning, bring to a boil and serve as extra-delicious broth—or with the clams. Broth may be thickened slightly with butter-flour roux and served as sauce over clams.

Clam Souse

For 2 or maybe 3, dice 1½ dozen good-sized clams, 1 medium onion, 1 firm tomato, 1 sweet pepper. Add 2 tablespoons olive oil, 2 tablespoons vinegar, 2 teaspoons Worcestershire sauce, and 3 tablespoons lime juice. Toss the whole shebang well. Add salt and cayenne pepper to taste. Chill the souse for at least 2 hours—the longer the better. Serve it on a bed of water cress or coarsely shredded lettuce.

Clams a la Baltimore

For 4, mince 30 clams. Mince 1 onion. Delicately brown the onion in 2 tablespoons butter. Blend in 2 tablespoons flour. Add the minced clams and season with ½ teaspoon cayenne, ½ teaspoon dry mustard. Cook over a low fire for 30 minutes. Meanwhile, sauté 12 fresh mushrooms in butter. Beat 4 egg yolks with 2 tablespoons ice water. Add the yolks to the clams, stirring constantly. Remove from fire and spoon to a heated platter. Garnish with the mushrooms. Sprinkle lightly with chopped parsley. Serve with toasted and buttered crackers, radishes, spring onions, sliced tomatoes, and —if you are wise—plenty of cold ale.

Baked Clams

For 4, open 24 live clams, chop meat, and place back in half shell. Mix: 1 tablespoon chopped garlic, 1 tablespoon chopped shallot, 1 tablespoon chopped parsley, 1 tablespoon chopped chives, 3 tablespoons grated Parmesan cheese. Place a bit of this mixture on top of each chopped clam; top each with a piece of butter. Bake in a hot oven for 10 minutes. Serve very hot with a piece of lemon.

Crabs. Hard-shelled: Wash off all dirt and seaweed; better handle them with tongs! Drop them head first into boiling water, seasoned with salt, lemon, or vinegar, bay leaf, onion slice; boil, covered, for about 5 minutes, then turn down flame and simmer until they are red—another 10 minutes or so. Or steam them on a rack over (not in) a little water, wine, or beer—until their tail-aprons rise, or about 30 minutes. Drain and plunge them into cold water. When cool enough to handle, clean them: break off the apron (the part that folds under the tail); pulling upward from the tail end, separate the top shell from the bottom. Wash the top shells carefully if you're going to stuff them—otherwise, toss them out. Pull or scrape off and discard all the orange-colored stuff and the spongy lungs. Cut off the membrane and pick out the prize: the meat in the two body cavities. Crack the claws and legs and pick out the meat. Do this with about 14 crabs and you'll have a pound of fresh lump crab meat.

Soft-shelled: The soft-shell crab is usually the blue crab caught immediately after molting and before the new shell has hardened. Use only live crabs. With a sharp knife, cut off the apron or flap that folds under the rear of the body. Turn the crab and cut off the face at a joint just back of the eyes. Lift each point at the sides with the fingers, clean out the gills, and wash the crabs in cold water. When cooked, the entire body, including the legs and claws, is eaten. The crabs can be sautéd, with or without a breading.

Crab Meat Deluxe
For 3 or 4, mash 2 hard-cooked egg yolks with 1½ tablespoons flour, a sprinkle of nutmeg, ½ teaspoon salt, ¼ teaspoon paprika, and 2 tablespoons butter. Slowly stir in 1½ cups top milk. Cook over low fire, stirring constantly, about 8 minutes, or until smooth and thickened. Add 1½ cups crab meat and ¾ pound sautéd mushrooms. Reheat. Just before serving, stir in 3 tablespoons sherry and 1 or 2 raw egg yolks. Cook and stir until well blended, then serve in pastry shells.

Skipper's Crabmeat Delight
For 3 or 4, combine ¾ pound crabmeat, 2 cans (1½ oz. each) condensed chicken gumbo soup, ¼ cup milk, ¼ cup cream, ¼ cup sherry, ½ teaspoon curry powder, and ¼ teaspoon Worcestershire sauce in top of a double boiler and cook over simmering water until thoroughly heated. Serve in soup plates or bowls.

Spaghetti and Crab
For 5 or 6, braise ½ cup chopped onion, 1 teaspoon chopped garlic, 1 teaspoon chopped parsley in ¼ cup olive or salad oil until golden brown. Add 1 cup solid pack tomatoes, 1 cup tomato sauce, 1½ cups water, and 1 teaspoon black pepper and 2 teaspoons salt. Simmer for one hour. Add 1 pound crab meat and ¼ cup sherry and simmer a few minutes. Cook 1 pound spaghetti. Drain but do not wash. Add to sauce and mix well. Pour on platter and sprinkle with grated cheese. Serve immediately.

Lobsters. The best weight for a lobster is 1¼ to 2½ pounds; heavier ones are apt to be coarse or watery, leaner ones tough. During February and March, when the lobsters are breeding in their peculiar fashion (the male swimming before the female, never really coming in close contact), the meat is not so tender as during the rest of the year. The female lobster, prized over the male by many gourmets, is distinguishable by the softness of her uppermost "fins." Both sexes are a mottled blue-green when alive; their shells turn red when cooked. Keep your lobsters alive until the moment of cooking.

To tell if a boiled lobster was alive when cooked, straighten out its tail. The tail will spring back. To kill a lobster for broiling, thrust a sharp pointed knife into its back, where the body and tail meet, and cut its spinal cord. To clean a lobster, before broiling or after

156

boiling, slit the soft shell on the underside. Lift up the tail meat and remove the intestinal vein that runs down the back. Find and remove the "lady," a hard sac near the head. Don't tamper with the rest: the greenish liver and the pink-colored coral are delectable; you'll eat around the spongy lungs but need not remove them in the kitchen.

Boiled Lobster

Choose a pot large enough to hold your live lobsters. Fill it with enough water to cover the lobsters. Add thyme, bay leaf, salt, and pepper. Bring to a full, rolling boil. Drop the live lobster into this court buillon, head first. Let the water come back to a boil before adding a second lobster. Time the cooking from the moment the water boils after the last lobster is added; allow about 20 minutes for a chicken lobster to cook at a full boil. Remove from fire and let the lobsters cool in the liquid.

Lobster a la Newburg

Boil one lobster, 1½ to 2 pounds, for each person. When cool, dice meat and add plenty of hot, clear butter, salt, and ground pepper. Fry without allowing it to take on color. Add 1 tablespoon lemon juice, cover with fresh cream, and reduce volume a little over low fire. Add 1 tablespoon Madeira for each lobster and bring to a lazy boil. Remove from fire. Thicken with 2 beaten egg yolks and same volume of cream, adding a little at a time and stirring briskly. Reheat without boiling, season with a pinch of cayenne, and salt to taste. Serve at once over wedges of toasted bread.

Lobster with Norwegian-style Mayonnaise

Cover live lobsters with cold salted water; add enough lemon juice to make slightly tart, season well with a few coarse celery stalks, bay leaf, tarragon, plenty hand-milled black pepper, and 1 grated medium onion for each pair of lobsters. Boil up gently, simmer only 15 minutes or so. They're done when red—don't overcook, as most professional chefs do. Split, discard dark sections and small sac behind eyes. Crack claws well. Serve with any good mayonnaise pointed up with freshly grated horse-radish to taste, a little finely chopped dill and one half as much thick sour cream. Mix well; chill well. Chilled Chablis with this.

Oysters. Like clams, make sure the shells are closed tight. Scrub them carefully. Open them over a strainer over a bowl, so you can catch the juices. To open, poke a sharp knife into the hinged or pointed end of the oyster; push until you manage to cut the center muscle that holds the shells together. When the shells begin to separate, run the knife around the shells to finish the job. The deeper of the two is your "half shell." Look the oysters over for bits of shell before you proceed with your recipe. (You may also encounter tiny transparent crabs—very much alive—inside the oyster shell!) Incidentally, oysters are not dangerous to eat during the months without an R; they *can* be eaten in the middle of summer. But eastern oysters spawn in the R-less months and are therefore weaker, thinner. Spawning often continues through a warm SeptembeR, too, but a good oyster is good any time.

Dutch Oysters

Dry oysters well, then roll them in beaten egg yolk, dip them in bread crumbs, salt and pepper them. Let them stand half an hour, if you have time, so the breading will adhere better. Then fry them in butter. Service with melted butter on the side.

Oysters Mignonette

Put fresh-shelled oysters without liquor in bowls surrounded by fine ice. Serve with this Mignonette sauce: 1½ teaspoons cracked white peppercorns, ¼ cup each of vinegar, fresh lemon juice, dry white wine. Add 1 scant tablespoon grated onion pulp, 2 teaspoons finely chopped chives, 1 teaspoon fresh-grated horse-radish, salt to taste. Blend and chill half hour before using.

Moules Mariniere for Mussels

For 6, wash and brush thoroughly 6 dozen medium-sized mussels, pulling off all the seaweed. Better use a scrubbing brush. Put them in a large saucepan or soup kettle. Add: 1 pint good dry white wine, ¼ pound sweet butter, 8 chopped shallots (or 2 large onions, cut in half so they can be removed before serving), a pinch of salt and your favorite herbs: parsley and chives for a start. Cover the pan closely and cook until all the mussels have opened, usually about 10 or 15 minutes. Remove the mussels and keep hot in soup plates. Reduce the remaining liquid to about half its volume by boiling. Now, you may:

    ... serve as is, pouring the liquid over the mussels

    ... add a little lemon juice and pour liquid over mussels

    ... add a pint of cream and serve as soon as the cream is hot

    ... add a lump of butter and a ladle of Hollandaise sauce, mix with a beater, season to taste, and pour over the mussels.

Shrimp. When a shrimp tastes tough and leathery, chances are it's been overcooked. Cook a shrimp a bare 2 minutes if you are going to give it further cooking in a sauce or casserole; don't precook it at all if you're going to bake, broil, or fry it. Five to 10 minutes cooking, depending on the shrimp's size, should do it for shrimp that you'll use without further cooking or heating. The shrimp is done when it's pink, opaque, and firm.

Experiment a little to find out which basic method of shrimp-cooking you prefer.

Boiling? Cook up a pot of water or stock containing flavoring materials—lemon or vinegar, onion, garlic, bay leaf, celery, salt, and pepper. Use only enough water to cover the shrimp; let the liquid take on flavor through boiling for 15 minutes before the shrimp go in. Then drop in the washed shrimp, shelled or unshelled, and simmer covered until the shrimp are pink. Remove shrimp from liquid immediately or they'll go on cooking.

Steaming? Put shrimp on a rack over boiling water and cook them covered for a few minutes.

Baking? Lay shrimp in a single layer in buttered pan, season, dot with butter. Pour in just enough liquid to cover the bottom of the pan and bake for 15 minutes in a moderate (350-degree) oven.

Broiling? Same preparation as for baking, but no liquid. Broil 5 minutes or so, about 3 inches from a moderate flame or 6 inches from a very hot broiler.

Frying? For deep-fat frying, coat the shrimp with a batter. The batter will stick better if you chill the shrimp for half an hour after coating. Heat to 350 degrees enough fat to submerge the shrimps. Fry the shrimp a few at a time, so as not to cool the fat, for about 3 minutes, or until brown. For skillet frying, use just enough fat to cover the bottom of the frying pan; heat it to the smoking point. Fry the shrimp, stirring and turning often, for about 5 minutes.

Galley Cleanup Tricks

If it's true that pride strides the quarterdeck, it should be true that an equal pride will prevail in the galley and that all cooking equipment be in top condition at all times. All cast iron or steel (except stainless steel) pots, pans or utensils should be thoroughly dried after washing. Cast iron frying pans should be lightly rubbed all over with a rag moistened with vegetable oil to prevent rust during those frequent periods of non-use when the boat lies in her slip unattended. Some cooks prefer the old fashioned cast iron frying pans and stewing pots simply because they are heavy enough to stay put in all but real rough weather, durable enough to outlast the cook and dependable for first rate cooking. Today, of course, cooking pots, frying pans, and griddles are available in a wide variety of styles; inexpensive aluminum cookware is fine because of resistance to corrosion at one end of the scale; copper-bottomed stainless steel is the deluxe end. Incidentally the latter can be polished with a slice of lemon and salt.

Dishwashing aboard is a job that can be done with a minimum use of fresh water (always desirable aboard a boat) and a minimum amount of drain-clogging left-overs in the dish-water by the simple expedient of scraping all plates and pans before washing them. In this regard, an ordinary ten-cent-store, rubber plate-scraper is an invaluable tool.

Whatever amount of dishwater is used, it should be boiling hot. Scraped dishes and silver-ware should be placed in the galley sink and an appropriate amount of detergent added before the boiling water is poured into the sink. This will greatly reduce the actual washing job since the combination of boiling water and detergent will remove most grease and will effectively sterilize all tableware.

A second pan of hot water should be placed nearby to use as rinse water before draining dishes and tableware. A wooden-handled dish-mop will serve to keep the hands out of hot water and will greatly speed the chore itself. All dishes, pots, pans and flatware should be thoroughly rinsed before drying to prevent a detergent haze forming, which, though harmless, is not in keeping with a well-run galley.

Allowing all kitchenware to drain before being dried reduces the use of dish towels and the accompanying hazard of handling slippery equipment. A dish-draining trick: use a tray, and one of the rubber-coated storage racks (Rubbermaid has an excellent small one). Larger drain racks take up too much space.

A plastic garbage can, with a tight lid, is a good way to cope with garbage and wrapped refuse. But, there are few irritants that can stall a master cook quicker than being in the middle of preparing a feast only to find the garbage can full to overflowing—it being unthinkable to wade astern through the guests, toting a pail full of unlovely trimmings, onion skins, potato-peels, and perhaps the shells off a batch of steamed shrimp. One answer to this problem is to make sure before beginning a meal that all garbage containers are empty. Secondly, have on hand in the pot-and-pan locker at least one outsized pot with a lid on it. This will serve as an extra container for those odd times when the trimmings seem larger than the meal itself.

THE COCKTAIL FLAG IS FLYING

Many a mediocre cook has risen to fame through the simple but marvelously effective expedient of serving cocktails prior to sounding the dinner gong. In addition cocktails afloat have special meaning. When your yacht flies the cocktail flag while in a strange anchorage, fellow yachtsmen will raft alongside, and you'll make new acquaintances. Fly it when cruising with a group from your yacht club, or in home waters, you'll make better friends.

But just as good cooking afloat requires that certain ground rules be observed, so are there right and wrong ways of serving good cocktails. The following should be kept in mind:

    1. Always use a jigger (1½ ounces) to measure liquor, while a dash equals 6 to 8 drops. Follow exact measurements in recipes. Too much of any one ingredient can ruin the flavor of your drinks.

2. Although ice is generally scarce, never stint on it; use lots of it in your drinks. Because cocktail parties are held only when you're docked or tied up at a mooring or when anchored—or at least, they should be—it's often possible to get ashore and get an extra supply of ice. For this purpose, it's a good idea to carry an insulated bag aboard. Sometimes your dockmaster or yacht club steward can have ice cubes or a chunk of ice delivered to your yacht. Remember that ice is the bartender's best friend. In a Martini or Manhattan, for example, it's the chilling and slight dilution contributed by the ice that makes a smooth drink.

3. Use shaved ice for drinks to be sipped through a straw; cubed ice for highballs and the Old Fashioned; cracked ice for the in-between. (If you don't have an ice crusher aboard, use a cloth bag and mallet or buy cracked ice along with the shaved ice.) Drinks go flat from excessive dilution; don't let them stand too long with ice. Remember also, that nothing absorbs odors more readily than ice in the making. If exposed to foreign odors while being frozen, cubes will transfer these odors to the drinks. Ice should be clear, hard frozen, taste-free.

4. Shake all cocktails that contain fruit juices, eggs, cream or any other ingredients difficult to blend. Others should be stirred. The length of time a drink is stirred is important, too. Too much dilutes the drink or if a carbonated drink, it makes it go flat more quickly; too little fails to mix and properly chill the ingredients. Cocktails that require shaking should come out creamy, so shake well.

5. In mixing drinks, put in the less costly ingredients first—thus if you make a mistake you can start again with a minimum of loss. Also, for the sake of chemistry, when mixing drinks containing fruit juices, and/or sweetening, always pour the spirits last. Sugar always goes into the shaker before the liquor. Always use fine granulated sugar to avoid caking, and to insure thorough dilution. Don't use confectioners' sugar.

6. Cocktails taste better in chilled glasses. Therefore, if at all possible, chill the glasses in the refrigerator or ice box, or bury them in crushed or shaved ice just before using. Keep unused, empty glasses right-side up. Otherwise, soap fumes, which can be retained after washing, may ruin the drink's flavor. Rub the top edge of bottles with waxed paper when you open them, to prevent dripping. When opening soda, tilt bottle to conserve the sparkle. Some skippers pre-chill the liquor, too.

7. During a cocktail party afloat, the average guest will consume three drinks in the one and a quarter hours that he or she is present. For every six people invited, one fifth of gin or whiskey will vanish (seven people will consume a quart).

8. In order to accommodate requests for Martinis and Manhattans, have one bottle of French (dry) Vermouth on hand for every three bottles of gin; one bottle of Italian (sweet) vermouth for every three bottles of whiskey. *Remember this*—don't limit your cocktail party to Martinis and Manhattans only. Many people prefer whiskey on-the-rocks, highballs long or short, etc.

Here are some of the time-tested recipes for some of the more popular drinks:

Manhattan
To a mixture of one-third Italian vermouth and two-thirds blended whiskey, add one dash of bitters. Stir in cocktail shaker with cracked (not crushed) ice and strain into glasses. Add cherry.

Old Fashioned
One-half lump of sugar, 2 dashes of bitters, one teaspoon of water. Muddle thoroughly to dissolve the sugar, then add one jigger of blended whiskey, ice cubes. Stir a few times and decorate with half orange slice and cherry.

Martini
The standard formula for dry martinis is known as the "one-to-four" mix, meaning, one part French vermouth to four parts of gin. This proportion should be stirred in a cocktail shaker with cracked (not crushed) ice and strained in cocktail glasses. Serve with olive, or lemon twist.

Daiquiri
To one jigger of rum add the juice of one half a lime and one teaspoon of sugar. Shake well with cracked (not crushed) ice and strain into martini glass.

Orange Blossom
This is best enjoyed when the mixture is 50-50, half orange juice and half gin stirred with cracked ice and strained into martini glasses.

Highballs
In a highball glass, pour one jigger of whiskey over cubed ice and fill with club soda, ginger ale, or plain water.

Screwdriver
Place two ice cubes in 6-oz. glass; pour in one jigger of vodka, add orange juice, and stir.

Gin 'n Tonic
Squeeze the juice of a ¼ of a lime over ice cubes in 8-oz. glass; add rind of lime, one jigger of gin (or vodka or tequila), and fill with tonic (quinine water), stir.

Tom Collins
Put the juice of one lemon, a teaspoon of sugar and one jigger of gin (or whiskey) into a cocktail shaker filled with cracked ice. Shake well and strain over cubed ice in 10-oz. highball glass. Fill with club soda and decorate with cherry.

Whiskey Sour
Put one jigger whiskey, ½ jigger of lemon juice, a good ½ teaspoon sugar into a cocktail shaker with cracked ice. Shake well and strain into sour glass. Garnish with slice of orange and cherry.

Bloody Mary
Add one jigger vodka, two jiggers tomato juice, ⅓ jigger lemon juice and a dash Worcestershire sauce. Salt and pepper to taste. Shake with cracked ice and strain in 6-oz. glass.

Rob Roy
Mix ½ jigger Italian vermouth, one jigger Scotch and a dash of bitters, and stir with cracked ice. Strain and serve with twist of lemon peel.

Cuba Libre
Squeeze the juice from ½ a lime over ice cubes in a tall glass and add the rind. Put in 1½ jiggers of rum, fill with cola and stir.

Hot Toddy
Place one lump of sugar, two cloves and one jigger of blended whiskey in a toddy glass or cup. When sugar has begun to dissolve, pour in hot water while stirring. Serve hot.

Many cocktail drinks are available at your local liquor dealer in already prepared form. To serve, only the ice has to be added. A bottle or so of these ready-mixed cocktails are handy to have aboard when friends tie alongside unexpectedly. There are, of course, the new instant cocktails. To use, just take an individual service packet of one of these cocktail mixes, add the proper amount of the appropriate spirit, and you can serve up to order (and in seconds) your guests' choice of four instant cocktails—Manhattan, Whiskey Sour, Daiquiri, or Martini.

Cocktail supplies—including the liquor, wine, soda, etc.—are usually in glass containers and must be stowed carefully so that they don't break. The easiest way to handle this is to build a special wine and liquor locker in the bilge of the yacht. Such a locker has two major advantages: (1) it doesn't take space from the galley chief, and (2) it keeps wines at a good drinking temperature. The locker can be made with compartments so that the bottles can't rattle or move about.

With the cocktail flag flying, snacks and appetizers are appropriate. Pretzels, potato chips and peanuts are always good to have on board. Miniature shrimp, cheeses, canned smoked oysters, and raw vegetables—cucumber slices, carrot sticks, radishes, cauliflowerettes— are also worth trying. Generally, this finger food should be very simple and made from ingredients that are easy to stow. But just as it's important to plan your meals afloat in advance, so it's wise to plan for cocktail parties while anchored or tied up in a harbor.

YACHTING ETIQUETTE

A great many of our yachting customs—and even some of the rules of etiquette of the sea—are rather meaningless in this new age of the sail because they have been handed down to us by older generations who lived at different times and sailed under different conditions. But, one of the first things you'll learn about sailing is that while we're in the new age of sailing, our sport is steeped in tradition. It is this tradition that has set aside the yachtsman from the rest of his fellow man. (Remember that you don't have to be a member of a yacht club to be a yachtsman. It is your actions in observing the customs and etiquette that have been set down that stamp you as one.) Thus, as you go afloat, you carry with you the reputation of your fellow yachtsmen. It's a most precious charge and one that must be safeguarded.

To be rated a 100 per cent yachtsman—in other words, a "seasoned skipper"—the owner or captain of a boat should know the proper etiquette of the various flags, what they mean, and how to fly them. In this connection, it has always been our feeling that most yachtsmen would gladly comply with the protocol associated with the display of flags if they understood it. In addition, there's no doubt but that flags make for a yachty appearance.

Flags. The ensign may be either the conventional fifty-star, thirteen-stripe American flag or it may be the special yacht ensign with the thirteen red and white stripes of the American flag and a fouled anchor encircled by thirteen stars. When a sailboat is underway, fly either ensign at the leech of the mainsail, or when there's more than one mast, at the leech of the aftermost sail, approximately two-thirds the length of the leech above the clew. Under power alone, or when at anchor or made fast, the ensign should be flown from the stern staff of all sailboats. On powerboats, the ensign is also flown from the stern staff. The ensign should be flown from morning to evening.

The club burgee is usually triangular in shape, but sometimes may be swallow-tailed. It is never proper to fly the burgee of more than one yacht club at a time. On any two-masted sailing craft the burgee is carried on the foremost mast and the private sign at the aftermost mast. For example, in a yawl, the burgee would be displayed at the mainmast and the private signal from the mizzenmast. On a sloop, a burgee is displayed at the mainmast when at anchor; the private signal is flown at the mainmast while under way. On power-boats the burgee is flown from the bow staff. In the case of both sail and powerboat, the burgee is normally displayed from morning to evening colors.

The owner's private signal, sometimes called the house flag, is usually swallowtail, some-times rectangular. Any yacht owner, whether or not he is a member of a yacht club, may design and carry a private signal, and have that signal registered in *Lloyd's Register of American Yachts*. If you don't have a private signal and wish to design one, obtain a copy of *Lloyd's Register* and check to see if any of the flags illustrated therein resemble too closely the design you have in mind. Since the basic purpose of the signal is to identify your boat, it should be as simple as possible so that it may be recognized easily at sea. This means that it is best to stick to a simple design, employing no more than three colors. The traditional colors used are dark blue, red, and white. The owner's private signal flag is flown from morning to evening colors. On sailing craft the private signal is flown at the main or aftermost truck, while on a power vessel from the masthead.

The flag officer's flag is rectangular, blue with a white design for a commodore; red with a white design for a vice-commodore; and white with a red design for a rear commodore. This flag replaces the private signal when it can be properly flown. In cases where the private signal can't be flown, such as a sloop under way, the flag officer's flag replaces the burgee. A flag officer never flies his private signal because he and his vessel now represent his club and not an individual. And when he pays an official call on another yacht whose owner belongs to the same club, then this owner should replace the club burgee with the flag officer's flag.

A fleet captain's flag may be displayed at the bow staff of a small boat from morning to evening colors when this officer is executing his official duties. Yacht routine regarding the fleet captain's flag may vary with the individual yacht clubs.

The absentee flag is a rectangular blue flag which is displayed from sunrise to sunset when the yacht owner isn't aboard. It is carried from the starboard main spreader of a sailboat or the starboard yardarm of a power craft, and is hoisted the minute the owner steps off the boat, and is kept flying until his return. The purpose of the absentee flag, of course, is to save a fellow yachtsman the long journey out to the boat to see the owner, when the owner isn't on board. It is part of the yachting tradition to lower away the absent flag the moment the owner comes on board and to hoist it smartly the minute he goes over the side.

The guest flag is a rectangular blue flag with a white diagonal stripe which is displayed when the yacht owner is absent but his guests are aboard. It is carried in the same manner as the absentee flag, but is displayed when under way as well as at anchor.

The owner's meal flag is a rectangular white flag which is displayed when the owner and his guests are at meals. It is carried in the same manner as the absentee flag, but only when the yacht is at anchor.

The crew's meal pennant is red and is displayed when the professional crew (or paid hands) are at meals. It is carried when at anchor from sunrise to sundown at the foremost port spreader of a sailboat or the port yardarm of a power craft.

The nighthawk or wind pennant is a blue pennant which is displayed at the mainmast from evening to morning colors, or at other times when no other flags are flown.

The United States Power Squadron flag with its thirteen vertical stripes may be carried as an ensign on yachts owned by members of this organization. If the national or yacht ensign is flown, then the USPS flag is flown from the main starboard spreader of a sailboat or the starboard yardarm of a power craft, except when the absent, owner's meal, or guest flags are flown.

Making Colors. This refers to the ceremony of hoisting or lowering flags. Morning colors are made at 8 A.M., evening colors are made at sunset. Time should be taken from the senior officer present. When in company of the United States Navy or Coast Guard, or a shore station of these services, or in the home anchorage of another yacht's club, time should be taken from such vessel, station, or club. In making colors, a yacht always represents the rank of her owner, whether he is aboard or not. Also remember, when making colors, that all flags should be hoisted at the same time. When this isn't feasible, the ensign should be hoisted first, followed as rapidly as possible by the burgee and the private signal. Flags are lowered in inverse order. Colors should be hoisted smartly but lowered ceremoniously. Flag officers' flags normally carried night and day may be lowered and hoisted at colors. The nighthawk is hoisted at evening colors.

Half-Masting Flags. The ensign is half-masted only on occasion of national mourning. On Memorial Day, the ensign is half-masted from morning colors to noon. On the death of a yacht club member, the burgee and private signal only are half-masted on his yacht. The yacht club may also order mourning for a member, in which case the club, other members' yachts at anchor, and other stations should half-mast the burgee only. Custom dictates that such burgees be two-blocked after the funeral ceremonies. The owner's private signal and burgee are lowered and not rehoisted. If not previously hoisted, flags should be mastheaded and then lowered. Before lowering from half-mast, the flag should be first mastheaded, then lowered.

Flag Salutes. This is one tradition that has been almost completely lost, and one that would add immeasurably to the color of the modern yachting scene. All the following salutes are made by dipping the ensign once. The ensign should be lowered to the dip and hoisted when the salute is returned.

Vessels of the United States and foreign navies should be saluted. When a yacht in which a flag officer is embarked comes to anchor, all yachts should salute, except where a senior officer is present. Also, when a yacht comes to anchor where a flag officer is present, such flag officer should be saluted. A junior officer anchoring in the presence of a senior should salute, and the salute should be returned by the senior only. Yachts passing each other should salute, the junior saluting first. The ensign should be held at the dip until the yachts pass clear. All salutes should be returned in kind. On yachts displaying no ensign, or displaying an ensign which can't be dipped, the owner renders and returns salutes by doffing hat or cap.

Guns may be fired to call attention to signals, but their use should be avoided as much as possible. Guns should never be fired on Sunday. Whistles are never used in saluting.

Lights. In addition to navigating lights that must be displayed by law from sunset to sunrise, the following lights may be carried from sunset to sunrise while at anchor to conform with yacht routine: Flag officers may display two lights, arranged vertically, in the same position at which the absentee flag is flown during the day. The commodore's lights should be blue; the vice-commodore's lights should be red; the rear commodore's lights should be white. A single blue light may be displayed in the same way when an owner isn't aboard. A white light may be displayed in the same way when the owner is at meals.

The Ship's Bell. It is perfectly proper to strike ship's bells every half hour while at anchor. It's by no means necessary to do this, but it is a very pleasant habit and should be encouraged. The time for the ship's bells should be taken from the senior boat in port just as the time is taken for colors.

A clock with ship's bells is an expensive item which many don't wish to acquire, but such a clock is found on many boats and in most yacht clubs. The meaning of the bells should be part of any yachtsman's vocabulary. The custom of telling time in this manner is one of the oldest traditions associated with the sea. Men aboard the naval and commercial vessels of long ago stood four-hour watches or turns of duty exactly as they do today. The first watch is from 8 P.M. to midnight, the midwatch from midnight to 4 A.M., the morning watch from 4 A.M. to 8 A.M., the forenoon watch from 8 A.M. to noon, the afternoon watch from noon to 4 P.M., and the dog watch from 4 P.M. to 8 P.M. The first half hour of each watch is designated by one bell, the second half hour, or first hour, by two bells, and so on. Thus one bell is rung at 12:30, 4:30, and 8:30, both A.M. and P.M.; two bells at 1:00, 5:00, and 9:00; three bells at 1:30, 5:30, and 9:30, and so on. Bells are struck in groups of two; thus 6:30 would be ding-ding, ding-ding, ding.

Bell Strokes	Clock Time		
1	4:30	8:30	12:30
2	5:00	9:00	1:00
3	5:30	9:30	1:30
4	6:00	10:00	2:00
5	6:30	10:30	2:30
6	7:00	11:00	3:00
7	7:30	11:30	3:30
8	8:00	12:00	4:00

In most instances in this book, as above, we have been guilty of using the landlubber's time system rather than the naval system, which is employed by most yachtsmen afloat. In the naval timekeeping system the hours begin with zero at midnight and run through 23. Thus 6:30 A.M. is simply 0630; noon is 1200; and 6:30 P.M. is 1830.

Good Manners Afloat

Everett A. Pearson of the Pearson Yacht Company lists the following points of etiquette and good manners afloat in his book, *The Lure of Sailing*, that immediately indicate a good yachtsman:

> 1. Never wait until the last minute to make clear your intentions of obeying Rules of the Road. Even when aboard sailboat and you have the right-of-way over powerboats, don't abuse this right by forcing them into a dangerous situation. Also, in the case of sailboats, never wait until the last minute to make clear your intentions of obeying the Rules of the Road.

2. Try to anchor clear of lines of traffic and outside of narrow channels. If forced to anchor in a narrow channel, take extra precautions should the tide or wind change. It's always best to anchor in an authorized anchorage or select an anchorage which allows room to swing without fouling other vessels already anchored. Always ask permission before picking up a buoy that doesn't belong to you. When sailing in a harbor, never have your tender on too long a line.

3. Navigate with care on well-known fishing grounds and keep well clear of fishing vessels. Don't run over fishing stakes or buoys.

4. Don't pass a vessel in distress. When you go out in your yacht, be on the alert and receptive to possible distress signals. In the case of small boats, it's a good idea to investigate any irregular motion or activity. It is better to know that you haven't passed up someone in trouble. Also, during the summertime most sailing areas are infested with young sailors who are attempting to learn our sport. Often they may be headed for trouble without knowing it, and it is your duty, as a yachtsman, to give them a word of advice or a helping hand. Remember that it's a tradition as old as the sea itself that mariners always go to the aid of those in distress.

5. Don't tie up to government buoys, or local navigation markers, except in emergencies. Actually, the law forbids any person to interfere with, remove, move, make fast to, or willfully damage any aid to navigation maintained or authorized by the Coast Guard. Violation of this law subjects that person to a fine up to $500.

6. Don't throw garbage or refuse overboard in harbors, or near beaches, or in lakes used for drinking-water supply. (Use shore disposal facilities.) Never throw cans overboard, even in open water, unless punctured at both ends so they'll sink.

7. Always be on the alert when passing dredges where divers may be at work and keep away from areas indicated by the skin diver's flag.

8. Never land at a private dock or float without invitation, except in an emergency. If your yacht is berthed in a marina or yacht club, other members have equal rights with you, so don't interfere with their berthing spaces. When visiting another yacht club, pull up to the dock or float and inquire as to where you might moor your boat so that you're certain you don't interfere with some regular member's berth. Then properly moor your craft before going ashore. Avoid tying up across club floats. And when anchoring for a swim, or using the bathing facilities of a club, do so quietly, without screams or roughhouse.

9. Don't stare at other yachting parties or into cabins as you pass. If you see a beautiful yacht and wish to look her over, you may do so, but avoid being obvious about it.

10. Never anchor on top of another boat unless there is a good reason for such action. Don't caterwaul or permit your children to do so, and be sure not to keep your radio or phonograph going late into the night on quiet evenings in crowded harbors.

11. Always talk to other yachtsmen. Remember there is no snobbishness about our sport. Always greet other yachtsmen—and landlubbers, too—with a wave of the hand or a cheery "good day." Wish them luck and exchange opinions about the weather. To get the most fun from sailing you must enter into the camaraderie of the sport.

12. Never presume upon the courtesy of yacht clubs, unless invited, or unless they exchange courtesies with your club. If you desire to use the club facilities, inquire first of the steward or attendant as to the club rules and regulations. When you're coming in as a guest at a strange sailing club or yacht club, act as a courteous guest. In general, yachtsmen are quiet, gentlemanly folk. They don't call attention to themselves by loudness or rowdiness. Therefore, it's best not to make yourself obnoxious by being demanding, because even if their courtesy gains the upper hand and you are served as you wish, it will mark you for any future time you may wish to take advantage of the facilities offered by that club.

13. Visiting between yachts that are anchored within easy reach of one another is a common practice. But, there is a ritual to be observed about visiting. Never board another boat without a distinct invitation from the owner. If you don't know the skipper get close enough to his yacht and engage him in conversation, but don't attempt to board until he asks you. Never stay if you're interrupting the work of the vessel.

14. When you anchor in a small port, make friends with the local natives. Greet and talk with them while ashore. Their customs and manners are a great deal different from the people of a large city, who make it a rule never to speak to strangers.

15. Don't give uncalled-for advice while a guest on someone else's yacht. Take your orders from the skipper and never try to interfere with the way in which he handles his craft. Courtesy and common sense are the basis of yachting etiquette. If this is kept in mind, the sailor is well on his way to becoming a true yachtsman.

CHAPTER SIX:
BOATING SPORTS

Owning a yacht in any section of our country can extend anyone's enjoyment of water sports immeasurably. The fun of boating can add exciting new horizons to fishing, swimming, photography, skin diving and racing. Each of these can be done better with a boat, and some sports like water skiing can't very well be accomplished without some type of craft.

FISHING

Fishing up to a few years ago was the only reason an average man owned a boat. It is still the most popular of all boating water sports. But fishing falls into various categories. Fortunately, there is almost one for everybody. Yours might be the relaxed angler on a quiet inland waterway content to break the stillness occasionally by catching a flounder, or at the other extreme your meat may be battling a big game fish for hours. If you're in the latter category, the chances are that you've purchased a boat with a fly bridge, built-in bait boxes, outriggers, plus the other fishing gear that comes with a real fishing craft. However, part-time fishing is important. A few hours spent participating in this sport will relax the whole crew and may give everybody a good meal or two. Remember that even though you may not be an enthusiast, having enough tackle—even for your guests—and knowing how to catch a fresh dinner will offset the added room the gear takes on your cruiser. Incidentally, the easiest way to stow rods when not in use is to install rod holders. There are available several types of holders that can be placed along the sides of the cockpit or hung overhead in the cabin. Install a sufficient number for your rods and those of possible guests, with a couple extra. But, before doing any fishing in a given area, check local fishing regulations, and purchase a license if one is required.

Using the Depth Sounder

Saltwater gamefish are broadly divided into two types—pelagic fish such as the tunas, sailfish and marlin which wander open seas—and inshore species such as the flounder, weakfish, snook, snapper, and hundreds of other varieties that frequent coastal areas. It is the latter group which comes under the eye of the depth sounder.

Usually saltwater fish have exacting habitat requirements which vary slightly according to the season and geographical location. However, for all practical purposes these conditions are inflexible. In warm oceans, for instance, all kinds of snappers can be found on coral reefs. Such reefs may appear as "heads" or tables in surrounding deep water, or they may appear as drop-offs from long shallow areas. Barracuda and groupers are also reef dwellers and thus coral, which reflects a sharp signal, is an easily located fish factory. Northern anglers harvest big sea bass and tautog (blackfish) on rock and shell beds, while winter and summer flounders are hooked from mud bottoms. Thus the extremes in signal width indicate feeding grounds as well. In common with the black bass of freshwater, striped bass and channel bass forage along inshore trenches or gullies in comparatively shallow areas. These hotspots are easy to locate in any surf by the drop-and-rise reading on your depth finder.

Shipwrecks, which have their own peculiar kind of signal, depending on the construction and size of the remaining hull, are guaranteed to produce fish. You can find the general location of wrecks on nautical charts and pinpoint them with your depth finder. Although wrecks are marked (usually with a cylindrical or conical buoy showing horizontal red and black bands) if they are dangerous to shipping, the great majority along all coasts can only be located with a depth sounder. Gamefish find an abundance of crustaceans and forage fish living in wrecks, and as a result, broken hulls along the 10 to 20 fathom curve have built the reputation of many party boat skippers.

Although experienced yachtsmen rely on depth finders to follow fog-bound channels or to traverse unmarked waters, the precise location of channels is also valuable angling knowledge. Those species which invade the tide flats during high water periods such as flounder, whiting, pompano, ladyfish, and tarpon, will move back to the *edge* of a channel during low water. Channel edges are seldom clearly defined and a familiarity with navigation isn't enough to locate say, a lunker tarpon, when drift-fishing between buoys. Naturally, the main channel will at times hold large schools of fish, and generally the holes on saltwater flats provide cover for bluefish, spotted weakfish, snook, and redfish.

In freshwater, there's no absolute rule concerning the depth distribution of fish. Much depends on the water temperature, the type of bottom, chemical conditions of the lake, and the availability of food. When the ice is breaking up in the springtime, for instance, any of the *salmonoids* can be caught directly at the surface. But this is a transitory period of short duration. As soon as the water begins to warm, all trout and salmon go deep. Broadly speaking, in a large lake (one having thermally stratified water), sunfish, chain

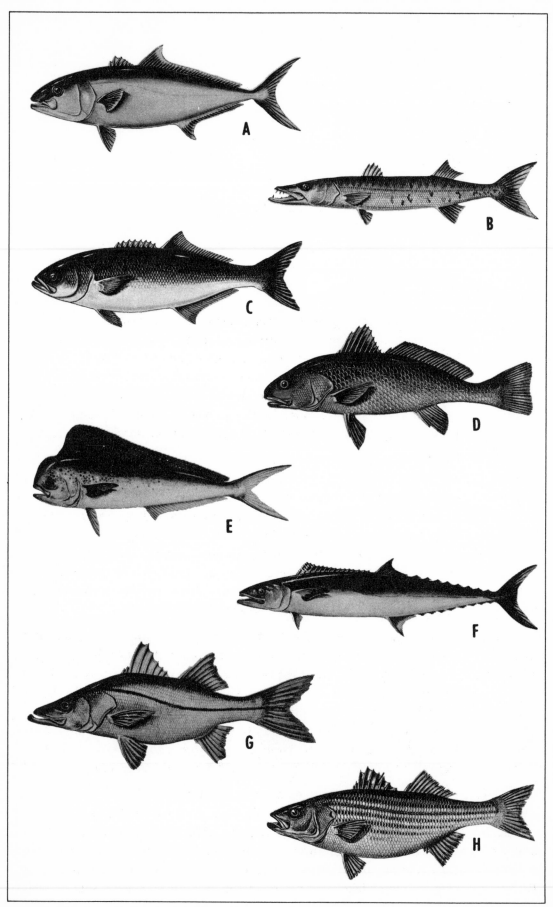

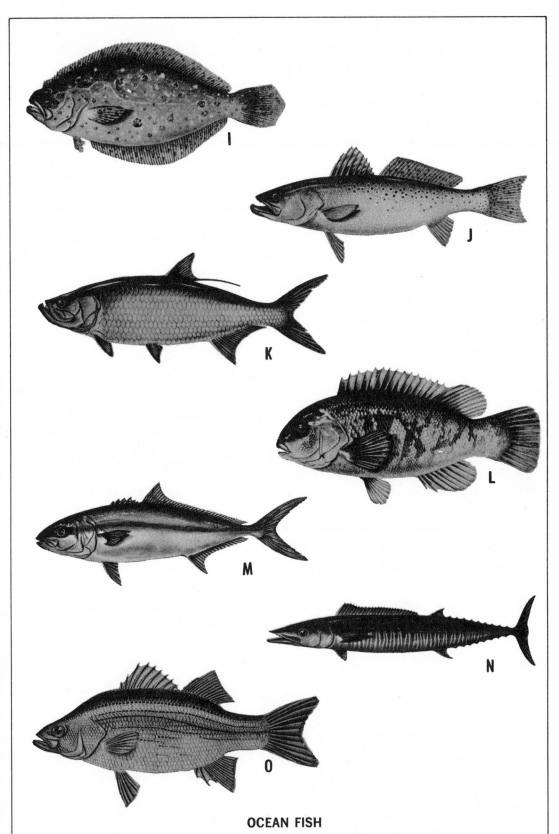

OCEAN FISH
A. Amberjack. B. Barracuda. C. Bluefish. D. Channel Bass. E. Dolphin. F. King Mackerel.
G. Snook. H. Striped Bass. I. Summer Flounder. J. Spotted Weakfish. K. Tarpon. L. Tautog.
M. Yellowtail (Calif.). N. Wahoo. O. White Bass.

pickerel, crappie, and northern pike will be found to depths of 10 feet. Young largemouth bass inhabit the same zone, but old lunkers will be on the slopes and in the holes between 10 and 30 feet down. Large northern pike and muskellunge are usually at the lunker bass level also. Walleyes, white perch, and smallmouth bass range between 15 and 35 feet, but they migrate shoreward toward evening. Rainbow trout invade the 35 foot level and also follow the brook and brown trout. Landlocked salmon, kokanee, and whitefish are found down to 40 feet or more below the surface. Lake trout and sturgeon are really deep— anywhere from 40 to 150 feet or more below the surface. Using these figures as a general guide, the depth sounder echoes absolute information to evaluate. On a strange lake, that can make the difference between success and failure.

Fishing Techniques

Most salt-water anglers caught their first fish by bottom fishing, as salt-water still-fishing is generally called, and the majority of these anglers continue to do so. They probably outnumber all the other types of salt-water anglers combined.

The tackle you use in bottom fishing varies, and includes anything from hand lines, bait-casting and spinning gear to elaborate and expensive big-game tackle. Most bottom-anglers use boat rods which usually come in two sections, although some are one-piece outfits. They run from 5 feet, 2 inches to 6 feet, 6 inches in over-all length and are made of tubular glass. These are good for general all-around bottom fishing in deep water, and can be used in bays and around piers. The heavier trolling or big-game rods are also used occasionally in bottom fishing for big fish such as amberjack, jewfish, rays, and sharks.

The reels used with the boat rods just mentioned hold from 200 to 300 yards of line. A free-spool, star-drag model is easier to handle than a standard freshwater bait-casting reel. Of course, with the trolling or big-game rods, you will use large salt-water reels which match the rod and the fishing. Either braided nylon or squidding line, or monofilament with reels designed for it may be used. The size depends mostly on the fish you're after, the weight of the sinkers used, the depth of water and the obstructions you are likely to encounter.

Probably the most important item of tackle in bottom fishing is the hook. Although you can catch a wide variety of saltwater fish on one kind of hook, specific designs have been developed for individual species. Local fishing stations and tackle dealers in the area you plan to fish will be glad to advise you on the hooks most commonly used in the vicinity. They will also suggest the best rig arrangement and bait to use to catch the fish you wish.

Jigging. Jigging is a time-honored method of fishing for weakfish inshore. It also takes other species—mackerel, striped bass, ling, and bluefish. As a matter of fact, jigging for blues in fast rips is one of the most productive forms of bluefishing. In this method, regardless of the species, the quarry is located by drifting the boat over deep holes and channels. In inlets and shallow water, small metal jigs—1 ounce or less—with a high shine are baited with worms or a strip of squid, or are left bare. In deeper waters, a heavy diamond jig is required. The line is stripped off the reel until the lure reaches the bottom. Then, with the boat drifting, the lure is "jigged" so that it bounces or dances through the water in a skipping motion a few feet off the bottom. This is accomplished by raising and lowering your rod's tip.

If you get no strikes at this level, repeat the procedure, but this time do the jigging a few feet higher; continue moving upward in the water until you connect. Jigging is usually a blind operation, without recognizable signs of fish. Diving gulls and terns often point out schools off-shore, but the inshore fisherman must find his own targets. You will ultimately locate your quarry at whatever level they are feeding. Mark the spot where the first fish hits, and remember how much line was out. Return to the spot and anchor (this is a good idea whenever you are drifting), jig at the same depth, and the chances are you will be working in a school. Where there is one fish there are usually plenty more.

Trolling. You can do light trolling with bottle-fishing tackle, but these outfits are too light for many inshore or near-shore species. It is better to use a boat-fishing outfit which will handle anything likely to strike. Remember that some of those inshore fish put on real weight—tarpon frequently weigh more than 100 pounds, and 40- and 50-pound channel bass are fairly common. You will need equipment heavy enough to stand up under the fast trolling of fairly heavy lures, a strain that would be too much for bay equipment.

For this heavy trolling, your leader should be stainless-steel wire in the smaller diameters, which will have all the test that you need. If you want nylon leaders, probably 15 pounds will be as low as you can safely go if you are after a big fish, with 30- and 45-pound test the best if you are trolling fast and expecting to take fish of 25 pounds or more. The length of the leader should be at least 4 feet, but many fishermen prefer to use a 6-foot leader to provide a wider gap between the line and the lure. Of course, the end of the leader next to the line must have a single-barrel swivel; snap swivels are good, placed next to the lure so that you can change lures quickly and lose less fishing time. Don't make the leader so long that you can't reel your fish near enough to the boat to net or gaff it.

Trolling lures are legion. Spoons, spinners, feather jigs, barracudas, plugs, strip baits—these you will probably use most frequently. One of the surest ways to take striped bass is with a smooth-running spinner whose trailing hook is baited with sea worms. Trolled slowly this is hard to beat. It will take weakfish, blues, and many others. Use a piece of pork rind or a thin strip of fresh-cut squid if you are caught without worms.

Your trolling speed should conform to the lure you use. You will note that each lure has its own best speed which gives it the most lifelike action. As a rule, you should troll fast (five to six miles per hour) for eelskin rigs and nylon or feather jigs. You'll need that speed to make the lure wiggle in the water. Even then, working your rod tip up and down continually will give the lure extra dive and flutter. A good strip of cut bait will wiggle more slowly (three to five miles per hour) and is especially popular on the Florida inshore reefs. Many spoons like those used for fluke give their best action at slow speeds (one and one-half to three miles per hour).

It is impossible to cover all the various techniques of catching fresh-water fish, as well as specific saltwater species. We would suggest, therefore, your reading a book or two on the subject of fishing such as the *Esquire's Book of Fishing.*

Crabbing and Clamming
If good eating is your hobby, then you'll want to do some crabbing and clamming. You'll find clams in the mud flats of sheltered shallow bays, in gravel-filled pockets in the rocks on tide-ripped headlands, or in the hard packed sands of our ocean beaches. Not only do the different varieties of clams live in different locations, but clam beds are not static. Populations may be decreased as a result of one digging; and clams often disappear in

173

unexplained cycles. Best sources of information on clamming areas along our coasts are the state fish and game departments. Local wardens, who patrol the coast, can give you more specific locations, proper clamming times, and the best digging technique, as can most local chambers of commerce. In popular clam areas, recipes that you should try with your freshly dug clams are usually available.

Good crabbing waters usually have rather definite characteristics. Look for a quiet bay or an open stretch of water with a gradually sloping bottom of clean sand or fine gravel. (Skip the place if fresh water or industrial waste empties into it.) The equipment used may vary from collapsible crab traps, scap nets, or simply lines for wading out to bottom grasses in your search for crabs. A spading fork or pitchfork, with the tines blunted with tape or rubber tubing, may be used to catch them in the latter method. But whether you use a trap, scap net, line, or fork, keep the crabs you catch in a large bucket of water. They'll scuttle off to one side, but they make no great effort to escape. How to prepare crabs and clams for eating can be found on page 155. But before you catch some nice fresh crabs, or dig clams, check for any local legal restrictions as to size and number, and also make sure no license is required.

PHOTOGRAPHY AFLOAT

The chances are that, if you aren't a camera fan already, yachting will make you one because owning a boat and taking photographs just naturally go hand in hand; for taking shots of your own craft to show to others; for keeping a picture record of a cruise; for snapping the often breathtakingly beautiful scenes you keep seeing on the water. But a few pointers about boating photography may be in order, even for the expert cameraman. Some are simple, common-sense precautions for the protection of equipment afloat. Others are related to lighting and picture composition situations that are peculiar to boating.

Photo Equipment

With more than a thousand different camera models now available to the public, which should you choose? This is a weighty problem, and your selection depends upon the use to which the camera will be put and the amount you can afford to pay. Of course, on a boat there is almost always motion. For this reason you should have a camera equipped with a shutter capable of speeds of at least 1/200 second or more. Usually cameras of this kind have fast lenses, a combination that costs somewhat more than a box Brownie. For average outdoor use, don't get a lens slower than $f/4.5$, and $f/3.5$ is even better. Big lenses are not essential, since some of your finest and sharpest pictures will be taken with apertures cut down to $f/11$ or $f/16$.

We recommend a camera no larger than 2½-inch square size (using 120 film) and not smaller than 35 mm. To many yachtsmen, 35 mm is the answer, since film costs are low and many pictures can be exposed with a single loading. A wide choice of 35 mm in color and black-and-white is available in this size. Because of the tiny frame, 35 mm negatives must be fine-grain developed and handled with care, since fingerprints, scratches, cinch marks and lint will show up prominently on enlargement. If you plan to shoot only color, 35 mm is ideal for a boating slide presentation.

If you have never enjoyed the thrill of composing your scenes on a ground-glass focusing screen before clicking the shutter, try one of the 2½ by 2½-inch size reflex cameras. This may be a dual-lens outfit in which sighting is done with the upper finder lens, or a single-lens reflex which permits sighting through the taking lens up to the moment of shutter-clicking.

Every boating camera should have a medium yellow filter to enhance sky, clouds, and water, rendering artistic effects. For color film, no filter will be required most of the time except on extremely clear days when the sky is a deep blue almost to the horizon. Then a skylight filter will help prevent an excessive bluish cast. A polarization filter will help darken the sky for better contrast between sails and background on a slightly hazy day. It also makes objects under the water's surface clear from above. Filters may be of the screw-on or slip-on type, and adapter rings are available to fit most any camera lens. In color photography, the polarizing filter is recommended for contrast.

One accessory every yachtsman should own is a lens shade to keep the glare out of the camera eye, thus insuring sharper photographs. For those who like compactness, there are collapsible lens shades to fit the skipper's pocket.

If you have difficulty judging available light or reading exposure guides and charts, an exposure meter may help to solve your problems. Today many movie and still outfits have tiny photoelectric meters built into the camera itself. Pointing the camera at the subject activates the meter which sets the lens opening automatically to match prevailing light. Because such built-ins are rather costly, the beginner might do well to start out with the normal camera and a hand-held meter to help him with his exposure so that he can master photographic fundamentals.

Another recommended accessory for the marine camera is a reliable flash gun. Flash not only permits shooting pictures around the clock, but greatly improves daylight shots where the extra boost of lights is used to brighten facial shadows and reach into dark picture corners.

If you want to insure good results, start with fresh film of popular make. Full panchromatic emulsion, sensitive to the full range of colors, will give black-and-white images with tone gradation of which you will be proud. With the extremely fine grain black-and-white films now on the market, such as Plus X, it's possible to make 16 by 20 inch enlargements from 2¼ inch negatives that look as good to us as the ones we used to get from our old 4 by 5 inch negatives. Fortunately, too, for us marine photographers color film's ASA rating has been vastly speeded up which brings it to a par with the moderate-speed black-and-white films.

Taking Pictures Afloat

While afloat, motion can be a problem. If your boat is under way, for example, be careful not to rest the camera on any part of the craft, and don't prop the camera with your

175

elbows. Instead, stand with your feet widely spread, knees slightly flexed to "ride" with your boat's movement. Don't let the camera touch your body either. Another trick to keep your camera steady if it has connections for a neckstrap is to either lengthen the strap or add on to it so that you can step on the free end and hold the camera—in picture-taking position—taut against it. This reduces the motion to the mere up-and-down motion of your cruiser and helps you prevent the tilting or swinging in an arc. Use 1/200 of a second for close-ups with a still camera. At 75 feet or more, 1/100 is usually fast enough. With a movie camera, expose at 24 or 36 frames a second, if possible, instead of the usual 16 frames. With inexpensive cameras that have a fixed shutter speed, there isn't much you can do except try to follow the scene as it moves past. Avoid taking close-ups (another boat, for instance) unless the subject is moving at the same rate you are. One trick to eliminate boat motion on rough water is to wait to shoot until the craft reaches the top or bottom of a wave. (Remember that any boat is momentarily motionless at the top of a wave or the bottom of a trough, while it's changing the direction of its motion.) The expert depresses his shutter a little bit (not quite enough to trip it) at each of these times—beating time with the action of the waves until the rhythm is set. Then, it becomes a simple matter to trip it at the proper time. Incidentally this will help cure you of any tendency to jab the shutter, a practice which has ruined many a picture.

When taking photographs of other moving boats try to shoot from a high level down onto the subject, since this will show more of the boat and the people on her. Pictures taken from near the water level will reveal only heads above the boat's sheer line, while spray from your own boat or the boat you're picturing may block out the subjects. Always be conscious of both the direction of the light source and the wind when shooting marine pictures. Avoid aiming your camera into a stiff breeze; otherwise your lens will become coated with spray. Even a single drop of water striking the lens may diffuse the light entering the camera and may alter the exposure or distort the picture.

To take the unusual picture, you must study the composition carefully before you shoot. When the horizon is part of the picture be sure to position the camera level so the subject doesn't seem to be sailing up or down hill. Pictures taken of perfectly calm water with no reflections are generally rather uninteresting. If the sun is such that you get no reflections, toss a stone or similar object into the water so ripples add pattern to the picture. Your camera will capture water texture best if the subject and water are side- or back-lighted so as to cast shadows. Marine pictures usually offer better water texture if taken when the sun is low. Speaking of water reflections, remember that water reflects far more light than do ground surfaces, and many beginning yachting photographers overexpose many pictures taken on the water. In general, if you don't have a light meter to establish an accurate reading, close down one f-stop smaller for marine photography than you would shooting under similar light conditions on shore.

Sailboats always make interesting photographs, but to take real good ones a little knowledge of sailing techniques doesn't hurt. For instance, sailboats are best shot from leeward with light from the direction the craft is headed. Wind of at least 10 to 12 mph will fill the sails sufficiently to give a good appearance of action. Try to expose when the boat is in a wave cycle, which will show her bow neither too high nor buried in the water. If the boat is racing, have her crew in the cockpit or along the windward rail. Sailboats look best when they are heeled toward the camera; there is more excitement then and masts look taller. With small sailboats, it adds to the picture if the crew is hiking. By the way, powerboats show up best when the bow isn't shaded and the light comes from ahead to highlight the cockpit.

To provide a complete record of your summer boating activities or a cruise, offbeat photos are a must. These are photographs taken during sunrise, sunset, rainstorms, or on dark, cloudy days. When you're working in low light, take a closeup or substitute reading of the brightest object in your scene. Then set your aperture with this reading against the top limit of your film speed range. With this setting, you'll take full advantage of the film's latitude and capture as many of the darker tones as possible. Sunrise and sunset pictures are most satisfactory on the water because it is so reflective. On land, it's hard to get such photos without having everything under the horizon go black. To figure your setting, point your camera or meter directly toward the sun and then directly overhead. The midpoint between these readings will give you a fairly reliable exposure.

Motion pictures are even easier to make than stills. With automatic cameras, one has only to wind the spring and press the release button. Several automatic movie cameras don't have to be focused and are completely self-setting. They tell you when you can't make a picture. Wide-angle, regular, and telephoto lens are permanently attached to the camera, and any can be selected with a simple twist of the fingers. If your motion-picture is fitted with a speed adjustment, increase the number of frames per second from 16 or 24 to 32. This will eliminate much of the jerky action from motion pictures taken under way, which is caused by shooting from an erratically moving platform. In motion-picture-taking you will create a greater feeling of action if you follow the subject coming toward you and pan more slowly than the subject, allowing it to move out of your field of view as you stop panning and hold your camera static.

Care of Camera

The boating photographer's basic problem is to keep salt spray—indeed, fresh-water spray, too—away from his equipment. Neglected droplets of fresh water will eventually cause trouble; salt water is far worse and will react quickly. So strive to keep your gear well guarded against the enemy, corrosion. For this reason, it's best to keep the camera in an "ever-ready" case which is tailored precisely to a particular camera and offers protection against jars and jolts, spray, and moisture from your hands. Also take care to keep your hands away from any portions of the camera not covered by the case. In either hot or wet weather, wipe your hands carefully with paper toweling before handling the little magic box. Carefully wipe down the camera with a thoroughly dry soft towel or clean linen hanky after each period of use before stowing away. Spray, rain drops, perspiration, dew, fog dampness—always wipe these carefully off. Use only lens tissue or the special camel's hair lens brushes on the lens itself.

Never leave camera and lens lying about on deck, or exposed to the sun. Direct exposure to hot sun can fog film already in the camera. Always use a neck strap, to keep the camera from accidentally flying overboard, and keep the lens cap on when not taking pictures. When shooting, it's wise to use a sunshade which acts as an air bell and will prevent a lot of mist from reaching the lens. Should that be a difficulty, put a filter on to protect the lens. When it's not in use, keep your camera gear and spare film protected from dampness in a Pliofilm bag.

Thoughtful selection of a below-decks stowage place comes next. Stow the case in a cool, dry, well-ventilated area down below. Dampish lockers won't do. Keep it away from engine heat, too. Always store film in a cool, dry place until it can be used. Be sure to have it processed as soon as possible after it's exposed, since color film, for instance, begins to lose its latent image and will deteriorate if left too long in the camera.

WATER SKIING

It is easy to understand the thrill of riding over the waves behind a fast-moving boat. But, if you can't swim, don't stretch your luck on water skis. Children as young as five and adults of almost any age can learn the fundamentals of this exciting sport with a minimum of effort. Usually, a simple lesson on fundamentals, lasting less than half an hour, is sufficient to enable the newcomer to remain upright on skis.

There are many types of water skis on the market, and each is a favorite with certain people. As an indication of the variety, the American Water Ski Association rules specify that skis used in A.W.S.A.-sanctioned tournaments shall be at least 4 feet long and 4 to 8 inches wide. As you become an expert water skier, you'll probably want to experiment with different types and sizes to find out which is best for you. The average skis however range from 5 to 5¾ feet long, and the actual length depends upon the weight of the skier. Skiers weighing between 50 and 120 pounds should choose skis 5 feet long; between 120 to 160 pounds, 5 feet 6 inches; and 160 to 220 pounds, 5 feet 9 inch skis. Skis about 6 to 6½ inches wide are considered best for general skiing and some tricks. It's easier to get up on skis that are wider, but they are harder to turn and maneuver with. The standard or all-purpose ski with adjustable aluminum and rubber bindings is best for the beginner, giving good control along with a quick-release feature.

If you are not a strong swimmer, be sure to wear one of the vest type of life jackets, or at least a life belt that has been specially designed for water skiers. These permit the free movement required for skiing, yet provide the protection needed in a spill. In addition, of course, a towline is needed. You can tow a skier with anything—even clothesline —but nothing will prove as satisfactory as a buoyant polyethylene tow rope about 75 feet long. It comes equipped with a handle. Don't permit anyone in the family to hook elbows through the handle or step inside it. Hang on with the hands only. The towline should be fitted properly to the boat. Don't settle for belaying the rope to a cleat on one quarter of the boat; the towing tension isn't evenly distributed, for one thing. Also, sometimes cleats pull out. Once you have assembled an outfit, it's time to go skiing. First, wet your feet, and fit them in the bindings so they are taut on your feet, but not tight. After you have donned the skis, sit down on them; hunch yourself down comfortably so you are squatting compactly on the skis. Do this on shore—not afloat.

Now extend your arms straight out in front of you—don't bend your elbows. Then have someone hand you the tow bar, and pull you upright. Let the towline raise you. Don't push yourself with your legs. Just follow the line's pull until you're upright. At this point, your knees should be flexed, and your body kept straight and braced against the pull.

After practicing this several times, you're ready to start in shallow water. Squat down on the skis and let your toes hold the ski tip up, so that the front of the skis are higher than the back, and the tips out of water. Grab the towbar so the line passes between the skis. When you're ready tell the tow skipper to "hit it" and brace yourself. Then you repeat the lesson learned on dry land; let the boat pull you up and out of the water.

Most people have little difficulty to make it up. However, they won't stay upright too long; most of them ski—at first—in an awkward position. Learn good posture right away. That is knees slightly bent, back straight, arms straight and relaxed. Practice this a few times, following in the middle of the boat's wake.

The direction of your skis is controlled by the turning of your foot. This is achieved entirely by ankle movement. To keep the skis directed straight ahead, point your toes in an imaginary straight line extending from behind the cruiser, and keep your knees directly over the skis. If the ski tips tend to cross rather than move parallel to each other, the chances are that your ankles are turned in and that your knees are touching. To correct this, spread your skis a little further apart (12 to 15 inches), and your skis will automatically right themselves. Remember always to keep your knees directly over your skis and your weight evenly distributed on both skis at all times. When you are up, keep in the wake of the cruiser. If you move to the side, the edges of the wakes will catch your skis and cause you to fall. Your boat driver can help you to keep inside the wake by adjusting his steering to your course.

Stopping is the easiest part of skiing. Signal to your boat driver that you want to stop, and he'll run the cruiser close and parallel to the shore line. Let go of the tow bar, spread your arms for balance, and you'll coast to a gentle stop quickly. Because your skis are buoyant, relax and float quietly until the boat driver can pick you up.

These are the basic techniques. To learn some of the advanced procedures and tricks, consult an expert, read one of the many books on the subject, or join the American Water Ski Association by writing them at 7th Street and Avenue G, S.W., Winter Haven, Florida.

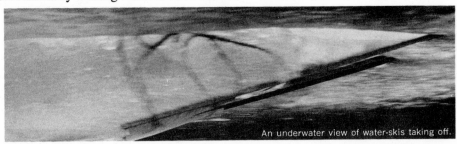
An underwater view of water-skis taking off.

The towboat operator's chief concern is to keep the boat away from the swimmers and bathers and congested waters so that the skier will have open water for maneuvering. The operator must remember not to make a sharp turn when the skier is already inside the turn since the strain on the side of the boat at a sharp angle can readily capsize the craft. Likewise, the skiing towline should not be made fast to the lifting handles at the transom, since the strain will be unbalanced. Remember that once the skier is up, he should always tell you how fast he wants to travel. He knows his own capabilities best; you, as the driver, can't know how fast he wants to go unless he instructs you. The skier's timing may be badly thrown off if he is required to move faster or slower than he is used to skiing. When you reach the speed the skier wishes, you should inform him of this and keep to it until he signals you otherwise.

By the way, safety in skiing and boat driving has its basis in the giving and understanding of hand signals. It is almost impossible to overstress the importance of signal communication between skier, boat operator, and other boats in the area. Study the illustrations shown here until you know the signals by heart—and see that each skier and crew member does the same.

The dry land technique can take the guesswork out of learning how to water ski and can be done almost anywhere, even in your living room. All you need is one other person (we'll call him an instructor), a pair of water skis, and a towline. First, take a few deep knee bends to sharpen your sense of balance and coordination. When putting on the skis adjust the bindings by sliding the heel piece forward. The fit should be snug, but comfortable. (If you're near water, wet your feet and the skis. Your feet will slip into the bindings easier.) Grasp the towline handle and your instructor lower you down into a sitting position. Stretch your arms out straight, knees between your elbows. (If done correctly the towline handle will be just in front of your knees.) Have your instructor pull on the towline, slowly raising you to a standing position. Don't try and stand up. Let the instructor exert the pulling force. (This simulates the manner in which you will be pulled to the surface when actually water skiing. Repeat this procedure several times.) Once you are in the water, review the dry land technique. Check the position of your knees and towline handle. If you've learned your lesson, you'll be flashing across the water on your first try.

Rules of Safe Water Skiing. There are only a few common-sense precautions to observe in the sport of water skiing. The following suggestions are the result of careful study by the American Water Ski Association:

1. Always have an extra person in the boat to watch the skier.
2. Always stop the motor when helping a skier into the boat.
3. When landing a skier, run paralled to the shore and come in slowly.
4. Stay away from solid objects, such as docks, other boats and sea walls.
5. Stay away from fishermen, swimmers and beaches.
6. Pick up a fallen skier immediately.
7. The boat operator should watch the water ahead at all times and never look back at the skier. That is the duty of the other person in the boat.
8. The boat operator should keep in the seat at all times; never on the gunwale.
9. Remember not to make too quick a turn as you may slow the skier down to where he sinks because the towline sags.

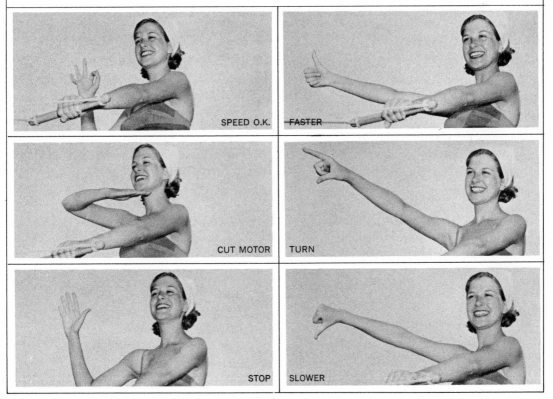

SPEED O.K.   FASTER

CUT MOTOR   TURN

STOP   SLOWER

Anybody who has ever tried swimming beneath the surface with eyes open has felt the first fascination of skin diving—the out-of-this-world sensation of underwater exploration. For a comparatively new water sport, skin and Scuba diving have gained in popularity that is nothing short of phenomenal. As with water skiing, diver clubs have sprung up so rapidly that one can find an organization of this kind in practically every section of the country. In many cases, the quickest way to get information about such clubs is through the local sporting goods dealer.

Basic skin diving equipment consists of just three inexpensive items. First is the face mask. This provides an air space between eyes and water, giving more comfortable and sharper vision. Be sure, when fitted to your face, that the mask is airtight so that when you inhale it stays on your face by suction alone.

The second item is fins for your feet. These greatly increase your swimming power and maneuverability. They should fit the feet properly; have open toes for comfort; enclosed heels for protection against hard surfaces; and skid-resistant soles for walking on slippery surfaces without constantly slipping and falling. While the fins should fit snugly, make certain they do so without chafing or interfering with circulation.

The third basic item is the snorkel, which is simply an air tube with a mouth piece. The skin diver breathes through the snorkel while lying face down on the surface, making it unnecessary to lift the head up into the air to breathe. When you dive below the surface, the upper end of the snorkel is sealed off automatically by a valve that keeps water from entering. Ear plugs should *never* be worn in diving.

With the three basic pieces of equipment, you're ready to enjoy the unique fun of skin diving. In a way skin diving is somewhat of a misnomer. A skin diver usually lowers himself into the water. He may sometimes jump in feet first, but he never dives while wearing mask and flippers. In fact, doing so can be dangerous.

Begin in a fairly shallow stretch of water that you are thoroughly familiar with. Start by simply floating face down; then try paddling underwater at depths up to about six feet for a closeup look at the bottom. When you're ready to go under, take a couple of deep breaths first, then an ordinary one for the dive itself. This is simply done by suddenly pushing your head down and flipping your fin-clad feet high in the air. Lifting so much weight out of the water will push you under. Once underwater, go down slowly. Be sure to "pop" your ears as you descend. Do this by holding the mask tight against your face and snorting through your nose at five foot intervals. This should clear your ears. If it doesn't or your ears hurt, don't go any deeper. In any event, never go deeper than 30 feet at any time.

Once you have reached your desired depth, you can arch upward to a horizontal position, and flutter along easily by using the fins. When it is time to come up for a fresh breath of air, you simply stop all motion and you'll slowly come to the surface. Hold your breath until the end of the snorkel is out of the water, then exhale sharply to rid the snorkel of water that has seeped in and clear it for your next breath.

After you have mastered skin diving, you may wish to use scuba (*S*elf-*C*ontained *U*nder-water *B*reathing *A*pparatus). This type of diving offers freedom from having to return to the surface for a breath of air, and it allows much more time to explore the underwater world. The diver can spend up to an hour underwater almost as comfortably as he would at the surface. However, because of the complexity of scuba equipment as compared to the simple skin diving gear, and the depths and distance its use invariably invites, beginners shouldn't purchase a scuba outfit and attempt to start out cold. First give the science serious study; then obtain individual instruction from an expert. Certified scuba schools and instructors can be located through your local skin diving shop or from the YMCA. A minimum diving course should consist of 15 to 20 hours equally divided between lecture and water-work. It is important for you to learn not only correct use of equipment, but also the laws of physics associated with pressure and underwater conditions. In other words, learn scuba diving from experts—by doing, and not by reading. But for the diving novice and expert alike, certain safety rules are basic. The following are seven of the more important ones:

1. Never skin dive alone. Take a safe, dependable companion, or "buddy."
2. Know the waters where you are diving, especially if they are influenced by tides or currents.
3. Have an operating base, preferably a tender, for a rest platform.
4. Know your own physical limitations and do not overextend them. Practice emergency procedures.
5. Have a skin-diving flag clearly visible to avoid danger from passing boats.
6. Be familiar with the sea life of the region.
7. Do not dive in areas where others are fishing.

Underwater Photography. This is a phase of skin and scuba diving that may hold a special attraction for you—particularly if you already are a shutterbug. There are several types of waterproof cases on the market especially designed for movie and still cameras. Less expensive is a plastic camera bubble with a water-tight seal, obtainable either at a sporting goods or camera shop. Taking good underwater pictures calls for patience and experimentation because the light-filtering effect of the water can change very swiftly. For example, if the surface is calm, only five per cent of the incident light may be lost by reflection. But let the surface become rippled by wind, current, or passing boats and the light loss may go up to as much as twenty or thirty per cent. Good color adds other interesting light problems. Fifteen feet of water filters out reds and yellows almost completely, unless some sort of artificial light is used.

Spear Fishing. This is another popular underwater sport. In many states spearing gamefish is a misdemeanor, but some regions permit spearing roughfish. Big gamefish are found, and catches allowed, in the following areas: California waters for big sea bass, Florida and the Bahamas for the giant grouper, or the biggest game of all—shark and barracuda. Some spear fishermen take on these tigers of the sea. But they are expert swimmers, in top condition, and know what they are doing. Despite their experience and skill fishermen have been injured when attacked by wounded shark or barracuda. Check local regulations carefully before investing in a speargun. Be especially sure you buy a legal gun. Some places will permit Hawaiian sling and spring- or rubber-powered guns, but frown on gas-guns.

PREDICTED LOG COMPETITIONS

Each weekend throughout the boating season at numerous yachting centers large fleets of one-design and cruising sailboats gather to race for silver mugs and brass plaques in predicted log competitions. Powerboats—both inboard and outboard—also take part in competitive yachting events to demonstrate the skipper's superiority in navigation and boat handling. Actually, the motive behind all yacht racing—both sail- and power-boats —is the competitive spirit to excel.

A predicted log competition is the only way so far discovered whereby powerboats of various sizes and various horsepower can race with each other on a fair and equal basis. Sail racing has its classes, such as Snipes, Stars, Blue Jays and Lightnings. Each boat in each class is built to specifications, has the same sail area as all others in the class, and participates on an equal basis with every other boat in the class. Skill in sail handling and maneuvering is a decisive factor. With power boats it is different, except for the souped up racing shells and certain inboard jobs built only for speed. In any predicted log contest, entries will include outboards from 18 feet up and inboards from 26 feet. There is no limit as to size. All that is required is that they all finish at a predetermined time. They are judged by the percentage of error in their calculations filed with the committee, for each leg of the contest. Errors range from as little as a fraction of one per cent to several percentage points.

Common Sail Insignia of One-Design Racer-day Sailers

Albacore	Arrow	Atlantic	Barnegat Bay Sneakboxes	B.B. 11	Beetle Cats
Beverly Dinghy	Blue Jay	Bull's Eye	Butterball	Cadet	Cape Cod Baby Knockabout
Capri 14	Celebrity	Checkmate	Chesapeake 20	CLIPPER	Coast 13
Cottontail	Cricket	Day Sailer	Dragon	Duster	Dyer Dhow
Dyersin (Class D) Dink	Eighteen Foot Knockabout	El Toro	Elvstrom Jr	Ensign	Enterprise
Explorer	Finn	Fireball	Firefly	Five-Point Five (5.5) Meter	5-0-5 Class
Flying Dutchman	Flying Fifteen	Flying Junior	Flying Scot	Flying Tern	Gannet

Each skipper who enters a contest spends hours figuring such problems as tide and wind. He estimates the revolutions per minute at which his engine is to run to take him over each leg of a six or seven-leg course, and which will bring him to the finish line at the predetermined hour. The course for a total run is usually from 30 to 60 miles. The more experienced the skipper is, the more time he spends on his predictions.

Each boat has an observer, who is officially a member of the race committee. Before the contest starts he checks that radios are silenced, that no instrument is visible to the skipper except his tachometer and compass, and collects all the watches. His is the only timepiece, and with it he notes the actual time at the end of each leg when the skipper cries out "Mark!" At the end of the race he compares the skipper's predictions with actual elapsed time for each leg and works out the percentage of error. That sounds very easy, something like a pleasant day afloat with nothing to do. But there's a lot more to it than that.

The secret of winning a predicted-log competition lies in how well you know your cruiser,

Common Sail Insignia of One-Design Racer-day Sailers

Geary 18	Gemini	G.P.14	Hampton	Highlander	Hornpiper
Indian	Inland Cat	Interclub	Interlake	International 14	International One-design
International 12	Javelin	Jet 14	Jollyboat	Knarr	Knickerbocker
Lark	Lehman Interclub	Lehman 12	Lido 14	Lightning	Little Bear
Luders 16	Maverick	Melody	Mercury (15 foot)	Mercury (18 foot)	Metcalf
Mobjack	Moth	Naples Sabot	Narrasketuck	National One-design	Nipper
O'Day 17	O.K. Dinghy	110 Class	Osprey	Osprey	Pintail

how precisely you figured the effect that tide, currents, and wind will have on the speed of your craft, and how accurately you have charted your course. Accurate calibration of your cruiser's speed well in advance of the contest is the starting point, and the best method of determining precise performance is to conduct speed tests over a nautical measured mile. In addition to the compass, the invaluable tachometer is the chief aid during the race, and knowing just how far your craft will travel at any given r.p.m. is fundamental to preparing estimated times.

After finding out exactly how your boat will perform over a measured mile, the U.S.C. and G.S. navigational charts, current tables, and tide charts covering the competition waters are employed to work out the predicted times. Knowing the finish time that the contest committee has set for the race and the length of the course in nautical miles, you will have to figure the effect that tides and currents will have on your cruiser. Using the performance figures you have obtained over the measured mile as a point of departure, you'll be able to estimate how long it will take to cover each leg of the course as well as

Common Sail Insignia of One-Design Racer-day Sailers

Pelican	Penguin	Pennant	Pilot	Pioneer	Quad Trainer
Rainbow	Raven	Rebel	Resolute	Rhodes Bantam	Rhodes 18
Rhodes 19	Rocket	Ross 13	Sailfish	S Class	Sea Shell
Seminole	Shamrock	Shields Class	Shore Bird	Six Meter	Skimmer
Snipe	Snowbird	Southeaster	Sprite	Star	Sunfish
Tallstar	Teal	Tech Dinghy	Thirties	Thistle	Town Class
Turnabout	Twelve Meter	210 Class	Vixen	Widgeon	Wayfarer

the entire course. It may sound a little complicated—it does require some application of navigation and mathematics—but the results are worth it. If navigation isn't your strong point, however, you can have a friend do the computing. Should you do this he must go along on the race as a member of your crew and act as your navigator. No professional help is permitted in such races.

At the beginning of the race, you have a choice of the method of starting. Most contestants prefer to get their craft to the chosen speed, then time their flying start so that they cross the starting line at just the right speed and exactly the right moment. You can keep your timepiece until you cross the line, then hand it over to the observer. He logs your exact starting time (though it doesn't affect your score as long as it's within two minutes of your prediction), and you're under way in the competition. Some contestants prefer to start from a standstill right at the starting line, having calculated the time it takes to accelerate to their chosen speed. The method you use depends on your preference, but it's a good idea to try both ways before making a decision.

Windmill	Wood Pussy	Y Flyer	Zephyr	Zip	

Common Sail Insignia of One-Design Racer Cruisers

Amphibi-Con	Amphibi-ette	Annapolis 30	Barnegat 20	Bay Lady	Bear
Bird	Bounty II	CALIFORNIA CRUISING CLASS	California 20	California 24	CALIFORNIA THIRTY TWO
Cap Vert	Chesapeake 32	Chinook	Coastwise Cruiser	Columbia 29	Controversy 27 (Mt. Desert 27)
Corsaire	Cutlass	Dickerson 32	Dolphin	Electra	FARALLONE CLIPPER
Frisco Flyer	Hinkley Sou'wester	Hinkley 36	Holiday Classes	Idler	Kestrel

Out on the course, everyone aboard can relax and enjoy the trip except the skipper, who must watch the performance of his craft most carefully. One of the real challenges of a predicted-log contest is compensating for unforeseen changes in weather, wind, and wave action, all of which will affect your running time. That's why you should run the measured course under as many different conditions and speeds as possible to learn to predict the unpredictable. Thus you'll learn to judge the wind and waves by sight and feel and will adjust your throttles accordingly. At control points along the course, you will tell the observer aboard your cruiser to stand by, then will give the exact passing moment by saying, "Ready . . . mark!" As you pass the finish point, you repeat your "mark" signal for the last time, and the competition is all over for you but the scoring.

Scoring is done by percentage of error. You take the difference between the actual time and the predicted time, in seconds, then determine the percentage of error by dividing the error, in seconds, by the predicted time in seconds. As an example, on a 3-hour predicted time, you missed your time by 5 minutes. The error, 300 seconds, divided by

K 40 Kettenburg 40	King's Cruiser	Lion	Maraudeur	Marlin and Fish Class	Maya
Meridian	New Horizons	Nomad	Orion	Polaris	PACIFIC CLASS
Ranger	RHODES 27	Schock 22	Schock 25	Seawitch	Signet
Swiftsure	Tartan 27	Thunderbird	Triangle 20	Tripp 30	Triton

Common Sail Insignia of Popular One-Design Racing Catamarans

Aqua-Cat	Catalina Catamaran	Cougar Catamaran Mark III One-design	DC-14	DC-14	Malibu Outrigger
Pacific Catamaran	Scamper	Shearwater III	Tiger Cat	Tiki II	Wildcat II

10,800, the number of seconds in 3 hours, gives you .0277. Multiply by 100 to get the percentage, and you have 2.77 per cent.

The official rules for predicted-log contests are set up by the Cruiser Commission of the American Power Boat Association. The rules are strict and precise for sanctioned contests by member groups, but are flexible enough to allow any group to modify them to any individual need. Any group that is an A.P.B.A. member can qualify for sanction, and the winner can be eligible for any of a large number of fine trophies offered by the association. For information on predicted-log contests and for the book, *Power Cruiser Contest Rules and Instructions,* you may write the American Power Boat Association, 2534 St. Aubin Avenue, Detroit, Michigan 48207. This book costs $1.00. It contains the complete rules, plus a lot of helpful data in the more complicated and complex calculations necessary for long events, and it also shows a sample log form.

SAILBOAT RACING

Sailboat devotees live in a world apart, a world in which wind and wave assume extra importance, in which the emphasis is on an entanglement with nature, either as an antagonist to be conquered or as a benign, relaxing agent to be enjoyed at leisure. With sailing on the upswing, more people are becoming interested in sailboat racing—either as a participant or as a spectator. Actually, watching a yacht race can be extremely interesting, whether it is the America's Cup races, a national championship regatta in a one-design class, or merely the Sunday race on the local lake. But, you have to know how to watch and what to look for. Most people, including many sailors themselves, don't know the mechanics of a sailboat race.

First, there are two major classifications of sailboat racing:
    1. Class sailboat racing—between boats of the same class, racing on even terms.
    2. Handicap racing—between boats of different types are handicapped by a time-allowance system which makes all boats as evenly matched as possible. With a system of handicap ratings, sloops, cutters, yawls, ketches, and schooners are then able to compete evenly against each other regardless of size.

Racing Courses. Most one-design class sailboat races, and a few handicap races, are held on a definite course. The majority of local regattas are held around triangular courses. Such a course is a good test of skill since it requires sailing to windward, reaching, and sailing before the wind. Boats start the race by crossing the starting line between a white flag on the committee boat or station and the starting mark, and they finish by crossing a line formed by a white flag on the committee boat or station and the starting mark. Generally the race course is so arranged that the first leg requires a beat to windward. This spreads the boats out a little and minimizes, to some degree, traffic jams at the first mark. Some courses are twice around the triangle.

One of the most popular courses, especially for class national championship, is the "modified Gold Cup" course, which consists of five legs, with starting and finishing at the same mark. The first three legs are generally around a triangle, starting with a windward leg followed by two reaching legs; the fourth leg is usually a repetition of the first leg to windward; while the fifth leg is a return downwind to the finish line at the starting mark.

Most handicap races usually take place over courses of varying lengths. Such events may

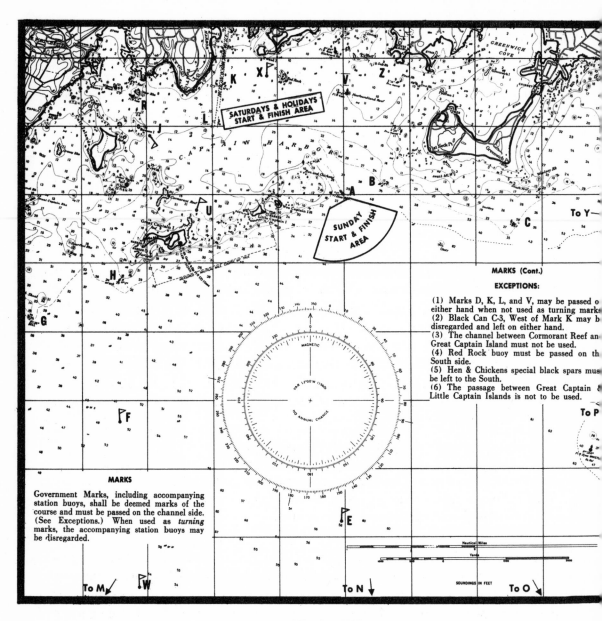

LIST OF MARKS

A Black Bell "1" (Flasher) Little Captain Island East Reef.

B Red Nun N "2," Flat Neck Point Shoal Buoy.

C Red Nun N "34," Greenwich Point.

D Red Whistle Buoy (Flasher) "32-A," Mid-Channel Buoy.

E Special YRA Permanent Mark, (180° Mag. from Mark "A," 2½ miles).

F Special YRA Permanent Mark, (225° Mag. from Mark "A," 2½ miles).

G Red Bell "36," Bluefish Shoal.

H Red Nun N "2," Great Captain Island West Reef.

J Special Indian Harbor Mark off Calf Island. (Spar)

K Red Nun N "4," Greenwich Harbor.

L Red Nun N "2," off Greenwich Harbor.

R Red Flasher "2," Otter Rocks.

T Starting Buoy, if other than a Government, YRA, or Special Mark. (For use as a turning mark.)

U Special Indian Harbor Mark, NNE of Great Captain Island. Light. (Spar)

V Red Buoy "4" (Flasher), Newfoundland Reef.

W Special YRA Tripod (208° Mag. from Mark "A," 3.4 miles).

X Special Indian Harbor Mark, South of Tweed Island. (Spar)

Z Starting Area R. Y. C. Dinghies, East Channel.

Marks off the chart which may be signaled — arrows show direction.

M Black Bell "21," Matinicock Point.

N Black Can "19," Oak Neck Point.

O Black Bell "17," Centre Island.
P Black Bell "15," Lloyd Point.

Y Red Bell "32," The Cows.

COURSE SIGNALS

Normally courses will be signalled as shown at right 10 minutes before start of that Division.

Courses may consist of 1, 2 or more Government, YRA or Special Marks.

I	II	III	IV
D	D	½ D	
F	J	K	
J	K		
K			

If shorter legs are indicated, the Committee may place a special turning mark on a line between Start and any one of the above Government or YRA Marks. Special turning marks will be flagged with the Code Flag of the letter assigned to that Mark, and a red or orange shape. The Committee Boat will signal such Marks, i.e.:

½ D— means Special Mark will be at ½ the distance from Start to "D."

All Marks signalled must be left on the same hand as starting Mark. Upon finishing, a yacht must cross finish line from direction of preceding mark.

STARTING TIMES
CONNECTICUT AREA

	TIME — P.M.	CLASS	SIGNAL CYLINDERS
WARNING	1:25		1 White
PREPARATORY	1:30		1 Blue
START, DIVISION I	1:35	Shields	1 Red
DIVISION II	1:40	L-16	2 White
DIVISION III	1:45	Quincy Adams	2 Blue
	1:50	Ensign	2 Red
DIVISION IV	1:55	Lightning	1 White
	2:00	Osprey, Cottontail, Flying 15 and Other Planing Boats	1 Blue
	2:05	Flying Scot	1 Red
	2:10	Rhodes 18	2 White
DIVISION V	2:15	Blue Jay	2 Blue
DIVISION VI	2:20	Falcon	2 Red
	2:25	Bulls Eye	1 White
	2:30	Mercury and All Other Classes	1 Blue

STARTING AND FINISHING LINES will be established between white flag on Committee Boat and adjacent mark or buoy.

Saturdays and Holidays — Inside Captain Harbor
Sundays — Outside Captain Harbor
(In areas shown on Chart)
Do not use "A" as Starting Mark

Yachts must not cross these lines except when maneuvering for a start or starting, or when finishing and clearing the line per rule 51.5, or when rounding the buoy which has been signaled as a mark of the course.

After the first Preparatory Signal, all classes must keep completely clear of the starting line until their own Preparatory Signal. The penalty can be disqualification.

NO RACE If no class has started by 3:30 P.M. all races for that day are cancelled.

TIME LIMIT 5:30 P. M. The finish of one yacht in a class by 5:30 P.M. constitutes a race for that class.

POSTPONED TIME LIMIT

6:00 P.M. For any class that has had a postponed start.

Yachts finishing after the Committee has left the line should take their time when they reach the finish mark or buoy and report same to the Committee.

SIGNAL SHAPES

ON STATION AT START (3 Red Cylinders, horizontal or vertical).

NO SPINNAKER SIGNAL (White Spinnaker Triangle.) When flown between Preparatory and Starting Gun of Class affected.

RECALL SIGNAL (White Cylinder with red band), with one blast of horn for each yacht recalled.

ON STATION AT FINISH (3 Blue Cylinders, horizontal or vertical).

SPECIAL CODE FLAGS

GENERAL RECALL SIGNAL (First Repeater) and 2 guns. Entire Class recalled for fresh Start *on next gun.*

COURSE CHANGE (Code Flag "L") Signal will be displayed until that Division has started. A Course Change cannot be made after the Warning Gun for that Class.

MISSING MARK SIGNAL (Code Flag M.) When displayed on temporary Mark, dory or launch, it means round this instead of Mark originally signalled.

SHORTENED COURSE (Code Flag "S") and 2 guns. May be used with 3 blue cylinders at any Mark of Course originally signalled.

POSTPONEMENT AND CANCELLATIONS

POSTPONEMENT (Answering Pennant and 2 guns). All Classes not started are postponed for intervals of 5 minutes. The next signals after a Postponement shall be the Warning, Preparatory and Start for that Class that would have started if there had been no Postponement.

PARTIAL CANCELLATION (Code Flag "O" and 2 guns.) All Classes not started are cancelled.

ALL CLASSES CANCELLED (Code Flag "N" and 3 guns). All Classes including those in progress are cancelled.

be one-day affairs, overnighter or rendezvous races; or may occupy several days and involve great distances such as Newport to Bermuda or San Pedro to Diamond Head. Distance races have little spectator interest, except at the start and at the finish lines.

The Race Itself

Whether you're a spectator or participant you should obtain a copy of the sailing instructions of the race. These sailing instructions, prepared in writing by the race committee, include the following matters: the starting signals and their scheduled times; starting line; finish line; the order in which the turning marks of each course are to be passed and the side on which each mark is to be passed, with a description of each mark. The instructions also cover: the date and place of the races; the classes to race; possible courses; eligibility and entry requirements; measurement certificates; the signals used to designate courses other than the only prescribed or regular course; any government buoys or other objects required to be passed on a specified side; whether buoys will bound the starting area (if so, they don't rank as marks); special method of recall; time allowance; special time limit; prizes; the scoring system; special time limit for protests; and any special provisions and signals. These written instructions make it possible for you to form a mental picture of the race course.

When a spectator at a race, it's nice to know who the participants are. In most major regattas, contestants lists are available, or at least the scoreboard can be copied.

The Race Committee is the official referee. A Race Committee boat flies the Race Committee flag and usually the burgee of the yacht club sponsoring the particular event. Plaques indicating the course to be sailed are displayed thereon. Signals for starting are made from the Committee Boat as follows:

> Warning signal   —One gun & White cylinder
> Preparatory signal—One gun & Blue cylinder
> Starting signal   —One gun & Red cylinder

These signals are made at five minute intervals. Each signal is lowered 30 seconds before the hoisting of the next.

In starting yachts by classes, the Starting signal for each class is the Preparatory signal for the next class. Various other signals are used under appropriate conditions. The starting and finishing line is established between the Committee Boat and a buoy or "stake boat." Marks of the course are usually Government or privately owned buoys. The first leg of the course is usually to a mark directly upwind from the starting line. The finish of each yacht is acknowledged from the Committee Boat by a blast of a horn or a whistle.

A yacht, when racing, is distinguishable because she usually flies a wind pennant from her mast head in lieu of any other signal. The courteous power boat and sail boat skipper, when recognizing a yacht racing, will do his best to keep well clear of the racer and to avoid creating a wake which might interfere with her progress. The racing rules of the N. A. Y. R. U. govern most races. These are available in booklet form for a small fee from the North American Yacht Racing Union, 37 West 44th Street, New York, New York 10036. Class rules can be obtained from the secretary of the class.

The Race Committee on the committee boat judges the finish, particularly when boats are fairly close at the end of the race. The committee must also act as judges for any protests which may be filed. The only requirements for finishing are that the boat must cross and clear the finish line, and that the first boat must finish within a prescribed time limit, usually designed to get boats home before sundown.

Most regattas and local races constitute no problem as far as observing them from your boat is concerned. Try to position your spectator boat on an extension of the starting line, so that you can see maneuvering that goes on at the start. But, make certain that you're far enough away so that you don't interfere with any of the contestant's pre-start strategy. Once underway remember that it's your responsibility to keep clear of the racing boats. Don't send disturbed wind or disturbed water toward the participants. Operate at slow speed so as not to create a wake. This is usually not a great problem since most sailboats will be moving along at less than seven knots for a major portion of the race, and five knots is a more probable average. Actually, the only time you're apt to turn to your power and throw up some wake is when you delay to watch the tailenders go around a mark, and then take off to catch up with leaders again. If you must do this, do so with extreme care, making sure that your wake doesn't hit the racing boat with force. Even small waves have been known to have knocked the wind out of carefully tended sails, and stop a light sailboat in her tracks.

Speaking of wind, keep in mind that your boat will cause the wind to flow around and over her, leaving a broken flow of wind and eddies to leeward and astern of her. This disturbed wind reduces the efficiency of a sailboat's sails greatly, and if you want to remain popular with the sailors, don't move along at the same speed as their sailboats while observing or taking pictures. While these are not set rules on how far you should be away from course so as not to effect the wind, we would suggest, when to windward of the fleet, *at least* ten times the maximum height of your boat. If you're to leeward of the fleet on the reaching and running legs of the course, it would be permissible to move *slightly* closer.

On a normal triangular course, you should stay outside the triangle. This means that you would be to windward of the fleet on second leg, and to leeward on the third leg. Watching these legs in this manner avoids crisscrossing the course. Even on the concluding leg of the race, keep outside the course so that the tail-enders have their full rights. At the finishing point, position your craft so that she is behind the smaller of the two official boats on the finish line, or in back of the buoy if there is no boat other than the committe boat at the finish. Whatever you do, however, make sure you don't impede the committee's sighting line.

As you become proficient at watching races, you will find yourself learning the rudiments of the right-of-way rules and brushing-up on tactics. You gradually learn the inside dope of the sport, and by that time you're liable to be so interested in sailboat racing that you're just apt to give it a try yourself. To learn more about sailboat racing, we would suggest reading one or more of the following books: *Techniques of Small Boat Racing* edited by Dr. Stuart Walter; *Latest Yacht Racing Rules & Tactics* by Gordon C. Aymar; *Race Your Boat Right* by Arthur Knapp, Jr., and *Sailing to Win* by Robert N. Bavier, Jr.

APPENDIX A:
YACHTING
LANGUAGE

The language of the sea is spiced with terms and phrases so trenchant and vigorous that "salty talk" is no idle figure of speech. Our yachting terminology of today has been handed down from an era of "iron men and wooden ships," when wind-bellied canvas drove tall sparred vessels to the ends of the Seven Seas. Take the word *knot*, for example, meaning a measure of speed. Ancients used to measure the speed of their vessels by dropping a properly weighted log of wood overboard to which was secured one end of a small line in which knots were tied every forty-seven feet, three-inches. Then, with the aid of a 28 second sandglass they counted the number of knots that passed over the stern as the vessel sailed on away from the log. Thus the question: "How many knots are we making?" was a valid contraction of the ancient method of measuring the vessel's speed. Today the word *knot* also is used to denote speed, though we have advanced considerably from the sandglass and the knotted line method.

The word *port*, meaning the left hand side of the boat, dates back to ancient sailing days, too. In that bygone era ships—such as they were—were steered by steering oars which always were mounted on the right hand side of the stern. Because of the steering oar, vessels habitually put into dock on the side opposite the steering oar to prevent damage to the oar—hence, the term *port side*. Likewise, the fitting that held the steering oar is called the *steerboard*, which has since been changed to *starboard*, meaning the right hand side of the boat.

On a modern boat the word *head* means toilet, and some of them are fancy enough to contain hot and cold showers as well as washbasins. But aboard the old sailing vessels no such conveniences were offered. Instead, sailors usually went forward to the bow of the ship where a sort of rope basket was slung to the bowsprit so the men could stand in it while taking in sail. Also in those days it was customary to have a figurehead on the bow of each vessel. So, when nature called, the sailors' saying was: "I'm going to the figurehead." Soon this was shortened and remains in use today.

Historians likely will have less trouble tracing the origin of our modern nautical terms since we are lovers of the "initial system" of demarkation. For example, the word *radar* —an electronic navigation instrument which can pierce fog, storm, or the black night— is derived from *radio direction and ranging*.

Mastery of nautical terminology is *not* a prerequisite of yachting enjoyment; however, the prudent and *correct* use of words and phrases used and accepted by mariners stamps a man as well-read if nothing else. Study the following glossary and you'll be able to hold your own in the best of company.

ABAFT   Toward the stern (rear) of a boat; behind.

ABEAM   At right angles to the fore-and-aft centerline of the boat. Off the beam or on the side of the boat.

ABOARD   On or in a vessel.

ABOUT   To change direction in sailing. When the wind fills the sails from the other side. To come about; change course.

ABOVE   On a cabin housing or above deck, nautical upstairs.

ABREAST   Side by side; alongside or abeam.

ADRIFT   Drifting, or broken loose from a mooring. Dragging anchor.

AFLOAT   A boat or object that is buoyant and will float on the surface of the water.

AFORE   Opposite of abaft, forward.

AFOUL   Entangled or snarled in any way.

AFT   At or near the stern of the boat.

AGROUND   When the hull or keel of a boat touches the bottom.

AHEAD   Toward the bow of a boat, or in front of a boat.

AHOY   Greeting used to hail another boat.

AID TO NAVIGATION   A chartered mark to assist navigators, such as buoys, beacons, lights, radio beacons, etc.

ALEE   The side of a boat or object away from the direction of the wind.

ALL HANDS   The entire crew.

ALOFT   Up above; as up in the rigging or up the mast.

AMIDSHIPS   Toward the center of the vessel.

ANCHOR   A device so shaped as to grip the sea bottom. From it a line to a craft so as to hold her in a desired position.

ANCHORAGE   A sheltered place or area where boats can anchor or moor without interfering with harbor traffic.

ANCHOR LIGHTS   Riding lights required to be carried by vessels at anchor.

ANEMOMETER   An instrument to measure the velocity of the wind.

ASTERN   To the rear of a boat or behind a boat.

ATHWARTSHIPS   At right angles to the fore-and-aft line of a vessel; across the vessel in a direction at right angles to the keel.

AUXILIARY   A power plant used as a secondary propulsion in a vessel. Also a small motor used to drive pumps, generators, etc.

AWEATHER   To windward, toward the weather side.

AYE   Yes; an affirmative reply to any order.

AZIMUTH   Angular distance measured on a horizon circle in a clockwise direction.

BACK WASH   The churning water thrown aft by the propeller.

BAIL   To bail a boat is to throw the water out of it.

BALLAST   Heavy material, usually lead or iron, placed in the bottom of some boats to give stability.

BALLOON JIB   Larger and looser cut than a genoa and is used on a reach or a broad reach.

BAR   A ridge or succession of ridges of sand or other substances, especially such a formation extending across the mouth of a river or harbor, and which may obstruct navigation.

BARK   A three-masted sailing vessel square-rigged on the fore and main, and fore-and-aft rigged on the mizzen. Same as a *barque*.

BARKENTINE   A three-masted sailing vessel, square-rigged on the fore while it is fore-and-aft rigged on the main and mizzen. Same as a *barquentine*.

BARNACLE   A small shell fish that enjoys the bottom of your yacht.

BAROMETER   An instrument for registering the atmospheric pressure.

BATTEN DOWN   To make water tight, said of hatches and cargo.

BATTENS   Thin wooden strips fitted into pockets at the after edge of a sail to keep it in shape. Also strips of wood or metal fitting over hatch coamings to secure a tarp.

BEACH   The shore gradually sloping to the water.

BEACON   A navigational mark placed on or near a shoal or on land to warn vessels of danger.

BEAM   The maximum width measurement of a vessel. Also, in radio, a signal transmitted along a narrow course for use in direction finding.

BEAM SEA   A sea at right angles to a vessel's course.

BEARING   The direction of one object to another.

BEAR OFF   To sail away from the direction from which the wind comes.

BEAT   To sail toward the direction from which the wind blows by making a series of tacks while sailing close-hauled.

BECALM   A vessel is becalmed when the sails hang limp and lifeless because of no wind.

BEFORE THE WIND   Having the wind coming from the aft.

BELAY   To take one or more S-turns with a rope around a cleat, set of bitts, or any other fixed point. Also to cancel an order.

BELAYING PIN   A wooden or iron pin fitting into a rail upon which to secure ropes.

BELL BUOY   A buoy with a bell actuated by the sea.

BELOW   Beneath or under the deck.

BEND   To secure or to make fast a sail to a spar. Also the knot by which one rope is made fast to another.

BERTH   A vessel's place at anchor or at a dock. Also sleeping accommodations on board a boat.

BIGHT   The bend or loop in a rope. Also a bend in a coastline or in a river.

BILGE   That part of the inside hull above and around the keel where water will collect. Also the space under a cabin floor, or floor boards.

BINNACLE   A stand with receptacle containing the compass and compensating magnets.

BITTER END   The extreme end of a line.

BITTS   Posts (generally in pairs) fitted into the deck for securing mooring or towing lines.

BLANKED   When a sail is between the wind and another sail, the latter cannot get the wind and is said to be blanketed. One boat can blanket another boat by sailing between it and the wind.

BOARD   A tack or leg to windward when beating.

BOAT HOOK   A device for catching hold of a ring bolt or grab line in coming alongside a pier or picking up a mooring.

BOLLARD   Single or double cast metal posts or wooden posts secured to a pier and used for mooring vessels by means of lines extended from the vessel and fastened to the post.

BOOM   The spar to which the foot of the sail is attached either with a lacing or by slides.

BOOM CROTCH   A frame in which the boom rests when the boat is at anchor.

BOOM VANG   A tackle secured to the boom to prevent it from lifting on a reach or run and to flatten the sail.

BOOT TOP   A narrow stripe of paint at the waterline.

BOS'N'S CHAIR   A piece of canvas or wood on which a man working aloft is swung.

BOW   The forward end of a boat.

BOW BREAST   A forward mooring line used in docking.

BREAKERS   Waves caused by ledges, bars, and shoals.

BREAK OUT   To unfurl; to remove from its storage place.

BREAKWATER   An artificial embankment to protect anchorages or harbor entrances. Also a low bulkhead forward to prevent seas from coming aft.

BREAST LINE   A mooring line leading at an angle of about 90 degrees from the fore-and-aft line of the vessel to the dock or to another vessel.

BREAST THE SEA   To meet a swell or waves head on.

BRIDGE   A short deck running from side-to-side of the vessel, fitted out for control and navigation of the craft.

BRIGANTINE   A two-masted sailing vessel, square-rigged on the foremast, fore-and-aft rigged on the main mast, sometimes carried a square main topsail.

BRIGHTWORK   Varnished wood and polished brass or chrome.

BROACH   A vessel running downwind swings broadside to the wind. Dangerous in high seas.

BROADSIDE   The entire side of a vessel.

BULKHEAD   Any partition or wall in a boat.

BULWARK   The extension of the hull sides above the deck.

BUMBOAT   A peddler's boat that comes alongside in a port.

BUMPER   A resilient object or material on piers or landings to protect boats alongside from chafe or breakage.

BUNK   Sleeping berth; same as a bed.

BUOY   A floating piece of wood or cask attached by a rope to an anchor, to show its position. Also, floated over a shoal or other dangerous place as a beacon.

BUOYAGE   A system of buoys and marks to aid your course.

BURDENED VESSEL   A craft required to keep clear of a vessel holding the right-of-way.

BURGEE   A triangular flag used to identify a yacht club or an owner.

CABIN   A room or more used for living space.

CAN   A cylindrical black buoy having an odd number; found on the port side of a channel as you proceed away from the ocean.

CAPSIZE   Upset; turn over, said of a boat.

CAPSTAND   A mechanical device used for hoisting anchors or other heavy objects.

CARVEL   A smooth-planked hull.

CAST OFF   To let go of a line.

CATBOAT   A sailboat with a single sail.

CATAMARAN   A twin-hulled boat.

CENTERBOARD   A keel-like device that can be hoisted or lowered in a well or trunk to act as a keel in shoal draft boats.

CAULK   To make seams watertight by filling them with cotton, oakum, or similar material.

CAVITATE   The forming of a vacuum around a propeller, causing a loss in efficiency.

CHAFE   To damage by rubbing.

CHAFING GEAR   Canvas or other similar material secured about a line or sheet to protect it from abrasion and wear.

CHAIN PLATES   Metal plates bolted to the side of a boat to which stays are attached to support rigging.

CHANNEL   The deeper portion of a water area adequately marked, as a rule, with buoyage to guide boats with some appreciable draft safely through shoal water.

CHART   Marine version of a road map, showing buoys, water depths, shoals, etc.

CHINE   The line where the sides of a boat intersect the bottom. A "hard" chine is sharply angled; a "non-trip" chine makes the transition between vertical and horizontal in two bends; a "soft" chine is rounded.

CHOCK   A device affixed to the deck used as a guide for anchor or mooring line.

CHOP   Short, irregular waves, usually caused by meeting of tides; or meeting of current and wind.

CHRONOMETER   A highly accurate clock used by navigators.

CLEAT   A wood or metal fitting for securing a line without a hitch.

CLINKER   Lapstrake planked (hull), planks overlapping like clapboards.

CLOSE-HAULED   Sailing as close to the wind as possible.

CLOSE-WINDED   A craft capable of sailing very close to the wind.

COAMING   The raised protection around a cockpit.

COCKPIT   The space at a lower level from the deck in which the tiller or wheel is located.

COIL   To lay down a line in circular turns.

COLORS   The ceremony of hoisting the national flag at 8 A. M. The lowering at sunset is called *making colors.*

COMPASS   Magnetized needles attached to a circular compass card that tends to point to the magnetic north.

COMPASS CARD   A calibrated card which has the points of the compass.

COMPASS POINT   One-thirty-second part of a full circle or 11¼ degrees.

COMPASS ROSE   A graduated circle printed on a chart that has the points of the compass.

COMPENSATE   Correcting a compass from local magnetic attraction so that it will point as nearly as possible to the magnetic north.

CONSOL/CONSOLAN   A directional radio beacon in the 190- to 194-kilocycle band from which bearing information is obtained by counting the dots and dashes heard in a cycle of operation.

CORINTHIAN   An amateur sailor interested only in the sport without any thought of compensation for services rendered during a cruise or race.

COURSE   Direction sailed as measured by the compass.

CRADLE   A frame used to hold a boat when she is hauled out of the water.

CREW   People (in many cases, the family) who man the boat.

CRUISER   Any boat having arrangements for living aboard.

CUDDY   Small partitioned space under foredeck for storage.

CURRENT   The continuous movement of water in a certain direction.

CUTTER   A single masted sailboat in which the mast is set amidships. See *sloop.*

DAVIT   A crane used to hoist an anchor aboard. Also (in pairs), cranes used to lower a small boat from the deck of a larger one.

DAVY JONES'S LOCKER The bottom of the sea.

DAGGERBOARD A type of centerboard which does not pivot on a hinge, but is raised and lowered vertically in the trunk.

DEAD AHEAD Directly ahead of a boat's course.

DEAD ASTERN Directly astern of a boat's course.

DEAD RECKONING Piloting based on vessel's courses and distance traveled without reference to landmarks, celestial observations, etc.

DECK A platform covering or extending horizontally across a boat. The floor.

DEGREE One 360th of a circle.

DEVIATION Angular difference between compass bearing and magnetic bearing caused by the effect of iron aboard ship. Effect varies for each point of the compass.

DINGHY A small rowing boat that sometimes is rigged with a sail. Same as *tender* and *dink*.

DIP A position of a flag when hoisted part way. Also, to lower a flag part way and then hoist it again, as a salute.

DISPLACEMENT The weight of water displaced by a boat.

DOCK Properly the water next to a pier, but generally used to designate any platform—floating or fixed—at which boats may come alongside.

DORY A rowboat with a flat, narrow bottom and high freeboard noted for seaworthiness.

DOUSE To take in or lower a sail. Also to put out a light. Same as *dowse*.

DOWNHAUL A tackle or single line by which a sail is hauled down.

DOWN HELM To bring a boat up into the wind. Same as *up helm*.

DOWNWIND To leeward.

DRAFT Depth of water required to prevent running aground.

DRIFT The leeway of a boat.

DRAW A sail draws when filled with wind, while a boat draws enough water to float her.

EASE To slacken off.

EBB The outgoing tide.

EDDY A current of water or air running against the main current, especially one moving circularly.

ENSIGN A national flag flown on a boat.

EVEN KEEL Floating level.

EYE OF THE WIND The exact direction from which the wind is coming.

FAIRLEAD An eyelet fitting which changes the direction of a sheet or halyard led through it.

FAIRWAY A navigable channel.

FAIR WIND A favorable wind in direction of sailing.

FAKE To lay a coil of line in such a way that it will run out freely.

FAST To secure.

FATHOM A nautical measurement for the depth of water. One fathom equals 6 ft.

FEND To push off.

FENDERS Bumpers hung over boat's side to prevent chafing when tied up.

FETCH When a craft sailing to windward can make her objective without another tack.

FID A pointed stick or pin used in making rope splices.

FIT OUT Preparing a boat for launching or an extended trip.

FIX To find a boat's position by celestial or land observations.

FLOTATION Air tanks or other similar devices or materials which help to prevent a swamped boat from sinking.

FLOTSAM Floating debris.

FLYING BRIDGE A bridge mounted above the regular bridge.

FOLLOWING SEAS When the waves approach from astern of the boat.

FORE-AND-AFT Lengthwise of the boat; the opposite of athwartships.

FORECASTLE The forward part of the boat below the deck. Pronounced *fo'c'sle*.

FORE MAST Forward mast of a sailing vessel having two or more masts.

FOUL To become entangled or clogged. Not clean.

FOUNDER When a boat is swamped and begins to sink.

FREE Sailing with the wind anywhere from abeam to due aft. Also means to cast off, untangle, permit to run easily.

FREEBOARD The distance from the top of the hull to the water.

FURL To roll up a sail snugly on a boom and to secure it.

GAFF   Spar hoisted on the aft side of the mast to support the head of a sail, hence *gaff-rigged*.

GALE   A wind force measured in knots.

GALLEY   Sailor's name for kitchen.

GAM   A nautical talkfest. Also used as a verb.

GANGPLANK   A movable bridge on which to get from the dock or pier to a boat or vice versa.

GANGWAY   That part of boat's side where people pass in and out of the boat. Also, a command meaning "Get out of way of."

GEAR   A general term embracing all rigging or boating equipment.

GIMBAL   A device used for suspending the compass so that it will remain level.

GRAPNEL   A cluster of curved hooks at the end of a shank, the other end of which has a ring for the attachment of a line. It is primarily used for snagging and bringing up objects from the bottom.

GROUNDING   Running ashore.

GROUND TACKLE   Anchor, cable, etc., used to secure a boat to her moorings.

GUNKHOLING   Shallow water sailing.

GUNWALE   The rail of the boat at deck level.

GUDGEON   An eye fitting into which the rudder's pintles are inserted. Located on the transom of small sailboats.

GUY   A rope or wire used to steady or support.

HAIL   To speak or call to someone aboard your craft or another vessel.

HALYARD   A line used to hoist sails. Same as *halliard* or *haliard*.

HAND   A member of the crew.

HARD OVER   Placement of the wheel, or tiller, when it is put over as far as possible to one side or the other.

HATCH   An opening in a deck with a cover.

HAUL   To draw a boat out of the water on to land.

HAWSER   A heavy line or cable used in mooring or towing.

HEAD   A shipboard toilet.

HEADING   Direction of sailing.

HEADSAILS   All sails forward of the mast.

HEAD SHEETS   The sheets of the headsails.

HEADSTAY   Wire from the bow supporting the mast.

HEAD UP   To luff.

HEADWAY   Moving ahead.

HEAVE   What you do with a line—you do not throw it; you heave it.

HEAVING LINE   A strong lightweight rope one end of which is formed into a weighted ball or "monkey fist." The ball may be heaved over the water to another vessel, a dock, etc. After the heaving line has been caught, it is used to haul over a heavier "working" line.

HEEL   The tilt, tip, listing, or laying-over of a boat, usually due to the wind.

HELM   The tiller or wheel by which the rudder is controlled.

HELMSMAN   The person who steers.

HIKE   To climb or to lean out to windward to counteract excessive heeling.

HOLD   The interior of a vessel where the cargo is stowed.

HOOK   An anchor.

HULL   The main body of the boat. Does not include cabins and deckhouse. These are superstructure.

INBOARD   Within or part of the hull. Inboard engines are those permanently installed within the hull.

INSHORE   Toward the shore.

IN STAYS   When a boat is in the wind's eye while going from one tack to another.

IRISH PENNANT   An untidy loose end of a rope.

JACKSTAFF   Small flagstaff on the bow of a craft.

JIB   A triangular sail set forward of the mast.

JIBE   When running, to bring the wind on the other quarter so that the boom swings over. Same as *gybe*.

JIB-HEADED   A sailing rig that has all sails triangular. As *Marconi* and *Bermudian*.

JIB SHEET   The line that leads from the lower aft end of the jib to the cockpit. It controls the angle at which the sail is set.

JURY   A term used for making a temporary or makeshift rig. For example, a jury rig is any kind of a temporary rig that can be used to take a dismastered sailboat back to port.

KEDGE   A small anchor.

KEDGING   To move a boat by hauling on a kedge anchor.

KEEL   The backbone of a boat running fore-and-aft.

KEEL BOAT   A craft with a fixed keel that extends below the hull.

KETCH   A two-masted sailing vessel with smaller aftermast stepped forward of the stern post.

KNOT   A tie for fastening. Also a unit of speed equal to one nautical mile (6080 feet) per hour.

LABOR   When a boat rolls or pitches heavily.

LANDLUBBER   A short person, or a beginner in boating; one without nautical knowledge. Same as *lubber*.

LANDMARK   A distinct or familiar mark or object on shore.

LANYARD   A line fastened to an article, such as a pail, whistle, knife, or other small tool, for purposes of securing it.

LASH   To bind or secure an object with a line.

LATITUDE   Distance north or south of the equator.

LAUNCH   To set a boat afloat. Also, a small boat usually used for transporting people within a harbor.

LAY   When a craft is held windward without moving except for drifting.

LAY-UP   Protecting the boat during winter storage, etc.

LAZARETTE   A small space below deck, usually aft, where spare parts are kept.

LEAD   A small piece of lead, or other heavy object used in determining depth of water by dropping it to the bottom; has marked-off line attached.

LEE   The side sheltered from the wind. This side away from the wind on a ship is called the *lee side*.

LEEBOARD   A wide board secured on pivots to the side of a boat to reduce sideways drift when the boat is under sail (similar to a centerboard). The boards can be removed for beaching.

LEE HELM   When the position of the helm necessary to keep a boat on her course is toward the lee side.

LEEWARD   The direction which is away from the wind.

LEFT RUDDER   The command to turn the wheel to the left.

LIFEBOAT   A small ship's boat for emergency use.

LIFEBUOY   A ringbuoy for saving lives, usually made of cork.

LIFELINE   A wire or rope rigged around the deck of a vessel for the safety of the crew.

LIFE PRESERVER   A buoyant safety device worn by a person to keep afloat; may be belt, cushion, jacket, or ring.

LIMBER HOLES   Holes bored horizontally on the frames of the boat near the bottom to allow water in the bilge to drain to the lowest point where it can be pumped out.

LINE   A term for any rope used aboard a boat.

LIST   A boat is said to *list*, or be *listing* when it is leaning at an angle due to excess weight on one side.

L.O.A.   Means *length over all* and refers to the longest measurement of the boat as compared to the length at the waterline.

LOCK   A compartment in a canal which is used to bring a vessel to a lower or higher level.

LOCKER   A storage compartment on a boat. A box, wardrobe or chest. A *chain locker* is a compartment where chain cables are kept, while a *boatswain's locker* is where rigging and small stuff are kept. A *hanging locker* is a closet sufficiently large for hanging of clothing.

LOG   A speed measuring device which when hung astern rotates and registers on a dial.

LOGBOOK   Record book or sheet of a vessel's activities: course, destination, time, speed, distances traveled, fuel consumed, weather, wind, and other items of importance.

LONGITUDE   A measurement of distance expressed to degrees East and West of the meridian of Greenwich, England.

LOOKOUT   A crewman positioned in the bow or aloft for the purpose of observing and reporting conditions and objects seen.

LOOSE   To unfurl a sail.

LORAN   A system of long-range radio navigation based on the measurement of the difference in time of reception of signals from shore station transmitters in pairs. Measurements are made with a special loran receiver.

LUBBER LINE   The mark on a compass which indicates the fore-and-aft line of the boat.

LUFF   The forward edge of a sail. When

sailing sharply into the wind, the luff of a sail trembles, or *luffs*. *To luff* is also to bring the boat's head to the wind.

LURCH   The sudden rolling of a boat.

LYING-TO   Keeping a boat stationary with her head in the wind, usually by means of a sea anchor.

MAIN   The most important, such as main deck, mainmast, mainsail.

MAIN DECK   The highest deck going the full length of the vessel.

MAINSAIL   The sail (fore-and-aft) that is set to the mainmast.

MAKE   To set sail is to make sail.

MAKE FAST   To belay or secure a line.

MARCONI RIG   A rig using triangular sails hoisted on the mast and stays. Other names are *jib-headed* and *Bermudian*.

MARINA   A place that offers dockage, services and facilities to all types of pleasure craft.

MARK   Markings on a lead line which show the depths visually or by feeling.

MARLINE   A tarred, small line used for lashings, whipping, etc.

MARLINSPIKE   A pointed wooden or steel instrument used to open up the strands of rope and wire.

MAST   A vertical spar to support rigging, yards, and sails.

MASTER   The captain or man in charge of a boat. Same as *skipper*.

MASTHEAD   The top of a mast.

MATES   Master's assistants. On a family boat, the first mate is usually the wife.

MEND   To refurl an improperly furled sail; to rebend a sail to a boom.

MERIDIAN   A measurement of geographical location; any point on a half circle drawn between the north and south poles.

MESSENGER   A light line used to haul over a heavier rope or cable.

MIDSHIPS   The middle of a vessel's hull, or widest part. Same as *amidships*.

MILE   At sea the nautical mile is one minute of latitude at the equator, or 6,080 feet; used as a measure of distance.

MINUTE   One 60th of a degree of latitude or longitude; also, one 60th of an hour.

MIZZEN   The shorter mast aft on a yawl or ketch. Same as *mizzenmast*.

MIZZENSAIL   The sail set from the mizzenmast.

MONKEY FIST   A knot which is worked in the end of a heaving line.

MOOR   To secure a boat between two posts, to a dock, or to a buoy.

MOORING   A place where a boat is permanently anchored. It consists of a heavy anchor, chain, shackles, swivels, a mooring buoy, and pennant of rope.

MOTORBOAT ACT   Regulations covering handling and equipment of small craft.

MOTORSAILER   A vessel combining the features of both a sailboat and a motorboat.

MOUSE   To turn small stuff around a hook to prevent jerking out of its hold.

MUSHROOM   A heavy anchor used as a permanent mooring, shaped like an upside-down mushroom.

NAUTICAL   Anything pertaining to the sea.

NAVIGABLE   Water that is deep enough to permit passage of boats.

NAVIGATION   The science of determining a boat's position and safely conducting it from one place to another by means of charts, instruments and/or the stars.

NUN BUOY   A conical buoy, colored red, that is always on the right hand or starboard side of a channel when entering from seaward.

OAR   An implement used for propelling a boat. *Oarlocks,* or *rowlocks,* are fittings on the side of a boat used to hold and guide oars.

OFFSHORE WIND   The wind when it is blowing from or off the shore.

OILSKINS   A term generally used for all waterproof clothing.

ONE-DESIGN CLASS   A number of sailboats that are built exactly alike.

OUTBOARD   Outside of the hull itself. Outboard motor is attached (generally temporarily) at the stern or transom, outside the hull.

OUTRIGGERS   In sport fishing boats the term refers to the lightweight spars or poles having fittings on the tips to lead fishing lines beyond the sides of the boat while trolling.

OVER-ALL   The boat's extreme length. Abbreviated *LOA*.

OVERBOARD   Over the side of a boat.

OVERHANG   Any part of a boat extending beyond the waterline at the bow and stern.

OVERHAUL   To overtake or gain on another vessel at sea. Also to repair an engine or boat.

OVERSTAND To sail beyond an object, such as a buoy.

OWNER'S FLAG The private signal of a boat owner; usually of his own design.

PAINTER Bow line by which a small boat is towed or made fast to a mooring.

PARACHUTE A spinnaker cut so as to resemble a parachute.

PARALLEL RULES A pair of straight-edges fastened together so that the distance between them may be changed while their edges remain parallel. Used for transferring lines from one part of a chart to another.

PARALLELS Lines of latitude going around the earth's surface parallel to the equator.

PART To break a line.

PAY OUT To let out a line.

PELORUS A compass card fitted with sighting vanes and used for taking bearings.

PENNANT A length of line. Also, a small, narrow flag.

PIER A structure built out into the water to serve as a landing place for boats. Same as *jetty* or *wharf*.

PILING Vertical timbers or logs driven into the water's bottom to form a support for a dock or to act as a breakwater.

PILOT A man qualified and licensed to direct ships in and out of a harbor.

PITCH The fore-and-aft motion of a boat. Also, the angle of the propeller blades.

PLANING When a boat rides on top of the water.

PLANING HULL A hull that is capable of planing.

POINT One thirty-second of a circle.

PORPOISE When a boat rides with the bow up out of the water.

PORT The left side of a boat, looking toward the bow. Also, a harbor or place where vessels enter and leave, as for commerce.

PORT CAPTAIN The official at a port who is in charge of all harbor activities.

PORTHOLE Hole or window in the side of a boat.

PRAM A small dinghy, usually rectangular in shape.

PRIVILEGED VESSEL One which has the right-of-way.

PROPELLER The device, when turning, that moves the boat through the water.

PROW The part of the bow which extends up and out from the waterline.

PULPIT The platform at the bow of fishing type of boat.

PUNT A small, rectangular, flat-bottomed boat or dinghy.

PURCHASE Any rigging consisting of two or more blocks used to hoist a heavy weight.

QUARTER The after part of a boat's side; that part of a craft which lies within 45 degrees from the stern, known as the port quarter or starboard quarter.

QUARTERS Living and sleeping portions of a vessel.

RACE A very strong tidal current created when two tides of a different level meet.

RADAR The detection of objects and measurement of their bearing and distance by their reflection of radio signals.

RAIL The outer edge of the deck.

REACH All sailing points between running and close-hauled. *Close reach,* sailing nearly close-hauled with sheets just eased. *Beam reach,* sailing with the wind abeam. *Broad reach,* sailing with the wind abaft the beam and with sails well out on the quarter.

REEF To reduce sail area by partly lowering sail and securing the surplus material to the boom. Also a chain of rock or coral, or ridge of sand lying at or near the surface of the water.

REEVE To pass lines through blocks or fairleads.

RHUMB LINE A course that crosses all meridians at the same angle.

RIDE To lie at anchor.

RIDE OUT To weather out a storm safely whether at anchor or underway.

RIDING LIGHT White light visible from all points showing a vessel at anchor.

RIG Arrangement of a boat's sails, masts, and rigging. Also to put in proper order for working or use.

RIGGING A general term applying to all lines, shrouds, and stays necessary to spars and sails.

RIGHT RUDDER The command to turn the wheel to the right.

RIPS Short steep waves indicating the meeting of two tidal currents or cross-currents.

RODE An anchor line.

RUDDER   A flat member attached to the stern of a boat which controls the course of the boat.

RULES OF THE ROAD   The international regulations for preventing collisions at sea.

RUNNING   Sailing before the wind.

RUNNING LIGHTS   Lights carried by a vessel under way; they are required by law.

RUNNING RIGGING   The lines, such as halyards and sheets, that are used in the setting and trimming of sails.

SCHOONER   A sailboat with two or more masts in which the mainmast is behind the smaller one or ones.

SCOPE   The length of mooring or anchor line in use.

SCREW   A term often used for the propeller.

SCULL   To impel a boat by one oar at the stern.

SCUPPERS   Holes in the deck or in a self-bailing cockpit to permit the water to drain overboard.

SCUTTLE-BUTT   Gossip.

SEA   Refers in this book to all sailing waters.

SEA ANCHOR   A drag device, usually canvas, used to keep a boat headed into the wind during very heavy weather.

SEA COCK   A through-the-hull fitting that can be opened or closed.

SECURE   To make fast.

SET   The shape of a sail.

SEXTANT   An instrument used in navigation by determining altitude of sun and stars.

SHACKLE   A U-shaped piece of metal with a pin across the open end.

SHAKEDOWN   A trial cruise to test boat's condition.

SHEET   A line used to trim a sail.

SHIPSHAPE   Well-kept, orderly, clean.

SHOAL   An underwater hill or sandbar whose top is near the surface. Also, shallow water.

SHROUD   Standing rigging, usually of wire, running from the mast to the sides of a boat to support the mast.

SKEG   The projection below a keel, usually supporting the rudder.

SKIPPER   Captain of the vessel.

SLACK   To ease off a line.

SLACK WATER   The short period of time when the ebb (low) and flood (high) remain stationary.

SLIP   The space between two wharves or piers where a boat can be moved.

SLOOP   A single masted sailboat in which the mast is set forward of amidships and, frequently, with a bowsprit.

SMALL STUFF   While it technically means any line or rope less than one inch in diameter, it usually implies twine, marline, etc.

SNUB   To check or stop suddenly, as a line.

SOUND   To get the depth of water.

SPAR   Term for masts, booms, spinnaker poles, etc.

SPAR BUOY   A tall buoy used as an aid to navigation.

SPINNAKER   A large, light sail used when a boat is sailing before the wind or on a reach.

SPLICE   To join rope by tucking the strands together, such as short, long, eye and back splice, etc.

SPRING LINES   Additional docking lines used to prevent a boat from moving.

STAFF   Upright pole on which a light or flag is affixed.

STANCHIONS   Any fixed, upright support.

STAND BY   An order employed to alert crewmen.

STANDING RIGGING   The shrouds and stays as well as other rigging which are not moved in working a boat.

STARBOARD   The right side of a boat, looking toward the bow.

STEADY   To maintain a given course.

STEERAGEWAY   Sufficient forward speed to allow rudder control.

STEM   More or less vertical timber at bow; boat's entering edge.

STEP   A socket that holds the base of the mast; hence, to step.

STERN   The after part of a boat.

STERNWAY   Backward movement of a boat.

STOW   To put away gear in its proper place.

STUFFING BOX   A device around a propeller shaft that permits it to revolve freely without letting water into the hull.

SWAB   Seagoing name for mop. You swab down, not mop up.

SWELL   Nonbreaking, long, easy waves.

TACHOMETER   An instrument used to record the r.p.m. of an engine; a nautical speedometer.

TACK   The lower forward corner of a sail. Also, to proceed to windward by sailing on alternate courses so that the wind is first on one side of the boat and then on the other.

TACKLE   A system of blocks and ropes arranged for hauling.

TAFFRAIL   The bulwark around a boat's stern.

TELL-TALE   A short piece of ribbon or string tied to a shroud to indicate the direction of the wind.

TENDER   A small boat employed to go back and forth to the shore from a larger boat.

THWARTSHIPS   At right angles to a center line passing through keel. Across the boat from side to side.

TIDAL WATER   Salt water being of, or having its source in, the ocean.

TIDE   Commonly, it is used to describe the inflow and outflow of water caused by the gravitational influence of the moon and sun. Better usage would restrict the term to the vertical rise and fall of water produced by these causes.

TILLER   A bar of wood or metal fastened to the head of the rubber post, by which the rudder may be turned.

TOPSIDES   That portion of the hull above the water line.

TRACK   The course of a boat.

TRANSOM   The board or boards forming the aft end of a more or less square-sterned boat. In outboard boats it is that part of the boat from which the motor is hung.

TRICK   A period of duty at the helm.

TRIM   To trim sails—to put them in correct relation to the wind by means of sheets. Also, the way a boat floats on the water—on an even keel, heeled over, or down by the bow or stern.

TRIMARAN   A term generally used to mean a craft that has three hulls.

TROLLING   To fish from a boat moving at a very low speed.

TROUGH   The valley between two waves.

TRUE COURSE   A course steered by a boat's compass that has been corrected for deviation and variation.

TURNBUCKLE   A device used to maintain correct tension on standing rigging.

TWIN SCREW   A term used to denote a boat that has two propellers.

UNBEND   To cast adift or untie.

UNDERWAY   A vessel when not aground, made fast to the shore, or at anchor.

UNFURL   To unfold a sail, flag, etc.

UP ANCHOR   Order to weigh or hoist up the anchor.

VARIATION   The difference in degrees between true and magnetic north.

WAKE   The eddies and swirls left astern of a boat in motion.

WASH   The waves made by a boat moving through the water.

WATCH   A tour of duty on board a ship.

WATERLINE   A line, painted or imaginary, around the hull at the water level. Also a line corresponding with the water level at various loads.

WAY   Movement through the water of the boat.

WEATHER   In the direction from which the wind blows.

WEATHER SIDE   The side exposed to the wind.

WEIGH   To raise the anchor.

WELL-FOUNDED   Well-equipped.

WHEEL   A revolving appliance connected with the rudder or tiller for steering. Also a name given to a propeller.

WHIP   To whip a line is to bind the strands of its end with yarn or cord.

WINCH   A mechanical device to give increased hauling power on a line.

WINDLASS   A winch for hauling cable, etc.

WIND'S EYE   Exact direction from which the wind is blowing.

WIND VELOCITY   Rate of motion of the wind.

WINDWARD   The direction from which the wind is blowing. The windward, or weather side of a boat, is that toward the wind.

YACHT   Geneal term for a boat used solely for the personal pleasure of the owner.

YAW   To swing off course (usually due to heavy seas) without regard for the position of the rudder.

YAWL   A sailboat similar to ketch but with smaller aftermast stepped abaft the tiller or wheel.

APPENDIX B:
ENGINE
CARE
AND
TROUBLE
SHOOTING

Dependability is the keyword in the design and construction of modern marine engines —both inboard and outboard. They will start faithfully every time and keep running in the roughest going, if given a minimum amount of regular checking and servicing. Some people turn the job of boat engine maintenance over to a trained serviceman in their vicinity; just as they do with the family car. Many, however, prefer to handle preventive maintenance themselves—not a difficult routine when the instructions in the engine builder's manual are followed.

Preventive maintenance for all engines begins with proper lubrication. Nothing else can do more to save repair bills and keep engines young for the longest possible length of time. With both inboards and outboards, the first essential of proper lubrication is the use of top quality motor oil that has been made specifically for marine use . . . which means an engine that has to work hard for long hours at a stretch. The following are the basic check points, beyond proper lubrication, that apply to sound preventive maintenance for both outboard and inboard engines:

Outboards
1. Check underwater gear units to be sure the supply of lubricant is up to level.
2. Check and lubricate as required swivel brackets, shift levers, throttle shafts and gears, carburetor and magneto linkage, any other points listed by the manufacturer for periodic lubrication.
3. Check remote control cables and linkages for steering, throttle and clutch.
4. Check gas lines and connections for absolute tightness.
5. Check electrical system, including spark plugs, battery, generator, voltage regulator, starter, lights, horn, windshield wiper.

Inboards
1. Check engine and gear case lubricant levels. Bring up to recommended levels as needed—*do not overfill*. Change all lubricants at recommended periods to avoid formation of sludge and other harmful deposits.
2. Check cooling system temperature gauge. A range from 165 to 180 degrees F. usually is recommended.
3. Check oil pressure gauge and ammeter readings regularly when running.
4. Before starting on a trip, check the power transmission line, including action of clutch, reverse and reduction gears; shaft alignment; thrust bearing and stuffing box.
5. Check cooling system piping and connections regularly for leaks. Check water inlet and by-pass valves; water pump; cooling water discharge. A closed, fresh-water cooling system should be protected by using a rust inhibitor to safeguard against corrosion, rust and scale.

6. Check electrical system, including spark plugs, distributor, starter, generator, battery, battery cables, lights, horn, windshield wipers, electric bilge pump.

7. Check fuel system regularly, including all lines, fittings and valves; tank shut-offs; filters; pumps; carburetors.

8. Water supply. Before starting on trip, be sure tank is filled; cap is on securely; all connections are tight.

9. Before each trip, check to be sure gasoline tanks are filled and tank caps are on securely.

TROUBLESHOOTING AN INBOARD ENGINE

A gasoline engine depends upon three main factors for proper operation: an unfailing fuel supply, uninterrupted ignition, and good compression. When any one of these is not present, or present only intermittently, engine failure will result. The following "trouble-shooting" information is designed to help the operator locate and overcome some of the most probable causes of engine failure or improper operation. Probable causes are listed in the most likely order of occurrence. Only one correction should be attempted at a time and that possibility eliminated before going on to the next.

Trouble	Probable Cause	Correction
Starter will not crank engine	Discharged battery	Charge or replace battery
	Corroded battery terminals	Clean terminals
	Loose connection in starting circuit	Check and tighten all connections
	Defective starting switch	Replace switch
	Starter motor brushes dirty	Clean or replace brushes
	Jammed Bendix gear	Loosen starter motor to free gear
	Defective starter motor	Replace motor
Starter motor turns but does not crank engine	Partially discharged battery	Charge or replace battery
	Defective wiring or wiring of too-low capacity	Check wiring for worn acid spots
	Broken Bendix drive	Remove starter motor and repair drive
Engine will not start	Empty fuel tank	Fill tank with proper fuel
	Flooded engine	Remove spark plugs and crank engine several times Replace plugs
	Water in fuel system	If water is found, clean tank, fuel lines, and carburetor Refill with proper fuel
	Inoperative or sticking choke valve	Check valve, linkage, and choke rod or cable for proper operation
	Improperly adjusted carburetor	Adjust carburetor
	Clogged fuel lines of defective fuel pump	Disconnect fuel line at carburetor. If fuel does not flow freely when engine is cranked, clean fuel line and sediment bowl. If fuel still does not flow freely after cleaning, repair or replace pump

Engine will not start (poor compression and other causes)	Air leak around intake manifold	Check for leak by squirting oil around intake connections. If leak is found, tighten manifold and if necessary replace gaskets
	Loose spark plugs	Check all plugs for proper seating, gasket, and tightness. Replace all damaged plugs and gaskets
	Loose seating valves	Check for broken or weak valve springs, warped stems, carbon and gum deposits, and insufficient tappet clearance
	Damaged cylinder head gasket	Check for leaks around gasket when engine is cranked. If a leak is found replace gasket
	Worn or broken piston rings	Replace broken and worn rings. Check cylinders for "out of round" and "taper"
Excessive engine temperature	No water circulation	Check for clogged water lines and restricted inlets. Check for broken or stuck thermostat. Look for worn or damaged water pump or water pump drive
Engine temperature too low	Broken or stuck thermostat	Replace thermostat
Engine will not start (ignition system)	Ignition switch "off" or defective	Turn on switch or replace
	Fouled or broken spark plugs	Remove plugs and inspect for cracked porcelain, dirty points or improper gap
	Improperly set, worn, or pitted distributor points. Defective ignition coil	Remove center wire from distributor cap and hold within ⅜ inch of motor block. Crank engine. Clean sharp spark should jump between wire and block when points open. Clean and adjust points. If spark is weak or yellow after adjustment of points, replace condenser. If spark still is weak or not present replace ignition coil
	Wet, cracked, or broken distributor	Wipe inside surfaces of distributor dry with clean cloth. Inspect for cracked or broken parts. Replace necessary parts
	Improperly set, worn, or pitted magneto breaker points (magneto models only)	Remove spark plug wire and hold within ⅜ inch of engine block. Clean sharp spark should jump between wire and block when engine is cranked. If spark is weak or not present clean and adjust breaker points

	Improperly set, worn, or pitted timer points. Defective coil or defective condenser	Remove spark plug wire and hold within ⅛ inch of engine block. A clean sharp spark should jump between wire and block when engine is cranked. Clean and set timer points. If spark still is not present when engine is cranked, replace coil
	Improper timing	Set timing
No oil pressure	Defective gauge or tube	Replace gauge or tube
	No oil in engine	Refill with the proper grade oil
	Dirt in pressure relief valve	Clean valve
	Defective oil pump, leak in oil lines, or broken oil pump drive	Check oil pump and oil pump drive for worn or broken parts. Tighten all oil line connections
Loss of rpm (boat or associated equipment)	Damaged propeller	Repair propeller
	Bent rudder	Repair
	Misalignment	Realign engine to shaft
	Too-tight stuffing box packing gland	Adjust
	Dirty boat bottom	
Vibration	Misfiring of pre-ignition	See correction under misfiring and pre-ignition
	Loose foundation of foundation bolts	
	Propeller shaft out of line or bent	
	Propeller bent or pitch out of true	
Pre-ignition	Defective spark plugs	Check all spark plugs for broken porcelain, burned electrodes, or electrodes out of adjustment. Replace all defective plugs or clean and reset
	Improper timing	Readjust timing
	Engine carbon	Remove cylinder head and clean out carbon
	Engine overheating	See correction under "Engine will not start" portion of this table
Backfiring	Insufficient fuel reaching engine due to dirty lines or strainer, or blocked fuel tank vent. Water in fuel tank	See correction under "Engine will not start" portion of this table
	Poorly adjusted distributor	See correction under "Engine will not start" portion of this table
Low oil pressure	Too-light body oil	Replace with proper weight oil

	Oil leak in pressure line	Inspect all oil lines. Tighten all connections
	Weak or broken pressure relief valve spring	Replace spring
	Worn oil pump	Replace pump
	Worn·or loose bearings	Replace bearings
Oil pressure too high	Too-heavy body oil	Drain oil and replace with oil of proper weight
	Stuck pressure relief valve	Clean or replace valve
	Dirt or obstruction in lines	Drain and clean oil system. Check for bent or flattened oil lines and replace where necessary
Sludge in oil	Infrequent oil changes	Drain and refill with proper weight oil
	Water in oil	Drain and refill. If trouble persists check for cracked block, defective head gasket, and cracked head
	Dirty oil filter	Replace filter

DIESEL ENGINE TROUBLE GUIDE

Ring Sticking
1. Distorted pistons or cylinders
2. High or low jacket water temperatures.
3. Worn pistons
4. Worn or weak rings.
5. Insufficient ring side clearance
6. High cylinder oil feed rate.
7. High crankcase oil level.
8. Poor quality oil.
9. Continuous overload operation.

Ring and Cylinder Wear
1. Improper filtration of air, fuel or oil.
2. Water in fuel or oil.
3. Corrosive fuel.
4. Low oil viscosity.
5. Insufficient oil.
6. Low jacket water temperature.
7. Blow-by.
8. Distorted pistons or cylinders.
9. Frequent cold starts.
10. Excessive piston clearance.

Crankcase Deposits
1. Improper oil filtration.
2. Improper combustion.
3. High oil temperature.
4. Low oil temperature.
5. Blow-by.
6. Condensation.
7. Leaking water jacket.
8. Excessive oil spray.
9. Clogged crankcase breather or vent.
10. Inadequate piston cooling.

Bearing Wear or Failure
1. Excessive bearing clearance.
2. Insufficient bearing clearance.
3. Misaligned bearings.
4. Distorted crankshaft.
5. Insufficient oil.
6. Low oil viscosity.
7. Contaminated oil.
8. Corrosive oil.
9. Water in oil.
10. Defective bearing construction.

High Oil Temperature
1. Clogged oil cooler.
2. Clogged oil lines.
3. Sludged crankcase.
4. Continuous overload operation.
5. Insufficient jacket water cooling.
6. Overheated bearing.
7. Incorrect oil viscosity.
8. Insufficient oil in sump or crankcase

Lack of Power
1. Improper combustion.
2. Insufficient air.
3. High back pressure.
4. Low fuel heat content.
5. Low compression pressure.
6. Leaking exhaust valve.
7. Tight bearings.
8. Improper lubrication.

9. Insufficient oil circulation.
10. Improper timing.

Combustion Chamber and Deposits
1. Improper air filtration.
2. Wet or corrosive gas.
3. Improper Diesel fuel filtration.
4. Improper combustion.
5. High cylinder oil feed rate.
6. High crankcase vacuum.
7. High crankcase oil level.
8. Worn or weak rings.
9. Low jacket water temperature.
10. Continuous overload operation.

Improper Combustion
1. Unbalanced cylinder head.
2. Sticking, leaking, or plugged injectors.
3. Unsuitable fuel.
4. Low injection pressure.
5. Incorrect injection timing.
6. Insufficient air.
7. Low compression pressure.
8. Leaking or sticking intake or exhaust valves.
9. Low load.
10. Low jacket temperature.

9. Leaking injectors.
10. Late timing.

High Oil Consumption
1. High cylinder oil feed rate.
2. High crankcase vacuum.
3. High crankcase oil level.
4. Leakage.
5. Worn or stuck rings.
6. Ineffective oil ring control.
7. Worn pistons or cylinders.
8. Excessive bearing clearance.
9. High oil pressure.
10. Low oil viscosity.

OUTBOARD MOTOR TROUBLE GUIDE

Trouble	Probable Cause
Motor Won't Start, or Misses	Gas tank empty. Fuel line shut-off closed. Motor not primed, or choked (if cold). Motor flooded (if warm). Fuel tank air vent closed. Dirt or water in carburetor, tank, screen or fuel line. Too much oil in fuel mixture (indicated by excessive smoke). Gaskets in crankcase, intake valves or carburetor blown.* Disconnected, loose, or broken spark plug wire. Spark plugs shorting to motor housing. Spark plug improperly gapped or dirty. Magneto coil, condenser, or magneto weak.* Spark plug insulation cracked or dirty. Magneto points improperly gapped or dirty.
Motor Won't Idle Smoothly	Incorrect carburetor idling adjustment. Spark plug type too "cold" or improperly gapped. Intake valve gasket blown.* Motor too deep in water.
Motor Loses Power or Slows Down	Carburetor main adjustment too lean (backfires and slows down). Carburetor main adjustment too rich (runs roughly and slows down). Spark plug type too "hot." Incorrect oil gas mixture. Motor overheating. Poor compression: scored cylinders; rings stuck in grooves; gaskets leaking or blown.* Gas line or screen dirty.
Excessive Motor Vibration	Incorrect carburetor adjustment. Clamp screws loose.

	Pivot bracket loose. Steering tension adjustment loose. Bent, broken, or fouled propeller. One spark plug not firing.
Motor "Knocks" or "Pings"	Propeller nut loose. Flywheel nut loose. Spark too far advanced. Carbon in cylinders.* Motor overheating, causing pre-ignition. Worn bearings, piston, cylinder, or loose rod.* Starter not properly centered.*
Motor Stiffens Up or "Freezes"	Rust on cylinder walls, rings or crankshaft.* No lubricant in lower unit gear housing. Fishline wound around propeller shaft. Bent propeller, driveshaft, or propeller shaft. Not enough oil in fuel mixture.
Motor Runs without Turning Propeller	Propeller shear pin broken. Propeller shaft, driveshaft, or propeller broken or propeller nut loose.
Motor Runs but Boat Scarcely Moves	Propeller blades bent. Lower unit foul, causing cavitation. Motor not deep enough in water. Rope or other obstruction dragging.
Motor Overheats	Water intake clogged. Water line leaking or broken. Gasket between power head and exhaust casing blown. Not enough oil in fuel mixture. Water pump clogged or worn.* Motor not deep enough in water.

*Authorized repair service is recommended.

APPENDIX C:
NAUTICAL CHART
SYMBOLS AND
ABBREVIATIONS

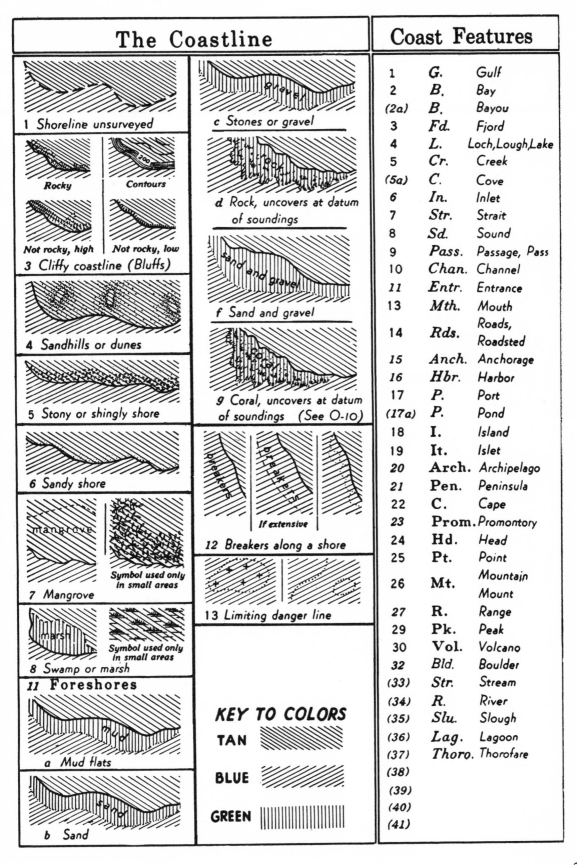

The Coastline

1 Shoreline unsurveyed

Rocky | Contours

Not rocky, high | Not rocky, low
3 Cliffy coastline (Bluffs)

4 Sandhills or dunes

5 Stony or shingly shore

6 Sandy shore

mangrove

Symbol used only in small areas
7 Mangrove

marsh

Symbol used only in small areas
8 Swamp or marsh

11 Foreshores

a Mud flats

b Sand

c Stones or gravel

d Rock, uncovers at datum of soundings

f Sand and gravel

g Coral, uncovers at datum of soundings (See O-10)

breakers | breakers | breakers

If extensive
12 Breakers along a shore

13 Limiting danger line

KEY TO COLORS

TAN

BLUE

GREEN

Coast Features

1	G.	Gulf
2	B.	Bay
(2a)	B.	Bayou
3	Fd.	Fjord
4	L.	Loch, Lough, Lake
5	Cr.	Creek
(5a)	C.	Cove
6	In.	Inlet
7	Str.	Strait
8	Sd.	Sound
9	Pass.	Passage, Pass
10	Chan.	Channel
11	Entr.	Entrance
13	Mth.	Mouth
14	Rds.	Roads, Roadsted
15	Anch.	Anchorage
16	Hbr.	Harbor
17	P.	Port
(17a)	P.	Pond
18	I.	Island
19	It.	Islet
20	Arch.	Archipelago
21	Pen.	Peninsula
22	C.	Cape
23	Prom.	Promontory
24	Hd.	Head
25	Pt.	Point
26	Mt.	Mountain, Mount
27	R.	Range
29	Pk.	Peak
30	Vol.	Volcano
32	Bld.	Boulder
(33)	Str.	Stream
(34)	R.	River
(35)	Slu.	Slough
(36)	Lag.	Lagoon
(37)	Thoro.	Thorofare
(38)		
(39)		
(40)		
(41)		

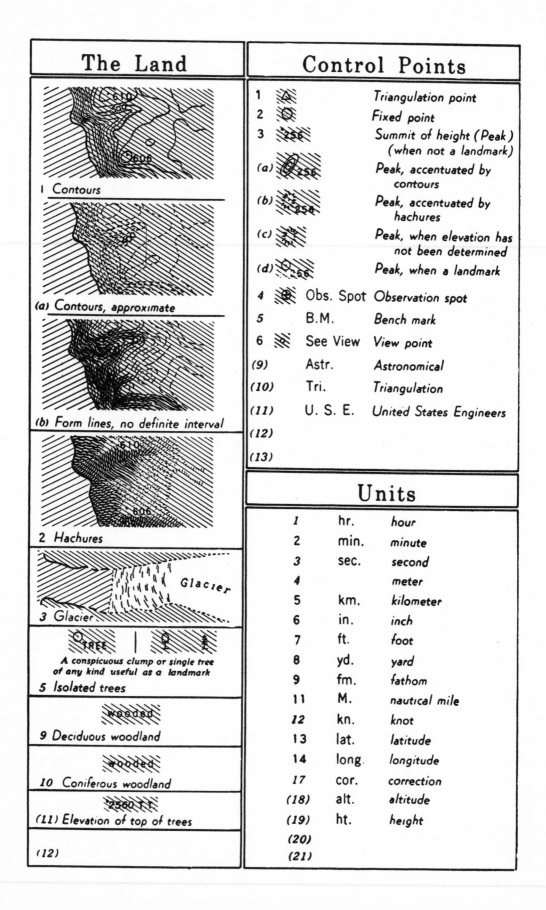

The Land		Control Points		

The Land

1 Contours

(a) Contours, approximate

(b) Form lines, no definite interval

2 Hachures

3 Glacier — *Glacier*

5 Isolated trees
A conspicuous clump or single tree of any kind useful as a landmark

9 Deciduous woodland

10 Coniferous woodland

(11) Elevation of top of trees

(12)

Control Points

1		Triangulation point
2		Fixed point
3	256	Summit of height (Peak) (when not a landmark)
(a)	256	Peak, accentuated by contours
(b)	256	Peak, accentuated by hachures
(c)		Peak, when elevation has not been determined
(d)	256	Peak, when a landmark
4	Obs. Spot	Observation spot
5	B.M.	Bench mark
6	See View	View point
(9)	Astr.	Astronomical
(10)	Tri.	Triangulation
(11)	U. S. E.	United States Engineers
(12)		
(13)		

Units

1	hr.	hour
2	min.	minute
3	sec.	second
4		meter
5	km.	kilometer
6	in.	inch
7	ft.	foot
8	yd.	yard
9	fm.	fathom
11	M.	nautical mile
12	kn.	knot
13	lat.	latitude
14	long.	longitude
17	cor.	correction
(18)	alt.	altitude
(19)	ht.	height
(20)		
(21)		

	Adjectives				Harbors	

Adjectives

and other abbreviations

1	gt.	great
3	lrg.	large
4	sml.	small
7	mid.	middle
9	anc.	ancient
12	conspic.	conspicuous
16	dist.	distant
17	abt.	about
(19)	aband.	abandoned
(20)	extr.	extreme
(21)	concr.	concrete
(22)	bet.	between
(23)	estab.	established
(24)	exper.	experimental
(25)	discontd.	discontinued
(26)	fl.	flood
(27)	mod.	moderate
(28)	maintd.	maintained
(29)	elec.	electric
(30)	priv.	private, privately
(31)	prom.	prominent
(32)	std.	standard
(33)	subm.	submerged
(34)	approx.	approximate
(35)	cor.	corner
(36)	Cl.	clearance
(37)	No.	number
(38)	Ave.	avenue
(39)	Hy.	highway
(40)	explos.	explosive
(41)		

Harbors

1	Anch.	Anchorage, large vessels (see P-12)
2	Anch.	Anchorage, small vessels
3	Hbr.	Harbor
6	Bkwr.	breakwater
8		jetty (partly below M.H.W.)
(8a)		jetty (small scale)
9	Pier	pier
11		groin (partly below M.H.W.)
12	Anch. prohib.	Anchorage prohibited
13		spoil ground
14		fish traps (actual shape charted)
(14a)	Fsh. stk.	fishing stakes when dangerous
16	Ldg.	landing place
18	Whf.	wharf
21	Dol.	dolphin
26	Quar.	Quarantine
29	Cus. Ho.	Customhouse
33	B. Hbr.	Boat Harbor
35		dock
36		dry dock (actual shape shown on large scale charts)
37		floating dock (actual shape shown on large scale charts)
39		patent slip (marine railway)
(39a)	Ramp	ramp
40		lock (point upstream)
45	Obsy.	Observatory
(46)		
(47)		

KEY TO COLORS

TAN BLUE GREEN

Topography

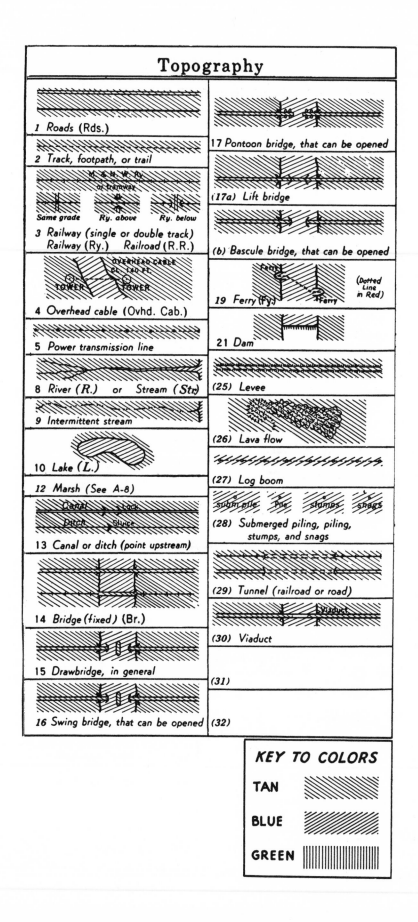

1 Roads (Rds.)

2 Track, footpath, or trail

3 Railway (single or double track)
Railway (Ry.)   Railroad (R.R.)
Same grade   Ry. above   Ry. below

4 Overhead cable (Ovhd. Cab.)
TOWER   TOWER   OVERHEAD CABLE CL. 140 FT.

5 Power transmission line

8 River (R.)   or   Stream (Str.)

9 Intermittent stream

10 Lake (L.)

12 Marsh (See A-8)

13 Canal or ditch (point upstream)
Canal   Lock
Ditch   Sluice

14 Bridge (fixed) (Br.)

15 Drawbridge, in general

16 Swing bridge, that can be opened

17 Pontoon bridge, that can be opened

(17a) Lift bridge

(b) Bascule bridge, that can be opened

19 Ferry (Fy.)   Ferry   (Dotted Line in Red)
Ferry   Ferry

21 Dam

(25) Levee

(26) Lava flow

(27) Log boom

(28) Submerged piling, piling, stumps, and snags
subm. pile   Pile   stumps   snags

(29) Tunnel (railroad or road)

(30) Viaduct
Viaduct

(31)

(32)

KEY TO COLORS

TAN

BLUE

GREEN

216

Buildings

When the buildings are prominent, they may be shown by landmark symbol with descriptive note. (See
The landmark symbol is used to indicate positions of objects when accurately determined.

1		City or town (large scale)	
(1a)		City or town (small scale)	
3	Vil.	Village	
4	Cas.	Castle	
5	Ho.	House	
8	Ch.	Church	
10		Temple	
12		Mosque	
13		Minaret	
14	Pag.	Pagoda	
16	Mony.	Monastery	
18	Cem.	Cemetery	
19	Ft.	Fort (actual shape charted)	
23		Airplane landing field	
24		Airport (large scale)	
		Small scale	
(24a)	(Red)	Airport (military)	
(24b)		Airport (civil)	
26		Street	
27	Tel.	Telegra.	
29	P.O.	Post Office	
30	Govt.	Government	
32	Hosp.	Hospita	
34	Magz.	Magazine	

35		Monument	
36		Cupola	
37	elev.	elevation elevator elevated	
40		Ruins	
41		Tower	
42		Windmill	
44		Chimney, Stack	
46		Oil tank	
47	Facty.	Factory	
(56)		Gable	
(57)	Sch.	School	
(58)	H.S.	High School	
(59)	Univ.	University	
(60)	Inst.	Institute	
(61)	Co.	Company	
(62)	Corp.	Corporation	
(63)	Cap.	Capitol	
(64)	C.H.	Courthouse	
(65)	Cath.	Cathedral	
(66)	Bldg.	Building	
(67)	Pav.	Pavilion	
(68)	Ltd.	Limited	
(69)	Apt.	Apartment	
(70)	Tp.	Telephone	
(71)			
(72)			

Miscellaneous Stations

2	Sta.	Station	19			Flagstaff
3		Coast Guard (similar to L.S.S.)	(20)			Weather Bureau Signal Station
(3a)		When the building is a landmark	(21)			Flagpole
6		Lifesaving Station (See No. J-3)	(22)			Flag tower
7	Rkt. Sta.	Rocket station	(23)			Lookout tower
8		Pilot Station	(24)			Standpipe
9	Sig. Sta.	Signal Station	(25)			On land
10	Sem.	Semaphore	(26)			

Lights

1		Position of light	(39)	min.	minutes	
2	Lt.	Light	(40)	sec.	seconds	
3	L.H.	Lighthouse	44		visible	
4	AERO	Aeronautical light	(44a)	M.	nautical mile	
5		Lighted beacon	47	Gp.	group	
6		Lightship	49	SEC.	sector	
7		Lighted buoy	61	Vi.	violet	
10	REF.	Reflector	63	Bu.	blue	
			64	G.	green	
			65	Or.	orange	
			66	R.	red	
(17)	Priv. maintd.	Private light (maintained by private interests; to be used with caution)	67	W.	white	
			(67a)	Am.	amber	
			68	OBSC.	obscured	
21	F	Fixed	69	(U)	unwatched	
22	Occ	Occulting	70	Occas.	occasional	
23	Fl	Flashing	71	Irreg.	irregular	
24	Qk Fl	Quick flashing	73	Temp	temporary	
(24a)	I Qk	Interrupted quick	80	Vert.	vertical	
26	Alt	Alternating	81	Hor.	horizontal	
27	Gp Occ	Group occulting	(82)	D.	destroyed	
28	Gp Fl	Group flashing	(82a)	Exting.	extinguished	
(28a)	S-L	Short-long	(83)	V.B.	vertical beam	
29	F Fl	Fixed and flashing	(84)	Exper.	experimental	
30	F Gp Fl	Fixed and group flashing	(85)	R.	range	
31	Rot.	Rotating	(86)	AERO	aeronautical	
			(87)			
			(88)			
			(89)			

Buoys and Beacons

On entering a channel from seaward, buoys on starboard side are red with even numbers, on port side black with odd numbers. Light on buoys on starboard side of channel are red or white, on port side white or green. Mid-channel buoys have black and white vertical stripes. Obstruction buoys are green, or have red and black horizontal bands. This system does not always apply to foreign waters. The dot of the buoy symbol, and the small circle of the light vessel and mooring buoy symbols ...i the center of the beacon symbol indicate their positions.

1	•	Position of buoy	24	Qr	Quar.	Quarantine buoy
2	Magenta disc	Lighted buoy (on magenta disc)	(27)	BW		Fish trap buoy (W. & B. H. B.)
3	BELL	Bell buoy	(28)			Anchorage buoy
(3a)	GONG	Gong buoy	(29)	Priv. maintd.		Maintained by private interests; to be used with caution
4	WHIS	Whistle buoy	31		H. B.	Horizontal bands
5	C	Can buoy	32		V. S.	Vertical stripes
6	N	Nun buoy	33		Chec.	checkered
7	SP	Spherical buoy	41		W.	white
8	S	Spar buoy	42		B.	black
(8a)		Checkered buoy	43		R.	red
12	Magenta disc	Lightship	44		Y.	yellow
			45		G.	green
14		Fairway buoy (B. & W. V. S.) (Mid-Channel)	(46)		Br.	brown
			(47)		Gy.	gray
18	RB RB	Junction buoy (R. & B. H. B.)	(48)		T.B.	temporary buoy
19	RB RB	Isolated danger buoy (R. & B. H. B.)	52	△ Red ▲ ▲ W.Bn. R.Bn. Bn.		Fixed beacons (unlighted daymarks)
20	RB G	Wreck or obstruction buoy (R. & B. H. B.) or (G.)	(52a)	MARKER		Private aid to navigation
22		Mooring buoy	53		Bn.	Beacon (See L-52)
			63	⊙		Landmark
			(63a)	○ Tank		Landmark, position approx
			(64)		REF.	Reflector
			(65)			

Note: Buoy and beacon symbols with topmarks may be shown on charts of foreign waters

Radio Stations

1	○R Sta.	Radio station
2	○R. Tp.	Radio telephone
3 Magenta	⊙R. Bn.	Radiobeacon
7	⊙R. D. F.	Radio direction finder station
9	○R. Tr.	Radio tower
(9a)	○R. Mast	Radio mast
(10)	○R. Tr. (WEAF)	Commercial broadcast
(11) Magenta	⊙Ra.	Coast radar station
(12)	⊙Racon	Radar responder beacon
(13)	Ra. Ref.	Radar reflector
(14)	Ra. (conspic.)	Radar conspicuous object
(15)	Ra. Mk.	Ramark

Fog Signals

1	Fog Sig.	Fog Signal Station
6	SUB-BELL	Submarine fog bell (mechanical)
7	SUB-OSC.	Submarine oscillator
8	NAUTO.	Nautophone
9	DIA.	Diaphone
11	SIREN	Fog siren
12	HORN	Fog trumpet
13	HORN	Fog horn
14	BELL	Fog bell
15	WHIS.	Fog whistle
16	REED	Reed horn
17	GONG	Gong
(18)	D. F. S.	Distance Finding Sta.
(19)	GUN	Fog gun
(20)		

Dangers

1 Rocks which do not cover; with their elevations above M.H.W.	**16** Sunken wreck, not dangerous to surface navigation or over which the depth exceeds 10 fathoms
2 Rocks that cover and uncover, with heights in feet above datum of soundings	**17** Foul ground
(3a) When rock of No. 2 is considered a danger to navigation	**18** Overfalls or tide rips — Symbol used only in small areas
(4a) Sunken rock	**19** Eddies
(4b) When rock of No. 4a is considered a danger to navigation	**20** Kelp, any kind — Symbol used only in small areas
(4c) Shoal sounding on isolated rock replaces symbol	*(20a)*
(6a) Sunken danger with depth cleared by wire drag (Feet or fathoms)	*(20b)*
10 Coral or rocky reef (below datum of soundings) See A-11g	**21** Bk. bank
	22 Shl. shoal
	23 Rf. reef
	24 Le. ledge
	25 breakers (see A-12)
11 Stranded wreck (any portion of hull above datum of soundings)	**27** Obstr. obstruction
	28 Wk. wreck
12 Sunken wreck with only masts visible	*(28a)* Wks. wreckage
	33 cov. covers
	34 uncov. uncovers
	35 Rep. reported
14 Dangerous sunken wreck with less than 10 fathoms of water over it (See No. 6a)	*(35a)* shoal reported
	36 Discol. discolored
	41 P.A. position approximate
(14a) A number of sunken wrecks	**42** P.D. position doubtful
	43 E.D. existence doubtful
	44 Pos. position
(14b) Obstruction of any kind	*(46)*
	(47)

Various Limits

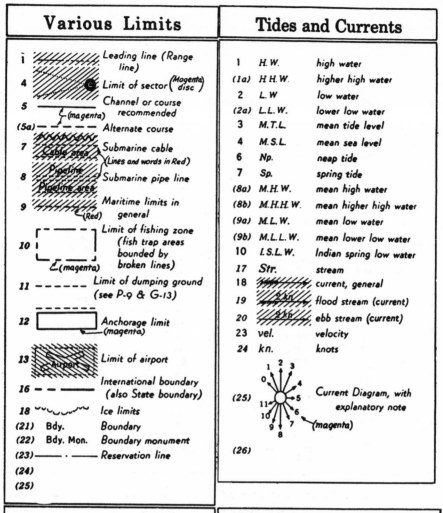

1	Leading line (Range line)
4	Limit of sector (Magenta disc)
5	Channel or course recommended (magenta)
(5a)	Alternate course
7	Submarine cable (Lines and words in Red) — Cable area
8	Submarine pipe line — Pipeline area
9	Maritime limits in general (Red)
10	Limit of fishing zone (fish trap areas bounded by broken lines) (magenta)
11	Limit of dumping ground (see P-9 & G-13)
12	Anchorage limit (magenta)
13	Limit of airport — Airport
16	International boundary (also State boundary)
18	Ice limits
(21)	Bdy. Boundary
(22)	Bdy. Mon. Boundary monument
(23)	Reservation line
(24)	
(25)	

Tides and Currents

1	H.W.	high water
(1a)	H H.W.	higher high water
2	L.W	low water
(2a)	L.L.W.	lower low water
3	M.T.L.	mean tide level
4	M.S.L.	mean sea level
6	Np.	neap tide
7	Sp.	spring tide
(8a)	M.H.W.	mean high water
(8b)	M.H.H.W.	mean higher high water
(9a)	M.L.W.	mean low water
(9b)	M.L.L.W.	mean lower low water
10	I.S.L.W.	Indian spring low water
17	Str.	stream
18		current, general
19	2 kn.	flood stream (current)
20	2 kn.	ebb stream (current)
23	vel.	velocity
24	kn.	knots
(25)		Current Diagram, with explanatory note (magenta)
(26)		

Soundings

2	No bottom sounding
5	Dredged channels (controlling depth may be shown in separate note) — 20 FEET MAY 1939
9	Swept areas (shown by green tint) (not yet covered by sufficient hydrographic surveys to show adequate soundings) — 17, Green Area
(9a)	Areas swept by wire drag to depth indicated — 22, 8
(16)	Stream — 6, 5, 2½
(17)	6 See general remarks 13
(18)	

Depth Contours & Tints

Feet	Fathoms	
0	0	.... GREEN ....
6	1	.... BLUE ....
12	2	.... BLUE ....
18	3	.... BLUE ....
24	4	.... LIGHT BLUE ....
30	5	.... LIGHT BLUE ....
36	6	— — — — — — — — —
60	10	— — — — — — — — —
120	20	— — — — — — — — —
180	30	— — — — — — — — —
240	40	— · — · — · — · —
300	50	— · — · — · — · —
600	100	— — — — — — — —
1,200	200	— — — — — — —
1,800	300	— · · — · · — · · —
2,400	400	— · · — · · — · · —
3,000	500	— · · · — · · · —
6,000	1,000	....
12,000	2,000	— · — · — · — · —
18,000	3,000	— · · — · · — · · —
Or 10 fathoms and greater		Or — BLUE —10— 100 — COLOR

Quality of the Bottom

1	Grd.	ground		35	Rd.	radiolaria
2	S.	sand		36	Pt.	pteropod
3	M.	mud		37	Po.	polyzoa
4	Oz.	ooze		39	fne.	fine
5	Ml.	marl		40	crs.	coarse
6	Cl.	clay		41	sft.	soft
7	G.	gravel		42	hrd.	hard
8	Sn.	shingle		43	stf.	stiff
9	P.	pebbles		44	sml.	small
10	St.	stones		45	lrg.	large
(10a)	Sp.	specks		46	stk.	sticky
11	Rk.	rock		47	brk.	broken
(11a)	Bld. (s)	boulder (s)		(47a)	rky.	rocky
12	Ck.	chalk		50	spk.	speckled
13	Qz.	quartz		51	gty.	gritty
14	Co.	coral		53	fly.	flinty
(14a)	Co. Hd.	coral head		54	glac.	glacial
15	Md.	madrepore		56	wh.	white
(16a)	Vol. Ash.	volcanic ash		57	bk.	black
17	La.	lava		59	bu.	blue
18	Pm.	pumice		60	gn.	green
19	T.	tufa		61	yl.	yellow
20	Sc.	scorice		63	rd.	red
21	Cn.	cinders		64	br.	brown
22	Mn.	manganese		66	gy.	gray
23	Sh.	shells		67	lt.	light
24	Oys.	oysters		68	dk.	dark
25	Ms.	mussels		(69)	Ca.	calcareous
26	Spg.	sponge		(70)		
27	Grs.	grass		(71)		
28	Wd.	weeds		(72)		
32	Fr.	foraminifera		(73)		
33	Gl.	globigerina		(74)		
34	Di.	diatom				

Conversion Tables

Meters	Feet			Meters	Fathoms			Meters	Fathoms	
				0.46	$\frac{1}{4}$	0.14		10.52	$5\frac{3}{4}$	3.14
0.30	1	3.28		0.91	$\frac{1}{2}$	0.27		10.97	6	3.28
				1.37	$\frac{3}{4}$	0.41		11.43	$6\frac{1}{4}$	3.42
0.61	2	6.56		1.83	1	0.55		11.89	$6\frac{1}{2}$	3.55
				2.29	$1\frac{1}{4}$	0.68		12.34	$6\frac{3}{4}$	3.69
0.91	3	9.84		2.74	$1\frac{1}{2}$	0.82		12.80	7	3.83
				3.20	$1\frac{3}{4}$	0.96		13.26	$7\frac{1}{4}$	3.96
				3.66	2	1.09		13.72	$7\frac{1}{2}$	4.10
1.22	4	13.12		4.11	$2\frac{1}{4}$	1.23		14.17	$7\frac{3}{4}$	4.24
				4.57	$2\frac{1}{2}$	1.37		14.63	8	4.37
1.52	5	16.40		5.03	$2\frac{3}{4}$	1.50		15.09	$8\frac{1}{4}$	4.51
				5.49	3	1.64		15.54	$8\frac{1}{2}$	4.65
1.83	6	19.68		5.94	$3\frac{1}{4}$	1.78		16.00	$8\frac{3}{4}$	4.78
				6.40	$3\frac{1}{2}$	1.91		16.46	9	4.92
2.13	7	22.97		6.86	$3\frac{3}{4}$	2.05		16.92	$9\frac{1}{4}$	5.06
				7.32	4	2.19		17.37	$9\frac{1}{2}$	5.19
				7.77	$4\frac{1}{4}$	2.32		17.83	$9\frac{3}{4}$	5.33
2.44	8	26.25		8.23	$4\frac{1}{2}$	2.46		18.29	10	5.47
				8.69	$4\frac{3}{4}$	2.60		18.75	$10\frac{1}{4}$	5.60
2.74	9	29.53		9.14	5	2.73		19.20	$10\frac{1}{2}$	5.74
				9.60	$5\frac{1}{4}$	2.87		19.66	$10\frac{3}{4}$	5.88
3.05	10	32.81		10.05	$5\frac{1}{2}$	3.01		20.12	11	6.01
	Meters	Feet			Meters	Fathoms			Meters	Fathoms

Compass

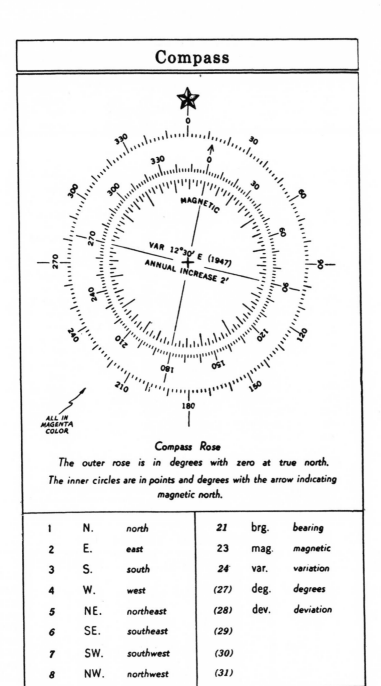

Compass Rose

The outer rose is in degrees with zero at true north.
The inner circles are in points and degrees with the arrow indicating
magnetic north.

1	N.	north	21	brg.	bearing
2	E.	east	23	mag.	magnetic
3	S.	south	24	var.	variation
4	W.	west	(27)	deg.	degrees
5	NE.	northeast	(28)	dev.	deviation
6	SE.	southeast	(29)		
7	SW.	southwest	(30)		
8	NW.	northwest	(31)		

VITAL STATISTICS OF YOUR YACHT

Yacht	Capacity of Each ....
Out of	Total Capacity ....
Registration Number	Water Tanks
Yacht Club	Number ....
Year Purchased	Capacity of Each ....
Year Built	Total Capacity ....
Type	Navigational Equipment
Designer	Compass ....
Builder	Serial No. ....
Rig	Log ....
L.O.A.	Serial No. ....
W.L.	Tachometer ....
Beam	Serial No. ....
Draft	Radio Telephone Make ....
Material Used	Model ....
Planking	Voltage ....
Deck	Serial No. ....
Fastenings	R.D.F. Make ....
Miscellaneous	Type ....
Working Sails	Voltage ....
Light Sails	Serial No. ....
Engine Make	Depth Finder Make ....
Type	Type ....
Serial No.	Voltage ....
Serial No.	Serial No. ....
Generator Make	Loran Make ....
Capacity	Model ....
Year	Voltage ....
Fuel Tanks	Serial No. ....
Number	Radar Make ....

Model ....

Voltage ....

Serial No. ....

Automatic Pilot Make ....

Model ....

Serial No. ....

Other Electronic Equipment ....

....

....

....

Radio Telephone License Number ....

Radio Telephone Operator's License Number

....

Ground Tackle ....

....

....

....

Engine Room Tools ....

....

....

....

Fire System and Extinguishers ....

Locations ....

Number and Location of Berths ....

Bedding Equipment ....

Toilet Equipment ....

....

....

....

Toilet Unit Make ....

Model Number ....

Toilet Operational Notes ....

....

....

....

Galley Gear

Stove Make ....

Type ....

Fuel ....

Ice Box Make ....

Type ....

Ice Capacity ....

Sink ....

Type ....

Operation ....

Galley Accessories ....

....

....

....

Dinghy

Type ....

Life Preservers ....

Outboard Make ....

HP ....

Serial No. ....

Miscellaneous Gear Aboard ....

....

....

....

COAST GUARD STATIONS

List below all the U.S. Coast Guard Lifeboat Stations in your boating area.

Name of Station		
Aerial Identification Number		
Descriptive Location		
Telephone Number		

STORM WARNING DISPLAY STATIONS

List all storm warning stations around your yachting area.

Station		
Location		
Signals*		

*Day (flags)—Night (lights)

PRINCIPAL FOG SIGNALS

List the location and signal of all fog warning devices in your area.

Type

Location

Signal Identification

LOCATION OF YACHT CLUBS AND MARINAS

List the Yacht Clubs and Marinas in your area.

Name

Location

Telephone Number

PRINCIPAL RADIO BEACONS

List the principal radio beacons in your area so that you will have the information when needed for the operation of the radio direction finder.

Beacon		
Location		
Freq. Kcs.		
Signal		
Schedule		

RADIOTELEPHONE WEATHER ANNOUNCEMENTS

List the marine radiotelephone stations that issue weather forecasts and storm warnings.

City or town		
Freq. Kcs.		
Call Letters		
Schedule		

PRINCIPAL COMMERCIAL BROADCAST STATIONS

Because they are useful for direction finding, list the following information on the principal commercial broadcast stations in your area:

City or town _____

Freq. Kcs. _____

Call Letters _____

Latitude N _____

Longitude N _____

AERONAUTICAL STATIONS

Name of field _____

Freq. Kcs. _____

Identification _____

Latitude N _____

Longitude N _____

MISCELLANEOUS NOTES

MISCELLANEOUS NOTES

MISCELLANEOUS NOTES

MISCELLANEOUS NOTES

MISCELLANEOUS NOTES

MISCELLANEOUS NOTES

ACKNOWLEDGEMENT

The success of any cruise depends on the help of your crew. And when preparing a book, an editor needs the cooperation of many people and organizations. I would like to thank the following for their help in this book: Everett A. Pearson of Grumman Allied Industries, Inc.; Jack B. Owens formerly of Owens Yacht, Inc.; Captain W. Thompson and Lieutenant Jack C. Goldthorpe of United States Coast Guard; William K. Carswell of Danforth-White, Inc.; Edward C. Denaple of Prince & Company, Inc.; James P. Reynold of E. I. du Pont de Nemours & Company; Ira E. Dowd of American Hydrofoils, Inc.; A. G. Turner of Standard Oil Company of California; Newell Garden and Captain Fred Lawton of Raytheon Company; Tom L. Fitzsimons of the Yacht Racing Association of Long Island Sound; Marine Office of America; S. L. Kaye Company, Inc.; College Hill Industries, Inc.; Mobil Oil Company; Walter Kidde & Company; and Wall Rope Works.